OF SWORDS AND RED BUTTERFLIES

Of Swords and Red Butterflies

A CHILD'S HEART SHALL ENLIGHTEN ALL WOMEN AND RESCUE HUMANITY

——•——

Robert W. Farrar

ISBN: 9780692515518
ISBN: 0692515518

Silver Entertainment LLC
(Johnny S.Baravong)
www.SilverEt.com
Jbaravong@silver-et.com
Cover design by Sonia Miller http://mysurewave.com/ mailto:sonia@mysurewave.com

For

Mom and Dad, who believed in me.

My wife Tammie and our wonderful kids Robert Jr., Chase, and Faith.

My beautiful granddaughter Safina.

My niece Carissa, whose star burned out much
too soon – we miss you so much.

My maverick childhood friend Johnny Baravong, who
somehow got me to do the unthinkable – write a book!

Love and thank you all.

TABLE OF CONTENTS

PROLOGUE

SWIRLING CLOUDS OF RED DUST dance in giant waves across the barren sky. Growing bigger and bigger, the clouds envelop everything in their path, until even the light of the sun is blocked out. A single red butterfly emerges from the massive red cloud. Descending toward the earth, she hovers before *you,* the "Chosen One."

Can you feel her in you? At this very moment, her mind is merging with yours. Her thoughts become your thoughts, and your thoughts become hers. Can you hear her voice?

*"My emerald-green eyes have seen through your eyes, and **your eyes will now see through mine.** At last, we're one!"*

Suddenly, every woman hears the voice. Day and night, the voice whispers gently—but firmly—in their minds. It awakens the infinite, latent powers deep within every woman. It is the voice of an unfathomable power—it is the universe itself. It speaks of an all-pervasive and uncompromising law of the universe: women and men are *equal* halves of the whole.

"With unwavering adherence to this universal law, women shall regain what is rightfully theirs. They will become an unstoppable force, like a gathering, fierce storm—a perfect storm, the likes of which humankind has yet to witness. The courageous actions of these women will unequivocally wash clean and permanently correct the evils and injustices perpetrated against them and their children through hundreds of thousands of years. United, and with complete conviction, they will be in alliance with absolute truth and the power of the universe. These women will finally reclaim their birthright as the equal halves of the whole…not just for themselves, but for the future of every child, woman, and man on the planet," says the voice.

CHAPTER 1

THE CHOSEN ONE

———◆———

SHE WAS TWELVE YEARS OLD when she assisted in the murder of her best friend. Although she wasn't the actual "ax man," she sometimes wondered if she should've been. At least then she wouldn't have given him false hope before slitting his throat. No, she was far worse. She was the one who played with him, sang songs to him, and showed him love. In return, he gave her joy and reflected the love back to her.

He trusted her.

Then came the snowy evening when she stood like a coward as her dear friend was taken away on a truck—along with all the other "undesirables"—to meet their bloody end. *Why didn't I do something?* she had thought. *I knew this day would come, yet I foolishly believed that somehow he'd be spared…that somehow he'd be good enough. Was it his fault he wasn't born with the genes necessary to be of value to those who judged? He wasn't especially handsome, muscular, or smart; but he was my friend, and, unlike me, he knew the meaning of loyalty. Why didn't I sneak him out the night before and set him free? At least then he might have had a fighting chance, a fair shot at this incessant masquerade called life.*

Ever since that dark day, she had wondered (or maybe it was more accurate to say had been obsessed with) exactly what had gone through her friend's mind during his final tour of the world. *Did he know of the atrocities that awaited him? Was he terrified? Did he soil himself like others did? Did he feel betrayed by me? Did he hate me as much as I hated myself?*

That she had the good fortune to be born a human being instead of a show pig was highly debatable to her now, especially as she lay bound and tied by her own captors.

My, how the wheel of fortune had changed! Unlike her dear friend, she knew what awaited her at the end of this ride through the long, dark night, and knew the answers to all those questions she'd had about his final thoughts on that cold, bloody Sunday a lifetime ago.

But before she returned to the River of the Great Spirits, she had passed on to you her story, so that, if worthy enough, a tiny sliver of her light may shine on through you.

Her voice—it had countless names, belonging to countless souls, over countless centuries; but in this case it had been given the name Kiwi, and she was the Chosen One. Kiwi was short for Kiwidinok, which was Chippewa for "woman of the wind."

Kiwi remembered, as a child, getting an uncomfortable feeling, bordering on a panic attack, every time a family member, friend, or tribal official referred to her by that title. It felt more like an unbearable responsibility than an honor. Everyone knew that the title of Chosen One was just another way of saying "our last hope" or "savior." The idea of her being anyone's savior scared the hell out of her. She just wanted to study medical books so she could find a cure for her mother's illness— and sometimes swim in the river or chase butterflies.

As she now lay bound by her captors, she remembered the first time she had seen a butterfly. She was in the fifth summer of her life, riding high on the shoulders of her grandmother, whom she referred to as Me'me'. They were on one of their special adventures at Yellowstone, and Me'me' was carrying her through an endless sea of wildflowers and but-terflies. She clearly remembered the potpourri of sights, sounds, colors, smells, and tastes of that moment. But she especially remembered the butterflies. It seemed as if for every flower there was a butterfly float-ing above it. She threw her little arms out as Me'me' spun her around and around. The butterflies danced in circles all about them—as if they knew the game. They didn't want to stop playing when Me'me' stopped, and the butterflies kept spinning around them.

Then, a big red butterfly landed right on Kiwi's lips! Her hands were clasped tightly on Me'me's head, but she wasn't at all afraid. She could see the butterfly's big eyes, which made her happy because they were the same mystical green as hers. But when she focused closer on those eyes, she saw every color of the rainbow.

The butterfly sat softly on Kiwi's lips, slowly flapping her silky, red wings. Kiwi decided the butterfly must be a girl because it was so pretty. She couldn't make out exactly what the butterfly's wings looked like, but to her they seemed to have strange patterns on them in the shape of eyes. The eyes had long eyelashes and somehow looked familiar to her.

Me'me' didn't know about the butterfly and continued walking through the field with Kiwi atop her shoulders. As the butterfly and Kiwi bounced up and down, Kiwi felt something she could only describe as dreamlike. She felt as if, for a moment, the red butterfly and she became one and saw the world through the same eyes. Something strange, warm, and beautiful entered her body. At first it was only on her lips and face, but then it poured down into her chest and stomach, then out to her fingertips and toes. To Kiwi, it was as though her new friend had given her something wonderful—like a beautifully wrapped gift. She felt a little bit sad because she had nothing to give the butterfly in return. Then, without warning, the red butterfly flapped her wings and lifted away into the big blue sky.

Later that day, Kiwi told Me'me' about her encounter with the red butterfly. Me'me' was overjoyed. She told Kiwi that some butterflies carried an extra spirit inside them, and that this special spirit was like a stowaway riding on the wings of its host. She said you would never know which butterfly carried this spirit, so it was important to be extra careful not to harm any of them. She told Kiwi that the purpose of this special spirit was to tell us something very important, something from beyond.

Kiwi told Me'me' about how the butterfly gave her a beautiful gift, but that she had nothing to give back.

"What was the gift?" Me'me' asked, and Kiwi's eyes filled with tears because she'd already forgotten.

Sensing the reason for Kiwi's upset, Me'me' offered, "You haven't forgotten, child. It will reveal itself at the exact moment when it's needed most."

From birth, Kiwi had what some of the elders called "forever memory." She could recall everything she read or saw in a book perfectly, as if it were right in front of her. She loved to read everything. Virtually every book in the reservation library was forever scanned into her brain.

Naturally, the news of her special gift spread throughout the tribe. She suddenly became the pride and savior of their insignificant yet devoted tribe.

She knew they all meant well by calling her the Chosen One, but she couldn't help but wonder, *What if they're all wrong? What if this Chosen One is someone else or doesn't even exist at all? Or worse…what if they're right?*

Growing up on the reservation, or what her people referred to as "the rez," wasn't most people's version of the American dream. But it was for Kiwi's parents. They wouldn't have wanted to raise their children anywhere else. Almost every family she knew hoped of having a special child who would break free from the poverty, isolation, and government stranglehold around the Chippewa.

To the elders, the unfavorable conditions were always a punishment by the Great Spirits for the younger generation's disrespect of their elders and culture. To the younger generation, unfavorable conditions were always the fault of bad decisions and lack of courage on the part of their elders. It was a vicious and destructive cycle. As a result, there always seemed to be a sense of hopelessness felt by all, but spoken of by few.

Kiwi's mother had finally succumbed to tuberculosis the day after Kiwi's fourteenth birthday. To Kiwi, her mother was the most beautiful woman she knew, and although she wasn't fully Chippewa, she had been accepted by the tribe as one of their own. But it wasn't so easy for her mother's mother, Kiwi's Me'me', because she was a full-blooded French woman from Canada. Me'me' had thick, wavy, silver hair and big blue

eyes and was once a journalist. She met Kiwi's grandfather while covering a story on Native Americans in Montana. Kiwi's grandfather was
the son of a well-respected tribal chief by the name of Bear's Paw. Her
grandparents fell in love, and her grandfather was pressured into leaving the tribe because he "married outside tribal blood." But because
her grandmother played such a crucial part in helping the Chippewa
gain back their tribal rights through her news articles, the tribal leaders agreed to make an exception for her, and Kiwi's grandparents were
allowed to come back to the rez.

That was how Kiwi and her mother came to be, and they looked a
lot like Me'me'. The women elders always said that Kiwi and her mother
had something they called "the curse of beauty." Kiwi was confused and
never understood what that meant, and it scared her. Her mother told
her to never mind the elders, that they were just jealous and that it wasn't
true. But still, Kiwi never quite shook their words from her mind.

The tribal medicine man did his best to keep Kiwi's mother's lungs
working long enough to at least make it through Kiwi's fourteenth birthday. She'd been in a partial coma, and they kept her locked away so she
wouldn't infect the others. Kiwi begged her father to let her spend the
day with her mother, but he insisted that she participate in the celebration because tribal traditions dictate that turning fourteen is a special
spiritual movement into the next chapter of a person's life.

The celebration didn't matter to Kiwi; she cried for almost the entire
day. After the opening ceremony, which consisted of full ceremonial
dress, her dad left the celebration and spent the rest of the day and night
with her mother. He was by her side when the Great Spirits came for her
later that night.

Kiwi's father, Red Dreams, was a man of few words, but to Kiwi and
most of her tribe, he was the bravest warrior they had. The story behind
his name is a strange one.

The name was given to him by the elders of the tribe. When his
mother, Kiwi's other grandmother, was pregnant with him, she had
strange dreams. These dreams would always be in red. She would wake

up from these dreams sweating and in a state of panic. The only thing she could ever remember about these dreams was that everything was bright red.

Needless to say, this was stressful to her and unnerving to family and friends. The tribal medicine man even tried to cure her of what he called "demon dreams" by giving her a concoction of herbs, human urine, and a bit of peyote cactus juice.

It was common practice that peyote, a powerful hallucinogenic, was often taken by tribal spiritual leaders, called shaman, in their quests for visions. After taking the peyote concoction, Kiwi's grandmother also had visions—except hers was all in red! After that incident, the tribal medicine man nervously left their home and never returned. Weeks later, Kiwi's grandmother died giving birth to her father. The tribal shaman said she died because the tribal medicine man messed up and gave her the special peyote concoction, causing her to have red visions. Apparently the concoction was only to be taken by the "vision seekers," like him—not by the common folk. They say that Kiwi's grandfather, the tribal chief at the time, was so angry that he stripped both the medicine man and the shaman of their titles and appointed new ones. As a result, Kiwi's father got his tribal name of Red Dreams, even though he himself never had a single dream in red.

Red Dreams was the police chief of the little reservation, and he had just two deputies to help him enforce the law. Law enforcement on the rez was usually a daunting task, to say the least. Back then, many adults on the reservations were addicted to alcohol or some type of drug. Fortunately, Red Dreams was very well respected by the tribe. He was known to be firm yet fair when dealing with any situation—and being the father of the Chosen One didn't hurt either. The only time Kiwi saw her father cry was at her mother's funeral. It was a shock for everyone there, which was almost the entire tribe, to see such a strong, mountain of a man like Red Dreams completely break down in tears.

Although medicines existed to treat tuberculosis at the time, they were very expensive. What was shameful and inexcusable to Kiwi was that the price of the medicines was so grossly inflated that most lower-income people, like those of her tribe, couldn't afford them. Her mother and many others suffered unnecessarily and died slow, painful deaths at the expense of greedy pharmaceutical companies and crooked politicians. Some politicians were paid off by big drug companies to protect them by not passing laws to prevent the deliberate overpricing of critical drugs.

After countless hours of research, Kiwi discovered that the United States was one of only a couple industrialized countries in the world that didn't have regulatory control measures set to ensure the affordability of critical drugs for their people. Americans paid two to three times more for the exact same cancer, tuberculosis, and other drugs sold by the same companies in other countries, like Canada or Mexico.

Kiwi's plans of becoming a medical doctor changed after her mother's death. Her only purpose in life became to correct the injustices perpetrated by both the billion-dollar pharmaceutical companies and the crooked politicians who made money protecting them. For her, this meant she needed to become a journalist like her Me'me' had been. She went on a mission to become the most influential journalist in the state of Montana—maybe even in America.

She finished high school early and was accepted into the University of Montana. It was three hours away from home, and she was more than excited for the change in scenery. At that time, being of Native American descent actually made it more difficult to be accepted into a predominately white college. But because she aced her college entrance exams, the university made an exception. She'd always been told she was exceptionally beautiful, although she could never see why. In fact, she rarely looked at herself in the mirror. This meant not wearing makeup and keeping a simple ponytail hairstyle. Deep down she suspected her social anxiety was a result of her fear of having "the curse of beauty" as the elders would say. In her multiple face-to-face interviews with the university dean, he made it quite clear about his interest in her "other attributes." But she didn't let his lack of integrity and male chauvinistic attitude bother her. She was in!

CHAPTER 2

SATAN'S SAMURAI

———◆———

A RED BUTTERFLY SWAYED GENTLY in the soft summer breeze as it clung to a leaf of a giant beech tree. It watched with a heavy heart as the dark figure low-crawled slowly toward the small cottage.

At exactly 02:22 hours military time, the man entered through an unlocked door at the rear of the house. Silver moonlight filtered through the kitchen windows, casting long shadows on the walls. A thick odor of cigar smoke hung in the air. Inhaling the musty air, the assassin made a mental note that he would not be able to rely on his keen sense of smell tonight. Loud snoring from the end of the hallway mixed with the sound of a blaring TV.

The shadow slithered by the living room. A tall slender woman was curled up on the couch under a blanket. Light from the TV danced on her young yet weathered face. The intruder confirmed that it was, in fact, the target's twenty-five-year-old German wife.

He glided softly past the seven-year-old child's room, moving on to the last room on the left. The door was wide open. With his back flat against the wall, the assassin carefully exposed part of his head into the doorway and scanned the room.

The target was sound asleep on his back at the right edge of the bed. An empty bottle of cheap wine sat on the nightstand, and next to the bottle was a P38 pistol. The room was fairly spacious, with minimal obstacles. The silky, transparent curtains glowed in the moonlight like floating ghosts. The air was permeated with alcohol, cigar smoke, and something else—something the assassin couldn't quite distinguish. The thunderous snoring coming from the gaping mouth of the target was a welcomed ally.

With one smooth soundless motion, the assassin unsheathed the long sword from the scabbard strapped to his back. He looked over his right shoulder at the empty hallway one more time, then turned and melted into the room. With all his senses wide open, the dark shadow crept along the wall until he was adjacent to the target and then turned to face his prize. Expertly and methodically, the assassin inched forward into position—toes, feet, legs, hips, torso, chest, shoulders, head, arms, hands, and fingers—everything in optimal balance for the fatal strike.

Light from an unseen sun bounced off the face of the lone witnessing moon, bathing the assassin's sword as it hung over its prey. He froze. Something was amiss. The assassin felt the air shift ever so slightly; a door somewhere in the house had opened and closed, creating a vacuum effect. He stood motionless with his eyes fixed on the target, while his other senses searched the home.

A scream came from the living room followed by the unmistakable sound of shots fired from a semiautomatic pistol muffled by a silencer. One shot was followed by two more.

Immediately the assassin knew. *How foolish!* he thought. Apparently members of the Russian secret service had discovered or had been given information about this mission and had their own agent track him to the target.

The charismatic neo-Nazi leader sprung upright from his bed in panic. He reached for his pistol just as the dark shadow's blade effortlessly severed his head and left arm at the elbow. A child hidden under the covers on the other side of the bed pulled them off her face in time to see a gushing stream of blood shoot from her father's neck and headless body.

Damn! How careless not to notice the child in the bed! the assassin cursed silently.

The tiny blonde girl let out an ear-piercing scream and froze in absolute terror. The assassin was instantly on the other side of the room crouched low in the corner; the child was oblivious to his presence. He heard someone clumsily making his way down the hall. *How reckless of this incompetent fool to make such noise!* he thought.

When the Russian agent entered the room, the child looked at him, screaming even louder. A red dot instantly appeared on her forehead. The agent swung his pistol from the child over to the headless body, then back to the child. The girl screamed for her mother, who was now lying in the living room with a missing lower jaw and two holes in her forehead.

The agent quickly assessed the situation and concluded that the man named Ukko (also known as Satan's Samurai), the legendary Japanese assassin working for the American CIA, had beaten him to the target and was most likely long gone by now.

The Russian agent was totally unaware that Ukko was lying flat on the floor just twelve feet from him.

How stupid this Jap is to leave witnesses, the Russian thought. *Besides, the girl is of Nazi blood, so why not exterminate the little devil now?*

The Russian walked over to the crying child, slapped his leather gloved hand over her mouth, and put his pistol to the back of her head.

"No," Ukko whispered just loud enough for the agent to hear him without being overly startled.

The Russian agent nearly urinated on himself and swung his pistol over to the dark corner of the room. He tightened his hold on the child's mouth and was about to squeeze off three rounds into the corner when his racing mind connected the dots.

It's Satan's Samurai!, he realized. It took the Russian a few seconds to gather himself. Then he thought, *Hell, I finally get to meet the bastard Japanese legend after all!*

He ordered Ukko to come out slowly with his hands up. Ukko appeared out of the shadows, as if vaporizing from thin air. Again, the agent was so startled he nearly soiled himself this time. Ukko was now on the other side of the room.

What the hell? How'd the bastard get over there?

The agent looked at Ukko, sizing him up and down. Standing before him was an almost imperceptible black shadow. *Where's his gun? What kind of weapons does he have? Where the hell are his damn eyes?*

The Russian took a slow, anxious breath. *Ah, the Jap's not so big. He doesn't look anything like the badass killing machine everyone talks about, does he?*

Ukko sensed the aura of hatred resonating from the Russian assassin. The agent snapped at Ukko with a thick accent, "Is the rest of the damn house clear, or do I have to do that, too?"

"Yes, all clear," Ukko replied.

The child was hyperventilating and began to go into shock. The agent moved his pistol back to the base of her head.

"No!" Ukko yelled. "Please. There's no need."

Through the black mesh on Ukko's mask, the men's eyes met. Ukko slowly shook his head, desperately hoping that this heartless, incompetent fool would not do it, wouldn't kill an innocent child for no reason whatsoever. Then, as their eyes locked in intense battle, Ukko saw it. Silver moonlight exposed the Russian's grinning white teeth. *This madman has made his decision. He is going to do the unthinkable!*

As Ukko was midway into his combat roll toward the Russian agent, time seemed to slow to a crawl. He saw his seven-year-old sister in the early morning light. His beautiful fiancée was holding her hand. His sister was picking white blossoms from a cherry tree. Soft butterflies floated all around them. His mother waved to them in the background; she always had the most radiant smile. They were all so happy, so content—life cherished them to the extent they cherished life. They saw him and waved. Suddenly, there was a blast of wind as the trees were stripped of their flowers and leaves. His sister, fiancée, and mother fell to their knees and looked up. The sky was on fire—everything was on fire.

Coming out of his combat roll, both hands gripped firmly on the hilt of his sword, Ukko saw the child's skull fragments explode from her forehead, followed by brain matter as white as the cherry blossoms his little sister picked on that bright morning. At the exact moment the child's blood and bones spattered on the far wall, the Russian assassin's head rolled off of his neck, bounced off his right shoulder, and came to rest at the very spot the little girl had slept just moments before—her doll pressed tightly against her heart, dreaming her childish dreams.

CHAPTER 3

GHOST

THE SOUND CAME FROM THE forbidden room, causing the woman downstairs to flinch and look up. Sara silently cursed herself for dropping the book and drawing attention to herself. A few minutes went by before she heard the *clumping* of footsteps making their way up the spiral staircase. Sara froze. *Oh God. She heard it. She knows,* Sara thought.

The woman reached the top of the stairs. "Hello?" she called. "Is someone there?" Then the woman cautiously checked each room until finally she stood in front of the mysterious forbidden door that joined the mansion to the attached guest house. The heavy oak door was double dead-bolted. She gently turned the doorknob to find it locked, as usual.

"I know you're in there," she said. "I've seen you standing by your window before. Are you okay? Why won't you come out when I'm here?"

Sara closed her eyes tightly, praying that her pounding heart wouldn't give her away.

"You don't have to be afraid," the woman said. "I promise I don't bite. It's just that it'd sure be nice to have some company while I clean this big old house, you know."

Sara didn't reply.

The woman let out a sigh. "Okay, have it your way. Just think about it, and maybe we'll try again next week. Bye, now."

Sara listened nervously as the woman gathered her cleaning supplies and left the big house. She heard the car start and drive off. The following week, the woman did her usual cleaning but didn't try to talk to Sara at all. She finished cleaning, and Sara listened intently as the doors of the mansion opened and closed. She let out a sigh of relief but at the same time felt a pang in her heart. She wanted desperately to have a friend, someone she could talk to besides the birds she watched through her window and the ever-present chatter in her head. For a minute, she allowed herself to indulge in the thought of making friends with the woman. *She seems nice enough, and her country accent is quite amusing,* Sara thought, but then she shuddered and quickly dismissed the idea.

Sara thought about the previous cleaning lady. *Whatever happened to that sweet old woman?* she wondered. One day she just stopped coming. During the entire time Sara was locked inside the mansion, the old lady never made any attempts to talk to her. Obviously, the lady was wise and valued her life more than this new cleaning woman.

What Sara missed most about the old cleaning lady were the gifts she'd slide under her door every few months. The first gifts were a small pocket-sized Bible and a beautiful rosary. After that came a pack of twelve sharpened pencils, a spiral notebook with lined pages, a pack of gum, a roll of Lifesavers, and a drawing pad with exactly twenty-four pages which, if she cut them in half and drew on both sides, would equal a total of ninety-six pages.

Sometimes she splurged and allowed herself three whole pages where she could draw her favorite birds outside her window, all the while watching with longing in her heart. Through the years, she'd managed to hide the artwork in a shoebox tucked high in the corner of her walk-in closet. She hid the Bible and rosary between the mattresses of her bed. On stormy nights—or days when she felt especially sad—she'd lie in bed wearing her rosary and holding the Bible next to her heart.

Sara decided she needed a long hot bath after the anxiety she'd just endured. She was so relieved the new cleaning lady didn't try to talk to her again. She ran the water and climbed inside the Jacuzzi-size tub.

The grandfather clock downstairs announced it was lunchtime. Sara was surprised; she'd fallen asleep, and nearly forty minutes had passed. She got dressed and made her way to the kitchen, hoping the American cheese had been restocked. She loved it in her sandwiches and instant noodle soups.

From behind the massive armoire, the cleaning lady watched, mesmerized, as the mysterious girl walked down the staircase of the attached guest house. The tall slender figure floated down the steps as if she were a ghost that had materialized from a dream. Over her head and face and covering the length of her long blonde hair was a white sheer see-through veil. Her white dress had a divine glow to it and enshrouded her petite body from her shoulders to her toes.

To the cleaning lady, there seemed to be an innocent melancholy etched upon the young girl's radiant face. She had that rare natural beauty admired by all. Her thick blonde hair was exquisitely French braided and hung to the side. Metal hair clips with bright flowers sat above each temple, and a larger clip sat perfectly at the bottom of her braided hair. Her eyes seemed unusually big and were the color of a crystal blue lagoon. Her nose was slender and her cheekbones prominent. Her complexion was a soft pale tone with just a hint of freckles.

Sara walked by—inches from the hidden woman—on her way to the kitchen. Her narrow lips moved as if she were quietly whispering a song to herself. The lady watched the girl make herself a sandwich, pour a glass of milk, and sit down at the breakfast bar.

The woman quietly stepped out from behind the armoire, "Well, what'd you make us for lunch?" she asked.

Sara gasped and knocked her milk to the floor. She was oblivious to the sound of glass shattering against the Italian marble. She pushed away from the counter and stood wide-eyed, panting at the intruder. There was only one escape route, and the lady stood in its path.

The lady held out her hand. "Now, calm down, girl. My name's Montana, and you ain't gotta be afraid of me. I promise I'm as harmless as a dove. I just want to be your friend. Will you let me be your friend?"

Sara heard her shaky voice finally squeak, "How…how'd you get in here?"

"Comes in handy to have a locksmith for a daddy," Montana said. "He taught me all there is to know about picking locks. You should see me hot-wire a car." Montana calmly walked to a chair at the dining table just ten feet from Sara and sat down. "My aunt used to be the cleaning lady here," she began, "but she died of a brain aneurysm, so now I'm her replacement. I sure hope you're okay with it."

Sara thought about the sweet old cleaning lady. The trembling slowly left her knees. She stood staring at the empty chair next to Montana. Her mind screamed at her, *Take advantage of the seated intruder and escape to your room now!* But her aching heart said, *No, stay—this is the moment you've been waiting for, the dream you've been dreaming of.*

The silence between the two women was awkward yet somehow comforting. It was the kind of connected silence only true friends experience. *But how could this be?* both women wondered.

Montana cleared her throat and spoke softly, "It really is okay. I promise. Can we just sit and visit for a while?"

Sara saw herself nodding as if in a dream. She walked to a chair at the far end of the table across from Montana. She sat and stared down at the lush patterns of the wood grain on the table in front of her. She noticed she could no longer hear her thundering heartbeat. For the first time in what seemed like forever, she felt a faint sense of security—as if somehow a protective barrier had been placed around her. *Is this really a dream?* Sara wondered. *If so, then please let me live and die in it so I don't ever have to wake up.*

"I'm sorry for scaring you like that and for ruining your lunch. What's your name?" Montana asked.

Sara looked up across the wide space of the dining table at Montana. "My name's Sara." The loud sound of her voice startled her.

"Well it's nice to finally meet you, Sara," Montana said with a relieved smile. "You mind if I join you for lunch?"

"No—" Sara shook her head and then caught herself. "I mean, I don't mind. What I meant is that I want to have lunch together—with you."

"Great! Don't move. I'll be right back." Montana went into the living room and returned with her lunchbox. "I feel like I'm in a whole different county sitting way over here. The seat next to you doesn't happen to be vacant, does it?"

Sara heard the sound of laughter escape from her mouth for the first time in too long. The muscles on her face relaxed and she felt something strange and distantly familiar stretch across her small pale face. The corners of her lips turned upward into a smile. "Sure, come on over," she said with a confidence she didn't recognize.

Montana picked up Sara's plate and brought it to her. She sat down next to Sara and handed her the extra can of Coke she'd just so happened to pack that morning. "Well then," Montana started, "I'd say we're officially two peas in a pod now, wouldn't you say?"

Five hours flew by in a flash. After the initial shock had subsided, Sara was astonished at how quickly her walls had come crashing down. It was as if she and Montana had known each other their entire lives—as if just yesterday they sat painting their toenails and discussing the latest school gossip. This was clearly uncharted territory for Sara and a place she'd longed for all of her life. The most unlikely of events had happened, and she couldn't help but pinch herself. Living suddenly seemed worth the effort again; and, for what to Sara was a lifetime ago, smiles and laughter resurfaced like tulips bursting through the icy snow.

It was obvious to Montana that there was something amiss about Sara's situation. Why was she locked inside a guest house attached to the side of a mansion? Why were there steel bars on every exterior door and window, but only on the guest house side? It was as if the guest house was made specifically to keep its occupants locked in. Why did Sara not want to be discovered? Why did she wear that white dress and a veil over her face—was it part of her religion or something? Sheer instinct told Montana something was very wrong, that she needed to find out the answers to these questions. But she also knew it would take time and patience to draw an explanation out of Sara.

During their second visit, Montana cautiously brought up the subject. Her first question was, "So, is there a special reason why you wear white clothing and have a veil over your face?" Sara clammed up and seemed extremely uncomfortable with discussing it. She told Montana that she wasn't ready to discuss it and begged her to keep their friendship a secret. She said that under no circumstances could the master of the house find out that they were communicating in any way. Montana heard the panic in Sara's voice and backed off the subject. It would take time, she decided, but eventually the frightened girl would open up to her. Montana decided that as long as there were no signs of physical abuse, she would be patient and find out what was really going on in this secluded mansion in the woods.

Over the weeks that followed, Sara and Montana became very close. They confided in each other and became the reason for the other's existence. It turned out that they were close in age, Sara having just turned eighteen and Montana being twenty.

Sara counted every agonizing minute between Montana's biweekly visits. She felt miserable when they were apart and made a list of all the things they'd talk about during their next meeting. They were grateful that the master of the house was rarely at home, and when he was, it was usually late at night. Montana gave Sara notebook paper and a pen so they could write letters to each other. They exchanged the letters during their meetings so they would have something to look forward to while they were apart. Sara even began drawing sketches of Montana and attaching them to her letters.

Over time, each shared with the other her deepest secrets and fears. Every minute they spent together was the steady stripping away of what wasn't real, until what remained was the only thing that mattered to them—their souls. It was at this point that Sara decided to do the unthinkable, to allow her mind to revisit the forbidden repository where her darkest memories had been entombed.

"I grew up in the projects of Detroit," Sara began. "Mama and I didn't have much, but we had each other, and that was enough. I never met my father, but Mama said not to worry 'cause I wasn't missing much. Still, I wanted to meet him at least once. I needed to know if there was anything good I could expect from myself from him because, like Mama always said, the apple doesn't fall far from the tree.

"Mama was a laundry maid at a big hotel, and she took the bus to work after she dropped me off at school. She made sure to get her work done in time to come back and pick me up after school. My teachers always told me I was an exceptional student. I wasn't quite sure exactly what that meant, but Mama and I were very proud of the fact that I made straight A's—that is, until my school got in trouble for giving false grades and passing students who couldn't read or write. The news said that the school did this so it would continue to get funding.

"Mama came to America from Ireland when she was a child, after her father was slain for being a member of the Irish Republican Army during 'the Troubles,' the war between the people of Northern Ireland, who are mostly Protestants, and people of the Republic of Ireland, who are mostly Catholics. She lived with her mother until the day she was caught having an affair with a Protestant man from Northern Ireland—my father. Her mother disowned her, saying she'd disgraced the honor of her father by 'sleeping with the enemy.' Mama said she was scolded and reminded that during the 1641 rebellion, Protestants massacred thousands of Catholics, some of whom were our relatives. What Grandma failed to mention, says Mama, was that the rebellion was a result of thousands of Protestants being massacred by Catholics because of their religious beliefs.

"Mama had red hair and was the most beautiful woman around. She denied it, and I think she always tried to hide her beauty with hats and scarves and big sunglasses. She said that she was through with men, that they were all male chauvinist pigs and that I was to never forget it. So it was just the two of us in a one-bedroom apartment. We had a television, but I accidentally broke the antenna, so it only picked up one channel. Mama started getting back into church when I was about six, and we went to Mass every Sunday and on holidays. She seemed to be happier and started smiling more. Mama volunteered at the church whenever she could, and in return, they helped us with things like clothes and food and holiday turkeys. Things started to look up for us over the next two years, and Mama gave all the credit to the church and to God.

"But then something happened...I remember it like it was yesterday. It was summer, and I was eight years old. We'd just left from Mama's annual confession at the church and were driving to the ice cream shop. Getting freshly made ice cream after Mama's 'reconciliation'— as the Catholic Church calls it—was sort of a tradition we'd started. I could tell she was in an especially happy mood that day...and so was I. I'd been confused about a lot of things, so I asked Mama if we could play the Q&A game. This was a game she and I played where I would ask her questions, and she would try to answer them as fast as she could.

"'Absolutely!' Mama replied. So we began our silly game, a game that would change our lives forever."

Sara then summarized their Q&A session, which went something like this:

Q: Is it true what the nuns in Sunday school told us about how God loves all his children unconditionally and that he is forgiving?

A: Absolutely!

Q: Then why do you still go to confession?

A: Because that's what God says we must do.

Q: Why?

A: Because confessing your sins wipes the slate clean again with God and gives your soul the purity required to enter into the kingdom of heaven.

Q: So people can do bad things over and over and still go to heaven as long as they go to confession?

A: Well, as long as they're really sorry for what they did, I guess.

Q: But what about God being forgiving and loving us all unconditionally?

A: That's true.

Q: Then why couldn't we just speak to God ourselves and ask for his forgiveness instead of going to the priest?

A: Because God gave only certain people in his church special powers, one of which is to forgive us of our sins in the name of God.

Q: Oh, so can I confess my sins to the nuns at my Sunday school when I reach that thing the church calls "the age of reason"?

A: No. Only mediators between us and God, such as Father Odiar, and bishops, cardinals, or the pope himself can forgive us of our sins.

Q: Are any of them girls?

A: No, honey.

Q: So only men can forgive us of our sins?

A: Well, I guess so, according to the Bible. Yes.

Q: So are all these men like God, then?

A: No. They're human beings like us, and so are sinners just like us.

Q: Well, wouldn't it be better to ask for forgiveness straight from God, because he's the only one who doesn't sin?

A: No, because it's written in the Bible that we must do it this way.

Q: Who wrote the Bible?

A: Prophets whom God spoke to. And they wrote it down in words, and the words are now what we call the Bible.

Q: What are the prophets' names?

A: Well, let's see…there's Peter, Mathew, Mark, Luke, and John, and others, I'm sure. But I can't remember them all.

Q: Those all sound like men's names. Are they all men?

A: Well, yes, dear. They are.

Q: How come? Doesn't God like to talk to girls?

A: I'm sure he does, honey.

Q: How do we know God's a boy…maybe he's a girl.

A: Because it's written in the Bible, Sara.

Q: But how do we know if the men who wrote it weren't like Billy in Sunday school and didn't respect girls and always wanted to control them? Maybe that's why they made God a boy like them, instead of a girl.
A: I really don't think that's the case, sweetheart.

"It was at this time that Mama gave me a stern look," Sara told Montana, "as if I were somehow challenging the word of God."

Q: Billy said God hates gay people—whatever that is—because they're sinners. And he said God burns them all in hell. I told him that he's a liar because God would never hurt anyone and that he must be confusing him with the devil. Isn't that so, Mama?
A: Well, the first part's kind of complicated, but the Bible says God will send his angels down to gather the sinners of the world and throw them into the fiery furnace, where there will be weeping and the gnashing of teeth. So, yes, I guess it's true.
Q: So God really does hate gay people?
A: No, sweetie. I don't think God hates anyone.
Q: Well then, how come the teacher at our elementary school told us that God didn't create people to be gay, so all gay people don't deserve to live? I thought God created all people.
A: I don't know why he's saying those things, honey. He's wrong. God loves all his children.

Sara turned from Montana and walked to a window. "I remember looking out my window at the approaching storm clouds. 'I think God really *is* loving and forgiving. And I think he's a girl instead of a boy,' I told Mama.

"'Now, that's enough, Sara,' Mama chided. 'That's blasphemy! There're some things we don't question, and the Bible is one of those things. Never say that again—do you understand me?'

"Mama seemed more fearful than angry, so I decided to ask one last question."

Q: How come Father Odiar, the man you confess your sins to, pulls me out of Sunday school sometimes and touches me...?"

Back in the present, Sara walked to another window and stared out blankly. "Needless to say, we never made it to the ice cream shop that day."

There was a heavy silence, and then Montana walked over and hugged Sara. "I'm sorry. That must've been hard on both of you."

"Yeah," Sara managed to say.

Montana held Sara's hand. "You don't have to answer this if you don't want to, Sara, but I have to ask. What did your mother do after you told her?"

Sara wiped the tears from her face. "It's okay. I want to tell you. Mama drove for a little while longer and then suddenly spun the car around and sped back to the church. As we were pulling up to the church, Father Odiar was standing outside the door speaking to two elderly women. He saw us and waved. Mama pretended she didn't see him. He held his hand out in front of the old women and made the sign of the cross to bless them. The women kissed his holy hand and left happy and content. The priest looked over at our car, then turned and went back into the church. I watched as my mother sat with her hands on the steering wheel. Her knuckles turned white, and she was shaking all over. Then she lowered her head and began crying. After a while, she started the car, and we drove away. We never set foot inside a church again."

Montana suddenly became aware of the crucifix hanging around her neck and touched it. "I think the nuns at your Sunday school church were the only ones who were right."

"Me too. Do you go to church?" Sara asked.

"All the time," replied Montana, putting her hand on her chest. "The church of my heart. I discovered a long time ago that's the only place you'll ever find God."

Sara smiled. "I like that."

"Anyway, Mama and I never spoke again about church...or God... or what Father Odiar did to me. It was all like a bad dream. Mama began getting sick, and she missed a lot of work. Some days she'd skip meals so that I'd have something to eat. That hurt me more than anything. She refused to ask for welfare. She said that we were Irish, and Irish folk don't take handouts. I couldn't wait to go to school so I could eat other things besides cabbage soup and peanut butter sandwiches.

"Eventually she got so sick she couldn't get out of bed. She developed an infection in her lungs and refused to go to see a doctor. She told me that it didn't matter—that she deserved to suffer. I slept on the floor next to her bed almost every night and cried myself to sleep. One morning she never woke up again. I knew all along that Mama's death was my fault. If I'd never questioned the Bible and told on Father Odiar, she wouldn't have gotten sick and died of a broken heart. I'll never forgive myself—maybe I deserve to suffer too."

Tears streamed down Montana's face. She walked over to Sara and wrapped her arms around her from behind.

"It wasn't your fault, Sara...or your mama's fault...or God's fault. If anyone is to blame, it's the man who molested you—he's the *only* one at fault."

After a moment, Sara continued. "A couple days before Mama died she told me that my father wasn't a bad man, that he was actually good, and that in the beginning they were full of love for each other. She admitted that she'd said all those awful things about him because she was angry and resentful. She said that he had a good heart, but he just couldn't take the relentless badgering from Grandma for being of 'Northern blood' any longer. One day he left and we never saw him again. The night before she passed away she held my hand and told me, 'Always remember that women see relationships, and men see body parts. Men want sex, and women want relationships. Men want flesh, and women want love.'

"I went to live with my aunt in Chicago until I was fourteen. We lived in a nice neighborhood, and I went to a nice school. I had a hard time making friends and was sort of a loner. One day when I was walking home from school, two men jumped me from behind and pushed me into a car. I was tied up, gagged, and blindfolded. We drove for what seemed like days, and then, during the night, I was taken into a house. The air was thick and musty, and I could hear whimpering and crying all around me. I was moved into a room and was left lying on the floor for hours.

"Finally, a man came in and sat me up against the wall. He told me that a woman was going to come in to give me a virginity test, but that before then, I had to tell him the truth about whether I was a virgin or not. He said it was okay if I was a virgin or if I wasn't one, but that if he found out I'd lied to him, I would be hurt real bad.

"Then he asked, 'Have you ever had sex? Has anyone ever entered inside you down there before?'

"I remember feeling like I was being strangled and couldn't breathe. I didn't know how to answer the question. Although I'd never had sexual intercourse with anyone, I wasn't sure if what Father Odiar had done to me was considered sex or not. Somehow I had the feeling that the answer I gave would determine whether I lived or not.

"'Answer the question!' the man yelled. I heard a girl scream somewhere in another room, followed by a loud slap. I frantically shook my head.

"He laughed and said, 'Okay then, we're gonna find out here soon, aren't we?' Then he left the room.

"A few minutes later, the door opened and shut. I immediately recognized the hint of perfume in the air. It was the kind my mother used to buy at the corner drugstore. For some reason, I was filled with a surge of hope. Although I knew it wasn't possible because I'd seen Mama's body in the casket at the funeral, in my mind it was Mama who'd just walked into the room. I was trembling, and she knelt down next to me. She whispered to me that we were the only ones in the room, and she was going to take the handkerchief off my mouth—but I mustn't scream.

"In a low whisper, she asked me my name. I told her. She said she was going to do a virginity test on me and that the test was simple and painless. She explained that the test was a common practice in some countries for women to be eligible for marriage or to qualify for certain jobs, such as policewomen. She asked me to be honest and tell her if I'd ever had sexual intercourse with anyone.

"I opened my mouth to answer her, but nothing came out. I began to cry. She put her arm around me; she seemed to know I was hiding something and asked me to tell her. I told her about what Father Odiar had done to me, that I didn't want to lie to her, and that I wasn't sure how to answer her question. She held my hand, and, for a moment, neither one of us said anything. I could tell she was crying and was trying to keep it from me.

"Then she cleared her throat and told me she was finished conducting the test and that I was still a virgin. She said if anyone asked me if she had conducted the test I must tell them yes or it would cost us our lives. I begged her to please help me. Her voice cracked as she told me that she would if she could, but that there was nothing she could do; my life was now in God's hands. This was what Mama used to say, and I began crying.

"The woman held both my hands and whispered close to my ear that the place they were taking me was like heaven compared to some of the places other girls went—and that the man who would own me was very powerful, rich, and extremely dangerous. She assured me he wouldn't hurt me as long as I remained a virgin. But the moment I lost my virginity he would kill me. She said the girl who went there before me made the mistake of talking to the gardener and was accused by her master of having sex with the man. The girl swore she hadn't had sex with anyone and that the two of them only spoke to each other on a few occasions.

"The woman said she was summoned to come to the mansion to conduct another virginity test on the girl and that her test showed that the girl was telling the truth. She was still a virgin. But the master wanted a second opinion and had a male doctor conduct the same test. The doctor determined the girl had lost her virginity. Both the girl and the gardener were never seen again.

"Footsteps were coming down the hall, and the woman placed the handkerchief back on my mouth. She kissed me on the forehead and recited a quick Hail Mary for me, a prayer Mama used to say every night. She quickly walked to the door, just as it opened. She told the man she'd finished with her test and that I was as pure as the driven snow.

"The man picked me up, carried me outside, and put me into a car. We drove for about an hour; when we stopped, he took me into this house.

"The first person I saw when the blindfold was taken off was Chopper, the owner of this mansion. His first words to me were, 'I'm your master now, and you belong to me. If you break my rules or try to escape, I will kill you myself.'

"Then he went over his rules. 'Number one, obey my orders without question or hesitation, or you will die. Number two, don't let anyone discover your existence here, or you will die. Number three, remain a virgin and always cover your entire body with the white clothing I've provided whenever you're outside of your bedroom, or you will die.'

"I remember completely breaking down at that point until his thunderous voice commanded me to shut up. To my surprise, I was able to do exactly as he said without hesitation."

Sara and Montana searched each other's eyes. Sara's were begging for her friend's acceptance after such a horrifying revelation, and Montana's were full of compassion, empathy, and determination to somehow save her friend from this madness.

"Now that I know why you always wear the veil over your face, do you mind if I ask you to lift it for me?" Montana asked.

Sara looked to the floor and then slowly lifted the veil.

"It's okay, Sara, you can look at me. There's nothing to be ashamed of."

Sara lifted her head to her friend and looked into her light brown eyes, and in them she found her heart.

Montana was awestruck. Sara's face seemed to radiate a soft glow of the purest light. She heard herself whisper, "My God, you're the most beautiful thing I've ever seen."

Sara's smiling cheeks turned red as she shyly averted her eyes from Montana's.

Suddenly Montana stood up and began pacing the room. Sara could see the anger etched across her face.

Montana stopped abruptly and turned to face Sara, "Has this son of a bitch ever...touched you, Sara?"

Sara was taken aback by Montana's sudden harsh tone and use of profanity. "Never. Sometimes he'll come into my room and sit on the chair or lie on the floor—usually for about thirty minutes, but sometimes for hours—and then he leaves without a word."

Montana cracked her knuckles and resumed pacing again. "And you've been dealing with this crap for over three years?"

"Yes. Please, Montana, I'm really scared for you. I'm afraid your involvement with me will cost you your life. I don't want you to end up like my mother."

"Ah horse crap, Sara. That ain't gonna happen. I'm not gonna let it. Don't you worry about a thing. I'm gonna figure something out, and we're gonna get you the hell outta this demonic nightmare!"

Sara stood up and stepped in front of Montana. "Please, I'm begging you! You don't understand. Chopper is a cold-blooded killer. I've heard him talking with his men. He's one of the biggest drug lords in this city. I've overheard them plan out the murders of people. He's even got the city police in his pocket. I've seen the police chief come here to drink all night and discuss business. You don't know what this man's capable of. I watched him kill my bird with his bare hands right in front of me."

Montana shook her head. "So he's an animal abuser, too, huh?"

Sara nodded. "They were parakeets. Chopper gave them to me after my first year here. Maybe it was his sick way of celebrating the anniversary date of my abduction. It didn't matter. I loved the birds as if they were my children. According to the *Encyclopedia Britannica*, the only reading material in the guest house, one bird was a male and the other a female. I remember how I would have to ration the birdseed because I never knew when Chopper would buy more. The three of us spent most of our days looking out my window at all those birds blessed with the gift of freedom. Whenever Chopper was out, I would prop the cage door open and allow my birds to come and go inside my room as they pleased. It was my gift of freedom to them.

"Then one day it happened—the day I stood too close to my window and was spotted by the pool maintenance man. Apparently, the man made the mistake of asking Chopper about me; he was never seen again. Chopper came bursting into the house, stomping his feet hard as he made his way up the stairs. I had a bad feeling, so I grabbed my birdcage, and we hid inside my closet.

"I remember trembling and trying to make my birds keep quiet, but they kept chirping. My bedroom door flew open. He must've heard my birds because he immediately opened my closet door. He yelled at me to get out of the closet and asked why I allowed myself to be seen through my window. I was so scared I couldn't speak and just stood there trembling.

"He snatched the cage from my hand. He reached in and grabbed my female bird. He closed the cage and flung it back at me, hard. I managed to catch the cage, but the male bird had injured his leg and was hobbling around on the bottom. Chopper held the bird with her little head sticking out from the top of his fist.

"My terrified bird chirped loudly and desperately bit his finger. I dropped to my knees, crying hysterically and begging him not to hurt her. I swore I would be really good and never go near my window again. I remember the cold look he gave me. He seemed to be enjoying the moment, and a sadistic smile crept across his pale, pockmarked face.

"I set the cage on the floor and held my hands together in prayer, begging him to please let my bird go free. Then I watched in horror as his fat fingers began to slowly squeeze. Like a balloon with a hole in it, air began leaving my bird's lungs. She eventually stopped chirping. I watched helplessly as her tiny beak quivered silently. I couldn't bear it any longer and lunged at him, but I was met with his large boot slamming into my chest, throwing me backward.

"All the air seemed to vanish from the room as my bird and I struggled to breathe. I got back to my knees and tried to beg him to have mercy for my bird, but the words wouldn't come out. I remember vividly the blood seeping out of my bird's gaping beak and how her eyes bulged outward. I knew that hope was lost for her...and I couldn't take watching any longer. I grabbed the cage and fell to the floor. I balled up into the fetal position, clutching the cage tightly to my stomach. I wanted to cry for the friend I'd just lost, but the tears never came. I could hear Chopper laughing and then the sound of my lifeless bird falling to the cold floor.

"As soon as he left the room, I ran to the window and opened it. I reached inside the cage and gently took my wounded bird out. I told him this was his only chance at life and how sorry I was. I kissed him on the head, held him out past the steel bars, and tossed him into the air. He instinctively flapped his little wings and then disappeared into the trees. I swore to myself right then that I'd never curse another soul by allowing it to come into my life."

Montana sat down. She had a better understanding now of why Sara was so gripped with utter fear of ever defying her captor. "I know this ain't gonna be easy, Sara, and we'll have to be real careful and patient and smart about it. But I also know that, together, we can do this—we *have* to do this."

Just then Sara and Montana noticed something outside the window. It clung against the glass on top of the windowpane. They walked over to it and kneeled down. It was a bright red butterfly. It seemed to be watching them as intently as they were watching it. They were mesmerized by its beauty and the brilliant colors. "Are those small eyes on its wings?" Sara asked.

Montana shook her head. "Don't know—I've never seen a butterfly like this before."

Sara carefully reached out her hand and placed the tip of her index finger gently against the glass directly over the butterfly. It didn't move. She looked to Montana with the giddy smile of a child. Montana slowly reached out and placed her index finger right next to Sara's. Immediately the butterfly began to flap its wings in a rhythmic pulse—up fast, down slow, up fast, down slow. Sara and Montana felt the pulse of their heartbeats in the tips of their fingers move as one with the butterfly—up fast, down slow, up fast, down slow.

The three souls gazed into one another's eyes. Then, with a flick of the wings, the red butterfly lifted off the glass, gave the women one last glance, and floated toward the heavens.

CHAPTER 4

HARD CHOICES

———◆———

KIWI'S NATIVE AMERICAN GRANT MONEY ran out after her second year in college. Although she had a 4.0 GPA and was excelling in every course, the university denied her applications for financial assistance. She was sure it had something to do with her rejections of the school dean's advances toward her.

She was already working nights as a waitress during the school year and two jobs in the summer, but the tuition was still more than what she could afford. For the first time since leaving the rez, she felt a gloominess begin to envelop her.

Then it happened; the first link in the subsequent chain of events unfolded. One summer night while waitressing at a small diner, a strikingly handsome, middle-aged gentleman approached her, carrying a briefcase and wearing what appeared to be an expensive suit. He had a British accent and introduced himself as Lawrence Richard Gold. He began by addressing Kiwi by her name, which was odd to her because she'd forgotten to wear her nametag that night. He complimented her on her "extraordinary exotic beauty and hypnotizing green eyes."

She'd grown accustomed to these types of flirts and come-ons, but, needing the tip money, she played along with his game. What was different this time, though, was that he didn't seem to be interested in a relationship or sex like the others were. He had a professional, businesslike manner. He asked whether she ever considered a career in the companionship business.

Exposing her naïveté, she joked, "Sure, if it pays well enough to put me through school without breaking my back in the process."

He seemed to sense her innocence and looked at her with the sweet smile you'd expect from a caring friend instead of a total stranger. He asked how old she was. "Nineteen," she told him. He explained that her work would involve catering to society's highest elite—men with great power and influence.

"They're the movers and shakers," he said. "They're the billion-dollar business owners, world leaders, royalty, and high-ranking politicians. They're the people who have the world by the gonads. Simply put, they're the people who have more money than they could possibly spend in a lifetime."

Kiwi caught on as images of a filthy, venereal-disease-infested brothel entered her mind. She promptly thanked him for the offer and told him he was definitely wasting his time with her. He smiled, asking her if making five thousand dollars a day—tax free—might help with college expenses. She began to walk away in disgust, but then she turned around to face him.

"You should be ashamed of yourself. The desecration of one's soul through the violation of one's body is in itself a terrible travesty, but it pales by far in comparison to the low-life scum unbefitting to be classified as human, who prey upon the hungry, weak-minded, and poor in spirit."

Kiwi was surprised at her uncharacteristic boldness. Her face felt hot as she quickly left the counter to wipe off an already clean table at the other end of the room.

The man seemed pleasantly amused. He sat down at the counter and continued sipping his coffee. It was obvious he wasn't giving up easily, so she spent as much time as she could away from the counter. Eventually, she had to return to make a fresh pot of coffee. When she did, he apologized for his "presumptuous demeanor and lack of tact, resulting in offending what clearly is a lovely and intelligent woman."

Is this guy for real? she wondered. He sounded sincere, so she accepted the apology. He sat in silence, sipping his cup as she made more. She felt bad for snapping at him and asked if he'd like a refill. He gratefully accepted.

Then he said, "I know this might be hard to believe, but I honestly agree with everything you just said. It appears the more I experience through my many travels around this little planet of ours, the more I confirm what my mother told me when I was a boy."

Kiwi's interest sparked, and she gave him a playful wink. "Mothers know best, right?"

He smiled and lifted his coffee cup, gesturing a toast.

"So what was your mother right about?" she asked.

"Well, as far back as I can remember, Mother would tell me our world was grossly out of balance. She said it was obvious to most intelligent and reasonable people that men and women completely depend on one another for the survival of their species. If suddenly all women were to fall dead this very moment, how long would men exist before the human race was completely extinct?"

She found the question fascinating and poured herself a cup of coffee in eager anticipation of the answer.

Mr. Gold continued. "My mother told me that some so-called experts had estimated that in the best-case scenario, the human race would continue for approximately another century, give or take a few years. However, she concluded, if you were to study what the great philosophers and spiritual leaders have taught, you'd know that both man and woman together make what we call a human being—the Yin and Yang, the sun and moon, if you will. In the absence of one, the other doesn't exist. Thus, the human race would instantaneously be nonexistent.

"Mother said this was because the human was the physical part of the being, and the being was the spiritual part of the human. This, she said, was an immutable law of the universe and, just like with other universal laws such as gravity and electricity, it benefitted us greatly when we were in harmony with it. If we weren't, it simply destroyed us without prejudice. So, Mother concluded, until both men and women evolved to the point of realizing this universal law and treated one another as equals, our planet would remain out of balance, and there would be no end to pain, suffering, and war."

Kiwi was taken aback. This was not what she expected to hear from a man she just chastised a few minutes ago for being what she thought was a male chauvinist pig. She felt bad.

"You see," he continued, "it began with women who empowered themselves. The movement had begun through protests, marches, and such, but sometimes the most effective and efficient way to move from point A to point B was directly through the source of power. This could be accomplished by gaining the ear of the person who holds that power. Throughout history, every great male leader, innovator, and visionary had behind him, in some way, shape, or form, the 'equal half of his whole.' If this were not so, the universe wouldn't have allowed any significant progress in the evolution of humankind. Of course, the equal half of the whole was a woman, but not just any woman. These women were also extraordinary leaders, innovators, and visionaries, perhaps even more so than the powerful men they counseled."

He took another sip from his cup and looked straight into Kiwi's eyes. "If you don't mind me saying so, I believe you could be one of these extraordinary women my mother spoke of."

There was only one other customer in the restaurant, so she decided to humor him, staying a bit longer to listen. "And what makes you so certain of this?" she asked.

He held out his cup for a refill. "Just an educated guess, you might say. Would you like to know more?"

She took a deep breath. "Who could say no to someone with such a lovely and intelligent mother?"

He smiled and thanked her for her kind words. "Kiwi, the work I was referring to involves your heart, spirit, and mind, not your body. I admit that physical beauty helps, but it's inner beauty that is paramount in this particular line of work."

He explained that the work didn't involve any type of nudity or physical interaction whatsoever. In fact, physical intimacy between client and employee was not only discouraged, but was grounds for permanent dismissal from the company for both parties.

"So exactly what do your employees do?" she asked, somewhat facetiously. "Give me an example of a typical day at work."

He chuckled, explaining that a typical "social meeting" involved an engagement with a client at a social event or public location, such as a party, wedding, or ceremony. It was always in a social environment with other people present—never alone.

"The location of this meeting may be anywhere in the world," he said. "If travel by plane is required, you'll be taken by our company jet. Upon arrival, you'll be met with a chauffeur and limousine. Everything is first class, no expenses spared. You'll never travel anywhere alone. A company chaperone must be within your sight at all times. This chaperone will serve as your intermediary and personal bodyguard. If you're required to stay overnight, the company will arrange top-class hotel accommodations.

"While you're with the client, you'll simply be his or her 'close acquaintance,' so to speak. You'll simply be friendly and sociable, doing things such as making small talk and exchanging pleasantries, that sort of thing."

"So, in other words, I'd be an arm ornament or trophy," Kiwi chided.

He grinned. "Well, you can choose to look at it that way. But remember that our clients are considered the world's most elite. To them, pretty faces are a dime a dozen. It's your mind, your grace, your inner beauty that they're most interested in and pay lavishly for."

"When you return from your social meeting, you'll be paid in cash or any other method you choose."

There was a moment of silence before she asked, "And what jet plane will fly me to and from work? I attend college here."

He quickly replied, "Mine." Then added, "You'd only work during the summer. And in that one summer, you could earn enough to pay all of your college expenses in advance."

Kiwi was shocked, then skeptical. "You're not serious."

"We wouldn't be having this conversation if I weren't," he replied.

The only other customer in the café was finished with his meal. He put money on the table, told her to keep the change, and left.

Kiwi thanked the customer and began cleaning the table.

The man watched her perform her duties. He could tell that she was deep in thought.

When she was finished she walked back to the counter next to the man. "I'm not so sure about all this; I'll have to think it over," she told him. He said he understood and offered her his card. He said he was leaving for Vegas in two days, and if she wanted, she could go with him to kind of check things out for herself.

"A trip to Vegas sounds exciting," she began, "but I definitely can't afford to take off work, let alone pay for the expenses."

He replied, in a businesslike manner, "All expenses are covered by the company, and lost wages will be paid in full."

Kiwi just stared blankly at him for a long while.

"So, what do you say?" he asked. There was no reply.

He sensed a certain fear in her he couldn't quite put his finger on and decided to change the subject to take the pressure off. "Have you ever heard of the Golden Ratio, Kiwi? It's the numbers 1.618, also referred to as Phi."

Kiwi gave him a perplexed look. "No, math's always been my nemesis. Why, what in the world is the Golden Ratio?"

"Well, according to legend, the Greek philosopher and mathematician Pythagoras discovered the concept sometime between 570 BC and 495 BC. It's considered one of the most mysterious and fascinating discoveries in the world. Some believe it's the universe's secret formula for beauty and perfection. It can be derived through mathematics and geometry, and it appears in plants, animals, DNA, the solar system, art and architecture, music, population growth, the stock market, and…the human body. And, I believe it's literally written all over *your* face."

A skeptical chuckle escaped Kiwi's mouth. "I'm sorry, Mr. Gold, but I really do have to compliment you on your originality and persistence.

I mean no offense, but you don't expect me to actually believe all that do you?"

"None taken, and yes I do expect you to believe it because it's true and I can prove it." The man opened his briefcase and pulled out some sort of measuring tool. "This is a Golden Ratio caliper. With it I can measure the distance between your eyes, nose, lips, and other points on your face to confirm whether or not you've been blessed with the universe's gift—the Golden Ratio. Would you mind if we have a quick peek at your beautiful face?"

Kiwi was taken aback; it all seemed to be happening so quickly, but he did spark her curiosity. *Who wouldn't want to know if they've got this "Golden Ratio thing"?* she thought. "Well, I guess it wouldn't hurt, considering you're the only customer right now and my manager has already left for the night."

"Excellent," he replied. He explained how the simple measuring device worked and asked Kiwi to stand in front of him.

The heavyset cook watched curiously through the open kitchen window.

Kiwi looked into the hand mirror he'd given her and watched as he measured certain points on her face. He explained exactly what he was doing as he went along. She couldn't help but feel like some sort of science specimen and found it hard to take him seriously.

"Relax your facial muscles, try not to smile," he said. He measured the width and length of her eyes, nose, lips, ears, chin, cheekbones, and forehead. Then he measured the angle and distances between these facial features in relation to one another. He asked her to open her mouth and even measured her teeth. "Ah-ha, okay, lift your chin, turn your head, and…we're done."

Kiwi chewed on her nails as the man put his measuring tool back into the briefcase, closed it, and turned to her.

"Well, what's the verdict, doc? Am I golden or not?" she joked.

He looked into her eyes with a seriousness not yet revealed, and then an immense smile spread across his face. "Ninety-nine point ninety-nine percent. I've taken hundreds of measurements all over the world. The measurement I took just now was honestly the nearest to the Golden Ratio I've ever seen. Hell, I don't know; maybe it was perfect but my hands were shaking so badly toward the end. Without question, Kiwi, the universe has blessed you."

Kiwi was speechless. Her stomach felt queasy. The words of the elders echoed over and over in her mind, "Poor child, she has the curse of beauty."

"Are you all right, Kiwi?" he asked.

"Yes, sorry—just a bit dizzy. Well, that's good news, I suppose. I really appreciate your offer, Mr. Gold, but it's a big decision to make, so will it be okay if I sleep on it and let you know in the morning?"

"Of course, sweetie. Just think it over and call me by this time tomorrow. Oh, and by the way, I wasn't kidding. We'll be traveling in *my* private jet." The mysterious man smiled as he dropped a hundred-dollar bill for his coffee on the counter, then left.

Kiwi's head was spinning all night. *Should I do this?* she thought. *What if my family finds out? There isn't really anything bad about the work, is there? It seems to be an honorable service, or is it? Mr. Gold seemed like a trustworthy person. I like him.*

College paid for in one summer? she pondered some more. *That would be a major stressor off my back!*

Kiwi unconsciously placed her hand at the nape of her neck and rubbed gently. It was what she did whenever she was undecided about something important; she believed it somehow summoned the help of her Me'me' and mother. I guess it wouldn't hurt to check it out. If after I see it in person I don't feel comfortable, I'll chalk it up as a learning experience and come back to working my butt off to pay for school. I'll call Mr. Gold tomorrow. I'm going to Las Vegas!"

CHAPTER 5

VOYAGE INTO EXILE

———◆———

UKKO SAT LOTUS-STYLE ON THE swaying deck of the enormous freighter. He was basking in the pouring rain as curious onlookers watched from windows and any overhead cover they could get under. Ukko loved the rain and had always felt a spiritual connection with it. It seemed to be the only thing capable of cleansing his troubled spirit. He looked to the sky, consumed by the cool soft liquid washing over his face. *Ah…rain from the heavens*, he thought. *You are my only lover now, and the only thing I count on for hope.*

As lightning streaked across the sky he recalled the reason his father, the one inaccessible enigma in his life, had named him Ukko, though it was not a Japanese name. His father's simple explanation was that in Finnish mythology Ukko was the thunder god, in charge of storms, lightning, and the harvest. The real reason had always been a mystery to his family and its secret went down with Ukko's father and the battleship he captained during world war two.

Somehow deep down he'd always known this day would come—that he'd do the unthinkable and leave his beloved homeland. He just hadn't known how, or why, or when it would happen. Ever since he was a boy, he'd had daydreams of a different world, a different life, a different purpose. Often a voice would whisper to him from the far reaches of his mind, luring him, seducing him. Or was it warning him? The voice was always comforting and seemed to him to be that of a child.

His mind drifted back to recent events. The killing of the Russian agent wasn't something the ultra-secret and virtually invisible Coded Files Department, or CFD, of the CIA could just ignore.

The CFD had been shrouded in myth and mystery since its conception. It was believed that the CIA had CFD cells on every continent in the world. It was said that these agents were a hybrid of ninja, samurai, and commando, and also scholars of ancient philosophy. They were considered to be warriors of the highest class, the perfect killing machines, and instilled fear in the hearts of their enemies. Some said that they had been stripped of the fear of death.

It was rumored that the qualification, selection, and indoctrination process was so secretive that the mere mention of it would put one in mortal danger. Still, rumors fly, and it was said that the candidates were carefully selected based primarily on the suffering they had endured in their lives. He or she had to have been between the ages of fourteen and seventeen, and have had a certain level of loathing that bordered on— but hadn't crossed over to—pure hatred for evil. This usually meant that the candidates had experienced some sort of tragedy in their lives so great that they had suffered the death of their mind, and only the body and spirit remained. This was important because the founders of the CFD believed that humanity's greatest affliction was when the spirit was displaced by the mind, the result being that the body became a tool for evil instead of good. In order to "reprogram" the mind, it first had to be wiped clean of its preconditioned thoughts.

It was said that there were three "gates," over a period of six years, through which a candidate had to successfully navigate in order to become a Ghost Assassin. It was believed that 99.9 percent would fail or die in the attempt.

The first gate, lasting one year, consisted of the complete and total breakdown of the physical body, followed by its resurrection. Candidates were continuously put through a gauntlet of forced marches, grueling runs, mountain climbs, and death-defying obstacle courses, all while enduring food and sleep deprivation. Only 1 percent of the group would succeed and advance to the next level.

The second gate required three years of arduous training in the skills of combat, mental toughness, and spiritual awareness. Early each morning the candidate went into deep mediation for an hour, followed by studies in ancient philosophy—the *Tao Te Ching,* Sun Tzu's *The Art of War*—and the seven virtues of Bushido. *Bushido* means "the way of the warrior" and is a Japanese word for the way of the samurai life. Afternoons were dedicated to grueling lessons in mixed martial arts, weapons, and tactics. At the end of each day, when the candidate's brain was at its lowest mental capacity, he or she was hooked up to state-of-the-art brain imaging machines to analyze and evaluate the quality of their cognitive functioning.

Candidates were also required to master the soroban, a Japanese modification of the Chinese abacus. After three years of practice, the candidate was required to mentally calculate mathematical equations consisting of ten to fourteen digits quicker than that of a person using an electronic calculator. For example, an instructor would read off the following numbers as fast as he could, *39,261,475,329 minus 8,149,382,075,963 plus 77,554,411,281,846 minus 2,397,886,498 plus 651,849,732,315.* The candidate was to mentally imagine a soroban so as to calculate the problem while the instructor read the numbers, and then provides the correct answer of 70,093,742,527,029 within six seconds after the final number is read. Another example the instructor read off was *963,712 multiplied by 59,738.* The candidate was required to provide the correct answer of 57,570,227,456 within three seconds; this was equivalent to approximately thirty separate calculations per second.

Only when a candidate mastered the power of the brain as well as achieved a balance between animal instincts and human compassion could he or she enter the "Crucible of Dark and Light." This test was a requirement in order to qualify for admittance into the third gate. The candidate was locked in a caged pit and endured six hours of hand-to-hand combat with Ghost Assassin instructors. The only rest was the five-minute intervals between instructor rotations, which occurred every thirty minutes. Most candidates did not last more than two hours. It was said that this is where candidates wielding only physical and mental strength will fail. Only candidates with extraordinary transcendental spirit *and* superior mental and physical strength could endure such suffering. And only 1 percent of the 1 percent was successful.

The final gate was believed to be where almost all of the few remaining candidates would go to die. Over a two-year period, the candidate served as an apprentice to Ghost Assassin agents. The candidate was required to shadow these agents on twelve real-world missions. It was rumored that if the candidate faltered in courage, discipline, or skill, they might be "decoded" by their own mentor, their body cremated and disposed of. Successfully completing twelve missions did not guarantee admittance. At the end of the gate, there was a vote by every Ghost Assassin agent who'd trained and served on missions with the candidate. If the candidate received a majority "thumbs down," they were immediately "decoded." If it was a majority "thumbs up," there was an initiation ceremony so secretive and bizarre that the only rumor about it was that it was a "bloody rebirth."

Less than 1 percent of 1 percent of the 1 percent graduated and became "encoded" into the life-long brotherhood of the Ghost Assassins. The elite membership was said to be permanent; there was only one way out.

Although many female candidates had met prequalification requirements and volunteered, only one had ever made it past the first gate. She went on to successfully complete the course and, like Ukko, was the only other candidate to receive a unanimous thumbs-up vote. She had acquired the code name Silver Lioness because of the silver kimonos she wore and the ferociousness of her fighting.

Legend had it she was as beautiful as she was deadly and was a descendant of the great Viking Rollo, the first ruler of Normandy. She also had coursing through her veins the blood of Hervor, the famous and fearless Viking warrior woman. Although highly skilled in many weapons of combat, her weapon of choice were the crossbow and the Gurkha blade, a Nepalese knife with an inwardly curved blade. Like Ukko, she was extremely reclusive, but it wasn't long before she fell deeply in love with the mysterious Satan's Samurai. They'd served on several covert missions together, and each was highly impressed with the other's unsurpassed skills and poise.

They say that Silver Lioness owed her life to Ukko, because he had risked his life to save hers. She had been tracking a vicious warlord in the Congo rain forest. The covert mission involved terminating the evil man because of his crimes against humanity, including murder, rape, sexual slavery, pillaging, and conscripting child soldiers. She had silently slit the mass murderer's throat one night when he went into the jungle to defecate. During the exfiltration she had been hunted by wild dogs in the night and inadvertently fell into a camouflaged pit used by the locals for trapping boars.

Ukko immediately volunteered for the rescue mission and had infiltrated the area of operation and moved to her last known location. The pit was empty except for the Wolf's Cross pendent she always wore to protect her in battle. It had apparently been ripped from her necklace by one of the pongee sticks. A splotch of blood had saturated the dark fertile soil in the corner of the pit.

Because she had been unconscious, Silver Lioness wasn't able to swallow her cyanide pill before her captors had arrived. She was bound and tied and taken to the warlord's headquarters. The warlord's brother had taken over command and became infatuated with her beauty, strength, and courage. He ordered his men not to harm her and had planned to make her one of his concubines for the purpose of bearing him a son. He was to rape her later that night.

Silver Lioness fought gallantly. Even with her hands tied in front of her and puncture wounds on her legs, she managed to kill one man and seriously injure three more. Eventually she was overcome by sheer numbers and was strapped down on top of a large wooden table. The new warlord entered the grass hut in the dark of night to feast on his prize. She stared up at the ceiling, depleted of all hope, as the monster stood over her. She swore that with the first opportunity she would have the man's head on a spike. Suddenly she noticed a black object suspended from the ceiling directly above the warlord. The light from the torches danced off the object's subdued black facemask, and she knew Ukko had come for her.

The tanto, a samurai dagger, exploded through the warlord's chest as death from above fell upon him. Within hours they were safe aboard a UH-1 Huey military helicopter.

Silver Lioness had withheld a secret from Ukko, which was that her birth name was Akka. She had always wondered if he knew that their destinies were intertwined and written in the stars; that according to Finnish mythology Akka, the Earth goddess was the wife of Ukko, the thunder god. She never made known to Ukko her feelings for him. She knew all too well his unyielding love for his deceased fiancée and the eternal loyalty he had for her. Still, she was determined to keep him in her heart and believed that some day they would be lovers, in this life or the next.

Ukko's superiors had come to the conclusion that the killing of the rogue Russian agent was justified, and perhaps even necessary under such brutal circumstances. Although known by their enemies as being *the* dream team of assassins, they were not heartless and certainly not in the business of murdering innocent children.

Still, because of political pressures outside their control, the CFD had to maintain protocol and administer some form of disciplinary action. So it was reluctantly decided that they would relieve their most effective and trusted agent of his duties and destroy all record of his existence with the organization. They would also have to fabricate his death and create a new identity and life for him in America. Only in the United States could the CFD of the CIA adequately protect him from those who would certainly seek retribution.

More importantly, it was the only way to monitor Ukko's actions in case he, too, went rogue and decided to divulge information about their ultra-secret organization and its not-so-politically-correct activities.

Ukko had immediately objected. "How could I be at peace knowing I'm living in the very country responsible for the murder of my entire family?" he argued. He assured his superiors he'd take care of their problem promptly that night. He'd rather preserve his honor and family name by committing seppuku.

Ukko's American superiors weren't accustomed to such extreme dedication to duty and family honor. They knew that, with this most unusual man, it wasn't a bluff. He would do exactly as he said, and any attempts to dissuade him would be futile. When they asked him why he would be willing to kill himself instead of starting a new life in another country, Ukko replied, "In truth, I died in Nagasaki in 1945 along with my fiancée, mother, and sister. There's nothing more to live for in this life."

The CIA assigned two CFD agents to shadow Ukko to the location in which the samurai suicide ritual was to take place. This was extremely rare, as the CIA could not afford to risk losing so many prized weapons such as the Ghost Assassins by placing them all in one location together. Still, this was an unusual situation for an unusual comrade, so the decision had been made.

Fortunately, one of the agents was also of samurai descent, and although his lineage was of a much lower rank than Ukko, he was very good with a sword and qualified for the honor of acting as Ukko's second.

He was prepared to behead his comrade quickly and cleanly after Ukko sliced open his stomach, disemboweling himself.

The second's code name was Tasmanian Tiger, and Ukko had an especially close bond with the man. Tasmanian Tiger had saved his life when he was a CFD candidate on his seventh mission in gate three. Ukko returned the favor two years later as a Ghost Assassin when he ran back into a hail of enemy fire to retrieve the Tasmanian Tiger's bullet-riddled body. Ukko was shot in the arm and leg during the extraction, but both men survived.

They had become best friends and confided in each other about their dark past. Tasmanian Tiger knew of Ukko's broken heart over the loss of his family and fiancée. Ukko knew of Tasmanian Tiger's resentment about the fact that he had always been considered a half-breed by the samurai community and, worse, his own family. His father was a well-respected Japanese with good samurai lineage. His mother was Australian, and he had been born in Sydney. The prejudice Tasmanian Tiger endured most of his life was too much to bear, and one day, at age fifteen, he ran away and swore never to return. Soon after, he found himself in a secret CFD compound attempting to achieve the unthinkable.

Ironically, Tasmanian Tiger was madly in love with Silver Lioness, and although she liked him very much and respected his skills, her heart belonged to Ukko. After many failed attempts by Tasmanian Tiger to win her love, she finally divulged to him that she was in love with Ukko and made it clear that there could never be another man in her life.

A bone-chilling breeze wisped down the mountainside, washing over the ritual site at the edge of the cliff. The air was permeated with the sweet fragrance of falling plum blossoms, a sign that it was midwinter with the promise of spring. The sun was well past its zenith, bidding its farewell as it began to dip below the dark silhouette of snowcapped mountains.

One of the agents was stationed midway down the mountain, respectfully observing the solemn event. Ukko sat on a white bamboo mat. His white kimono blended into the backdrop of the thick snow. A screech from a falcon circling high above pulled Ukko out of his meditative state. With slow, deliberate movements, he removed a piece of mulberry paper from a leather case and laid it before him. Then he reached down and picked up a goose-quill ink pen and bottle of black ink. With it, he wrote his death poem: "*When there are no dark clouds within, the world without is reborn.*"

He bowed low to the words and then placed the paper back into the leather case. He stared at his katana and wakizashi laid out before him. Slowly, he repositioned himself on his knees so as to sit on his heels. He then opened his kimono, exposing his rippled stomach. He picked up the wakizashi, unsheathed it from its scabbard, and wrapped the midsection of the blade in a white towel. Then he turned the sword toward his stomach and held it with both hands, the tip only inches from his skin.

Tasmanian Tiger, also dressed in a white kimono, stood behind Ukko with his katana held high above his head. He positioned himself in the optimum position to speed his friend off into the great void.

A thick clump of wet snow drifted down, landing near the tip of the sword in Ukko's hands. He watched in reverence as the snowflake changed form from solid to liquid and then dripped off the razor-sharp edge. He thought of his fiancée. *Don't cry for me, my darling. We will soon be in each other's arms.* He clenched his fingers around the towel-wrapped portion of the blade, stared straight ahead into nothingness, and said good-bye.

Nothing happened. One minute passed, then two, but Ukko sat motionless, the tip of the sword had nicked his skin and was now only millimeters away from his tight muscles. A small amount of blood had run along the length of the blade and dripped onto the mat.

Behind Ukko, Tasmanian Tiger's arms began to twitch and quiver from the weight of the raised katana. *What's he waiting for?* The agent wondered. *This should've been over by now. I can't hold this position much longer. Is it possible the great Satan's Samurai has changed his mind?* Beads of sweat ran profusely down the faces of both men.

First Ukko heard it, a sound like the flapping of wings, thousands, millions—no, billions—of tiny wings flapping together in unison. Then he saw before him a single cloud in the sky that began to turn different shades of red. The cloud grew bigger and bigger, and the low humming sound grew louder. The cloud and the sound were coming straight toward him.

His mind was racing. *What is this? Why is this happening?* Something descended from the cloud and landed on his hand. Moving only his eyes, he looked down to marvel at the object. It was a beautiful red butterfly!

Little sister used to love butterflies.

This butterfly was like nothing Ukko had ever seen before. Its wings were elegant yet large and powerful; the patterns on them were mesmerizing.

How incredibly beautiful the afterlife is, he thought. Suddenly, he noticed a few of the patterns on the butterfly's wings stand out to him. He stared at them in awe, until it struck him like lightning. They were the eyes of his mother, sister, and fiancée!

The red butterfly slowly flapped her silky wings. Her eyes were the greenest green and bore straight into his soul. Then he heard that familiar soothing child's voice in his mind: *Come to me, to the land far, far away. There is where you will help save humanity.*

The butterfly floated away and disappeared into the massive red cloud above. Ukko closed his eyes. When he opened them, he saw a shivering white ghost standing before him with its head bowed low.

"Is everything okay?" the ghost asked. "Is there anything you wish for me to do?"

Finally realizing the ghost was Tasmanian Tiger, Ukko slowly lowered his aching arms. It took a while to unclench his stiff fingers from the sword. It felt to him as if an eternity had passed by, that he was somehow transported somewhere distant yet deep within. Many lifetimes came and went, and then, against his will, he was persuaded to return to this one.

"I must go to America," he whispered.

Tasmanian Tiger helped Ukko down the mountain. He gave orders to the other agent to take Ukko back to the compound in one of the two vehicles they'd driven there, while he returned to sterilize the site. Tasmanian Tiger watched as the car drove off. He reached into his kimono and pulled out an empty glass vial. Carefully he collected drops of Ukko's blood still beaded on the surface of the bamboo mat. He stood, slid the vial into his pocket, and stared out over the cliff as the last rays of sunlight disappeared.

Two days later, Ukko was notified that Tasmanian Tiger had never returned from a covert mission somewhere in Northern China. They said that his microchip transponder implant had simply disappeared off the radar. It was as if he had suddenly vanished off the face of the planet. Silver Lioness volunteered for the search and rescue mission. She, too, fell off the radar and never returned.

The clouds had dispersed, and the sun was now low on the horizon. The ship was motionless, as if it were cemented inside the think humid air. Ukko stood and stretched his legs. Soon he would go below and eat a small meal of rice, fish, and pickled cabbage. Then he would retire for the night on the straw mat in the corner of the small room.

As Ukko lay studying his Japanese-to-English dictionary, he became transfixed on a black-and-white photo of a Japanese girl. She stood on a massive concrete dock with the Statue of Liberty behind her. The girl looked remarkably like his fiancée. Ukko felt a pang in his heart, and old feelings began to surface. For years, the anger and resentment had festered inside of him. They had eaten away at his heart until it was full of holes. There was no hiding the fact that he felt betrayed by the country he loved. It was their fault his mother, sister, and the love of his life had perished in the fires of hell on that August day in 1945. Unlike his father, who had died going down with the battleship he had captained, they had been innocent.

What possessed our so-called divine emperor to ally with a sadistic demon such as Hitler? This evil act sealed the horrific fate of the Japanese people! What convinced our so-called military leaders to believe they could just march into the lands of their neighbors and steal their possessions, their lives, their innocence? Cowardly thieves, all of them!

The majority of the Japanese people, including himself, had believed in the lies and propaganda force-fed to them by their leaders. They took the bait, that it was an absolute necessity for the Japanese people to sacrifice their ethical values and their lives for the honor of defending their homeland against what was labeled "mortal enemies." The few commoners and business owners who had questioned the morality of the Japanese military's actions in such matters as the massacre in China, also known as "The Rape of Nanking", were labeled traitors and swiftly disposed of by Kempeitai, the Japanese secret police akin to Nazi Germany's Gestapo.

The glory-lusting generals and admirals had raised their cursed swords in rhythm with the beat of the war drums and had declared "war necessary for the peace and honor of Japan," and the people had cheered in agreement.

Later, when these cowards were alone in their lavish offices, they toasted themselves for their excellent acting and salesmanship, resulting in the duping of so many ignorant people. The purpose was so that their own legacies would live on in the history books forever. *Yes,* Ukko thought. *You threw us all to the wolves. But I will return, leading the pack…*

But then, Ukko contemplated, *hasn't this same tragic story been written and played out ever since the first man picked up a stick or stone, realizing he could get what wasn't rightfully his by causing pain to another with his weapon? Is it true what Plato said, that "Only the dead have seen the end of war?"*

Ukko walked out onto the deck to get fresh air. He watched a group of young women huddled near the stairwell. It reminded him of the images he saw in newspapers of the so-called comfort women. Again, his blood began to boil. He remembered when he had first found out about the atrocities. It was unfathomable to him how the Imperial Japanese Army could commit such an egregious crime against women during the wars, forcing thousands, maybe hundreds of thousands, of women and children into sexual slavery. These women were either abducted from their homes or lured with promises of work in factories or other legitimate establishments. They were then incarcerated in "comfort stations" throughout Japanese-occupied territories and used as sex slaves for the soldiers.

Ukko knew the first comfort station had been in Japan. He considered all those women from so many countries, including Korea, China, the Philippines, Burma, Thailand, Vietnam, Malaysia, Taiwan, Indonesia, East Timor, New Guinea, Hong Kong, Macau, French Indochina, the Netherlands, and Australia.

The fate of those poor innocent women and children could've easily befallen upon Mother, my beloved Aiko and baby sister Chouko. The thought made him sick to his stomach. He swore to himself that, in honor of the women in his family, he would stand up and die if need be for all enslaved women of the world.

How on earth could these so-called men ever think such unspeakable crimes would go unpunished? Ukko pondered. *That the heavens wouldn't somehow know? That their own consciousness wouldn't betray them and tell all to the universe?*

Unfortunately, many thousands of good, innocent Japanese citizens had to pay the ultimate price for the selfish and cruel actions of an arrogant few.

What Ukko couldn't begin to comprehend was that, after the first bomb was dropped on Hiroshima, killing an unspeakable number of people, the grossly incompetent, arrogant, and heartless leaders of his country had waited until after the second bomb was dropped on Nagasaki three days later, killing thousands more, before swallowing their pride and admitting defeat. Ukko's entire family had been taken from him in one fell swoop in the second bombing.

Had he not been hundreds of miles away from Nagasaki that day training with the Japanese Olympic judo team, he, too, would've been killed—a fact for which he would never forgive himself.

CHAPTER 6

ESCAPE

THE PLAN WAS NERVE-RACKINGLY SIMPLE:

1. Pack bag.
2. Wait until Chopper left.
3. Get in car and drive.

Montana knew exactly where they would go—an abandoned farmhouse in the country. The house belonged to the deceased parents of her previous boss and was 122 miles away. She'd been given permission to stay there as long as she needed to. They would have well water but no electricity and would have to make do with using an outhouse.

The thought of escape was almost incomprehensible to Sara. It had hardly been thirty-six hours since she had revealed her predicament to Montana; yet in just a few minutes, she would be free. Montana had refused to wait one minute longer than necessary, because the situation was highly combustible and anything could happen to Sara at any time. She could be moved to a different location, sold to someone else, or even killed.

Sara was overjoyed with the prospect of freedom, but the thought of being caught paralyzed her with fear. Montana reassured her as best she could and emphasized that, for the remaining time she was there, she would have to act as normally as possible so Chopper wouldn't suspect anything.

Sara decided to stay out of his sight as much as possible. She prayed that he wouldn't come into her room or try to talk to her. She knew she'd always been a terrible liar and was terrified that if Chopper just so happened to ask her if she was planning to escape, she'd probably break down and cry. Then he'd know something was up and everything would be ruined.

Their plan was to live in the farmhouse for a couple of months until Montana could save up some money working at her old job. They decided they'd head west, eventually making their way to the state of Montana to live out their lives together. Their dream was to raise horses and have a big ranch by the Missouri River near the town of Fort Benton. It was where Montana's father had been born and raised—and where her imagination took her as a child whenever her dad told her stories of his upbringing in Big Sky country.

Although she'd never been there, her father had told her the name of the place he loved more than any other. Her parents' dream had been to return someday and raise a family in her father's hometown. A tragic car accident ended that dream when she was ten. Suddenly without parents, she had gone to live with her aunt.

Montana's mother and aunt had been hardworking immigrants from Mexico, and her father was German and had served honorably in the US Army. Her mother would tell her romantic stories of when her mother and father had first met, how each couldn't speak the other's language, but that "love had one language and the heart always found a way."

Montana's aunt had been Chopper's cleaning lady for more than ten years before suddenly dying of a brain aneurysm.

When Montana had gone to the residence to tell Chopper about her aunt's death, he had offered her a job to replace her. He'd seen Montana on several occasions over the years, sitting in her aunt's car, playing with her dolls or reading while her aunt had cleaned the house. Etched in Montana's memory was the day, when she was seven years old, when the big, scary blond man had stared hard into the car at her as he had made his way into his mansion. He'd reminded her of the menacing statues of gargoyles perched high on each corner of the mansion.

Chopper had explained that the only reason he was considering hiring her, especially at such a young age, was because he had appreciated in her aunt the only thing he respected—loyalty—and that out of respect and loyalty to her aunt, he would take his chances and give her the opportunity to continue her aunt's work.

Having just graduated from high school and needing work, Montana had taken the offer. Upon completion of the interview, which had felt more like an interrogation, she'd gotten the job. The sound of his deep voice now echoed in her head. *Number one, never, under any circumstances, enter the residence at any other time than your scheduled cleanings. Number two, never, under any circumstances, speak of things seen or heard at the residence. Number three, never, under any circumstances, communicate in any way to the occupants in or around the residence.*

Montana had thought these rules were a bit extreme. But the generous payments, always in cash, had been too good to pass up.

Two months after her first day, the unlikely convergence of two innocent souls would forever alter their lives.

It was now Wednesday, one of the three days of the week Montana was scheduled to clean the mansion. She watched from down the street as Chopper pulled out of the driveway in his black Jaguar. She waited for ten more minutes, just in case he'd forgotten something and turned around to come back for it. The coast was clear, and Montana drove through the enormous iron gate.

Sara sat nervously on her bed next to a bag she'd filled with her white clothes, white toothbrush, white hairbrush, and a folder containing all her sketches. She heard the door open and shut, followed by Montana's footsteps as she made her way through the mansion to make sure they were alone. When Montana was satisfied, she approached Sara's door and knocked once, followed by three more knocks to signal that Sara could come out. If there had been only one knock, Sara was to stay put. It meant something wasn't right. If for some reason Sara didn't come out after Montana's all-clear knock, Montana would know there was something wrong on Sara's end.

Montana watched the doorknob slowly turn and the door open. Sara was so relieved to see Montana's face that she dropped her bag and hugged her so hard Montana could barely breathe. She had to pry the scared girl off her, informing her that everything looked good and that they could continue with their plan.

The girls quickly made their way downstairs. Montana left the house first so that she could park in the circular driveway as close as possible to the front doors. She had decided the day before that it would be worth it to dip into her savings and have dark tint put on the windows of the car.

She reentered the house, giving Sara a thumbs-up. They both carried their bags to the car. Sara was so scared she became dizzy as soon as the bright sunlight touched her face for the first time in years. She crouched low in the passenger seat, shaking. She wore her rosary and held her Bible, reciting the Lord's Prayer as Montana calmly drove away from the mansion of gargoyles.

After driving for a little over an hour, Sara's nerves finally began to settle down, although she'd not yet let go of Montana's hand. She wanted badly to roll down the windows and take in the fresh air, but dared not reveal herself from behind the dark windows.

"How do you feel?" Montana asked. Sara looked over at Montana, and her lips began to quiver as tears rolled down her face. A feeling of overwhelming relief washed over her. "Thank you," she finally managed to say.

Montana's eyes misted and she smiled. "I know this is an awful lot to ask so soon, but I want us to do something special today before we get to the farmhouse," Montana said. "I've saved up a little extra money for us to commemorate this moment."

"Sure, I'll do whatever you say," Sara replied joyfully.

"I have a friend who does tattoos from his home," Montana said with excitement. "He's really good, and I trust him. I want us to get matching tattoos of that beautiful red butterfly we saw outside the window the other day. There was a reason it came to us—I'm sure of it. I figured since you're the artist here, you can draw a quick sketch of it before we get there. I'm gonna have mine put on the inside of my wrist, and you can have yours wherever you want. What do you say?"

A look of anxiety fell over Sara's face as images of sharp needles piercing and injecting ink into her skin flooded her mind. But then something happened. She decided she wasn't going to let her fear ruin everything—especially not on *this* day. She wasn't going to disappoint yet another person in her life whom she loved. From this moment on, she swore, she would not just be alive, but would live. "Let's do it. I'll have mine put on the inside of my wrist too!"

CHAPTER 7
THE NEVER-SETTING SUN

EIGHT WEEKS FLEW BY IN a blur—Kiwi had visited nine different countries on seven different continents. Taking the job in Vegas had definitely been the most exciting thing she had ever done. She had met the most fascinating people, from movie stars to sports celebrities to presidents and princes. On one occasion, she had even shaken the hand of a king! Her life felt like a dream. She experienced a side of life most people had only read about in books or watch on television. That an insignificant Native American girl from Montana was suddenly rubbing elbows with the world's most powerful and influential people was unbelievable to her. To her, the experience was even greater than what Mr. Gold had said it would be.

Upon her return from the Mediterranean, Mr. Gold—or Lawrence, as he asked her to call him—told her that she'd made such an impression on her clients that every one of them requested future meetings with her. He said that this was unheard of and that he'd never seen a success story such as hers. He also said that he wasn't at all surprised, which made Kiwi feel good, but at the same time it perplexed her that he'd think that about her. Apparently, in just one summer, she'd become the most sought-after social event companion in the company.

Kiwi didn't know how to respond to the announcement—except to wonder if it were really possible. *All I did was stand or sit next to the clients, smile a lot, make small talk, and shake hands with people*, she thought. She'd especially enjoyed the interesting conversations she'd had with them.

She was treated like royalty by everyone and truly enjoyed the brief visits with her clients and their families. Each client had taught her something valuable, and she sincerely thanked them for that.

Kiwi was amazed at how much more cultured she felt after such a short period of time. It felt to her as if lifetimes of experiences had been crunched together and poured into her mind.

Lawrence told her that one client—a prince, no less—wished to take her hand in marriage! She laughed, telling him he couldn't possibly be serious. It reminded her of the fairy tale the princess and the frog, except in this case she was the frog and he the prince. Lawrence smiled, saying that he would never joke about such matters, and that this prince in particular happened to be the heir to a multibillion-dollar company.

Really? she mused. *Why would a prince, with the entire world at his feet, want to marry a poor frog from Montana?*

Lawrence and Kiwi were standing in the company lobby. He whispered in her ear, asking if she would meet with him in his office later that evening. He said it was time for them to have a very important talk. Kiwi became a bit nervous, and he quickly assured her it was nothing bad but would require her full attention.

At exactly 7:30 p.m., they sat in his corner penthouse office overlooking the Las Vegas strip. The room was lavish and lit by natural light filtering through the enormous tinted windows. The hum of the air conditioner was quiet and soothing. A sweet aroma of pipe tobacco swirled in the air. Books filled the massive cases lining the towering walls. Impressive art from around the world sat or hung in just the right places about the room.

The sun had just disappeared behind the horizon, leaving trails of pumpkin orange and fiery red afterglow. Lawrence and Kiwi looked out his window at the stunning view of the famous paradise in the desert. *It's ironic,* Kiwi thought, *Death Valley, one of the hottest places on earth, isn't very far from here.*

"I'm starting to fall in love with these desert sunsets," said Kiwi in a failed attempt to settle her nerves.

"The sun never sets," Lawrence replied.

"Okay, is this the part where I take the bait and ask you what you mean?" she playfully asked.

He laughed and elaborated. "It's not the sun that sets. It's us and the planet we temporarily occupy spinning counterclockwise at one thousand and thirty-seven miles per hour and rotating around the sun that creates the illusion that the sun is setting, an illusion we believe to be real and are hopelessly imprisoned by." Lawrence seemed to mumble the last few words more to himself than to Kiwi. He looked as if he were searching for the words or a way to tell her something indescribable.

He spun around in his big leather chair to face her. "In fact, it's the trap of this illusion that I want to talk to you about today, Kiwi."

He said that he felt personally responsible for her health and welfare, and that he would never allow this type of work to taint her in any way. Kiwi felt a bit disconcerted by the statement and asked him what he meant by "this type of work."

He took a deep breath. "Kiwi, please forgive me. I seem to be in uncharted territory. I'll do my best to try to communicate my thoughts in a way that hopefully is discernible." He rolled his eyes to the ceiling.

"I don't know how to say this, so I'll just say it. You're in possession of the most powerful force in the universe."

Kiwi's jaw dropped as the tidal wave of Lawrence's words slammed into her mind. They sat staring at each other for a moment.

"This force is an extremely rare gift," he continued. "It can be compared to an incredibly powerful sword with a double edge. This gift is like a beacon in the night, a brilliant searchlight in a terrible storm. It's both the warmth and safety of a mother's womb and the merciless destroyer of anything that misuses or abuses it. Like a child, this blessing is pure and without prejudice. It can be compared to the way nature gives us the stunning sunsets you love so much and the life-sustaining rains, while it also gives us the earthquakes and tsunamis that wipe out entire cities and villages. This blessing is the unfathomable force that keeps the planets, moons, and stars in equilibrium. Without it, the cosmos would be chaos instead of a masterpiece.

"Because of your powerful gift, people and things are attracted to you, drawn to you like a moth to a light. You have what they desperately need, what we all need."

Again, Kiwi just looked at him blankly while the beating of her heart quickened. At this moment, she realized that the man sitting before her sincerely believed that every word he said was true. *But how could that possibly be? There must be some kind of mistake.*

"Kiwi, I'm going to tell you something I've never spoken about to anyone before. I hope it will give you a better understanding of what I'm trying to convey.

"As you know, I was born and raised in England, and I once had what you have now. You see, all children are born with it, but for some reason most children begin losing it around the age of seven. It's unknown why we lose it. Perhaps we're stripped of it by the nonbelievers of this world, people so devoid of this love-giving force that they resort to desperate measures to regain it. Of course, these people find out that the very act of taking from another what's not rightfully theirs becomes a moral thorn that will fester until it kills them."

Lawrence looked deeply into Kiwi's eyes. It seemed as if he was determining whether he should proceed, if what he just said resonated within her. He seemed satisfied and continued.

"As a young boy, I desperately tried to hold on to this gift, even as I could feel it seeping out of every pore in my body the minute after my seventh birthday. Little by little this wonderful magic, this love-giving force of the universe, was slipping away.

"I noticed that I began to think differently about people, animals, trees, plants, flowers—everything around me. I began to look at them as inanimate objects with only labels and names attached to them, instead of the magnificent and infinite beings they really are. I began to separate myself from the oneness connecting us all. I felt a fear I'd never felt before. I became anxious and self-conscious about my newly separate self.

"Something in my head, a voice I believed to be me, was constantly comparing, naming, and judging everyone and everything. This voice seemed to be predominately negative and critical. It saw the world as a means to an end, a problem instead of the answer. This voice, claiming to be me, pretended to look out for my health and welfare. I became convinced that without it, I was doomed.

"The sun's light seemed to dim, colors lost their brilliance, and things no longer had the newness and intrigue they once had. It was like I was suddenly transported to a different world that was sick and dying. I was confused and sad most of the time. I became desperate and asked my family and friends if they'd noticed anything different. I got the same odd or worried look from everyone. How could they not notice? Eventually, I couldn't bear it any longer.

"One night, I lay in my bed crying. I knew someday soon I would be just like 'them,' like my parents, my grandma and grandpa, my aunts and uncles, like all the others who'd lost their special gift. I would become just another judgmental, calculating, lifeless machine, another lost soul held hostage by preconditioned thoughts, emotions, and actions, just another nonbeliever. Over time I would forget I ever had such a beautiful gift. I would teach my children to see the world through my numbed heart and blind eyes, and the vicious cycle would repeat.

"I decided I'd rather die than give up this gift. Immediately upon making my decision, I felt a sense of peace. I would return to the source of this love-giving energy. It was summertime, and we were on break from school. My plan was to leave early in the morning, walk west down the country road for two miles, then follow the railroad tracks north for another three miles to the big railroad bridge. There, I would commit my body to the peaceful waters of the fast-flowing river below.

"Under the covers I whispered my farewells to my family and friends, to my dog and cat. I was finally happy again."

Kiwi's heart felt heavy, and tears rolled down her cheeks as she listened to Lawrence. She suddenly felt closer to him, as if she'd known him all of her life.

Or maybe it was in a previous life.

"But then something happened. I had the most intriguing dream that night. In the beginning, the dream was frightful. Everything was lifeless. The trees, the flowers, the dark clouds—all glowed in various shades of gray. I was walking on a railroad track in the countryside. The tracks were straight and seemed to go on forever in front of me.

"Ahead there was a light on the tracks, except the light seemed somehow tainted or deceitful. It was getting bigger and brighter as I walked toward it. I could hear the sound of the approaching train, could feel the rumble under my feet. I was scared, wanting to run away from the tracks, but I couldn't. I just kept walking toward the light. Up ahead, I saw a track to my left that connected to mine. Somehow I knew that this was my only way to get off the tracks I was on, the only way to escape the pain and suffering of this world.

"Just as I reached the perpendicular track, I noticed something on the tracks in front of me. As I got closer, I realized that it was a little girl in a white dress, maybe five or six years old. She had bobbed hair, and her eyes were the most brilliant blue. Everything was black or gray except for her brilliant white dress and her big blue eyes. She was standing between me and the menacing black train coming to devour us.

"I looked down at the tracks to my left. Just one short step to the side and I would escape certain death. *But what about the child in front of me*, I thought. I wondered if my life was somehow more important than hers. Would the little girl suffer and die because of this paralyzing fear inside me? My heart ached as it pounded through my chest.

"*What do I do? What can I do?* I wondered. I found myself sprinting toward the little girl. The light was blinding and almost upon us. I thought it was too late, that we'd never make it back to the safe track in time. My legs burned like they were on fire. Then I noticed that the tracks under my speeding feet were rolling like a conveyor belt. I was getting nowhere. I could see the rocks next to the tracks and the trees around me frozen in place.

"To my relief, I realized that the rolling tracks were also bringing the little girl to me; but my heart sank when I saw that they were also bringing the train of hate. When the child was within reach, I swept her tiny body into my arms. She stared at me with her piercing blue eyes. As we turned to run back toward the safe track, I noticed that the perpendicular tracks were within reach. A thunderous roar blasted by us at the exact moment I jumped.

"Everything was silent. We were standing in a glistening white fog. I felt the most profound sense of peace and love I'd ever known. There were no shapes or colors—only white. I was sobbing tears of joy. Then the colors began to return. Violet was first, then purple, blue, green, and yellow.

"When the orange and red colors appeared, the shapes of my surroundings came into view. Then came sound; birds were cheerfully chirping. Next were the senses of smell and taste. The aroma of honeysuckle permeated the air. I could taste the sweet nectar in my mouth. Then came the sense of touch. The little girl's hand was warm and tiny in mine. I noticed something odd—on the opposite side of the tracks, there were no colors. Everything was still a lifeless gray. The trees were bare; there were no flowers; the clouds above were dark and menacing. This was the life I'd just escaped from, I realized, and the side of the railroad tracks we were now standing on was the life I had known as a child.

"The little girl and I stared in awe at the miracle around us. Arching for hundreds of miles across the sky was a full double rainbow, the kind you hear about but aren't likely to ever witness in a lifetime.

"Everything around us seemed brand new. The colors were so vibrant. Graceful butterflies of every color danced above beautiful flowers. Magnificent trees stretched their long green limbs toward the heavens and seemed to be giving thanks for their existence.

"The world was right again, the way it's seen through the nonjudgmental eyes of a child. We were so happy. The girl let go of my hand. In her other arm was a brown box about the size of a grapefruit. With a smile, she handed the box to me and watched with eager eyes. The moment I opened the top a small red butterfly shot out from its prison. It danced quick circles above our heads and then lifted toward the big blue sky."

Kiwi unconsciously robbed the nape of her neck.

"Then the girl gave me a big hug and skipped away, giggling.

"At that moment I noticed it; I could feel it in every cell of my body. A little bit of the gift resonating from the girl had rubbed off on me. It was the child! She and all the other children of our world still have it; they possess the universe's love-giving energy. I knew emphatically this love was humanity's only chance, our one hope of surviving the madness of this world.

"When I opened my eyes, my cheeks were wet, and I felt something on my face I'd not felt in a long time—a heartfelt smile. The light shining through my window was bright again. The colors of the objects in my room seemed to pop out at me. My cat jumped onto my bed, and I saw the spirit inside her eyes again. I sat up in my bed, staring out my window as I petted her. I recalled my dream and tried desperately to cling to the wonderful feeling, but it was fading fast, the way a fog evaporates with the touch of the morning rays."

Lawrence spun around in his leather chair and stared out his window again. The hum of the air conditioner took over once more as they sat in silence.

"So what did you do?" Kiwi finally asked.

"I became obsessed. I dedicated my life to finding the cure for humanity's sickness. Why do we lose our way after childhood? Why do we forget that the source from which we came is love, and that this love is infinitely abundant and nurturing? Why do we forget we're all one? Everything came from one, will return to one, *is* one."

Lawrence sensed Kiwi needed a more detailed answer. He spun back around to face her. "After my dream I volunteered most of my free time to charity work, mostly at homeless shelters and orphanages. I did this on weekends and during my summer breaks. This provided me with enough of the love-giving energy while I devised a plan.

"The years flew by. I graduated with honors from Cambridge with a major in physics. Yet I found myself no closer to finding the answer. Frustrated, I moved to India. I was fortunate enough to get a job teaching at one of the largest universities there. Surrounded by more than ten million other souls, I found myself immersed in a wealth of the most diverse humanity. In my free time, I traveled by bus or train to many cities and towns. I felt a special spiritual connection to the people, to the culture, and to the earth beneath my feet.

"Then one day, two years, six months, and twenty-three days after moving to India, I literally stumbled upon the answer. It was during the rainy season, and water was coming down in a monsoon as if the ocean nearby had been turned upside down. I was running from a little store to my apartment. As I rounded the corner of the building, my legs tangled. I tripped and fell. My bag of fruit scattered all over the sidewalk.

"A man was sitting cross-legged with his back against the wall. I was dumbfounded. He was meditating in the midst of a rainstorm! The emaciated-looking, dark-brown man calmly got to his feet, apologized to me, and helped me up. I was amazed at the man's physical strength. He pulled me to my feet as if I were a child. He had the most infectious smile, and when I looked into his big brown eyes, I knew this man had the answers I'd been seeking.

"Rama was his name. He was homeless and survived by making straw sandals. He would gather wild straw from the countryside and weave it into the most beautiful and comfortable sandals. When he made enough to fill his bag, he'd walk back to the city, hunched over against the weight of the heavy bag on his shoulders. He gave the sandals away to as many shoeless people as he could find, particularly the children. In return, he would sometimes be offered money. He always refused the money, but would gratefully accept food and fresh water. I had seen the old man before, but hadn't taken notice of this saintly sandal maker.

"Now I could see the magnetic and mystifying quality he possessed. It was like being reunited with a very dear friend. Soon our relationship became that of teacher and student. I wondered how someone with so little and who had to deal constantly with hunger and the elements could be so happy.

"On several occasions I couldn't help but offer, and at times insist, that Rama accept a bit of my money—just to get him through the hard times.

"'Hard times?' he'd ask with a toothless smile. "Have you not noticed how magnificently blue the sky is today? How much water the heavens blessed us with last week? And the happy smiling children running all about?'

"After such comments, what could I do but shake my head in amazement and see the world anew?

"It was from Rama that I was given the valuable gift. I learned how to meditate deeply and how to liberate myself from the monster of my incessant mind. It took many years to learn, but the reward was priceless. Truthfully, it probably saved my life. It was within the short fleeting moments when I was able to free myself from my redundant and mostly negative thoughts that I was closest to the profound peace I'd felt as a child. Just a few seconds in this 'no-mind' state provided such a rejuvenating energy that the world became a friend again. People and things glowed and existed purely for the joy of being.

"But then the buildup of negative thoughts would return, and with it, dark clouds. Only now I knew how to sit in silence and wash my mind clean again with the purifying rain of silence.

"After ten years, three months, and twelve days living in India, I found the universe suddenly growing dimmer. The light from a great star had suddenly been extinguished. Rama had been beaten to death by two young hoodlums in a robbery attempt. The shop owners who stumbled upon his body. They said the gray-haired saint was lying in a pool of blood, with a peaceful smile on face.

"One of the thugs turned himself in to the police and admitted to the crime. He said when they realized the old man had no money, his partner became angry and began kicking him, then smashed a large liquor bottle over his head. The young criminal tearfully added that he'd thought about helping Rama because the old man had once given him a pair of sandals, but he was too scared to stand up to his bullying partner.

"Word of Rama's murder spread like wildfire through the streets, and the murderer was found two days later, hiding under a bridge. The angry mob literally beat the man to a pulp as the police turned their heads.

"I was overcome with grief and guilt and, I'm ashamed to say, hate. Why wouldn't I do more to protect my beloved teacher, my mentor, my friend? With the money I made at the university, I could've provided Rama with a small apartment and steady sustenance. I should've made him live there, regardless of his wishes to live on the streets. How could the animals who murdered Rama not realize that gentle souls like his are our only hope for salvation?

"I was angry at myself and bitter at the world. I felt a sense of satisfaction in knowing that, in the end, Rama's killer also became a victim of his own hate. But then this made me feel even guiltier for harboring hatred in my heart. It seemed as if all the wonderful things my beloved mentor had taught me were beginning to unravel. It was during these low moments when I was reminded of what Rama often said: 'Every human being is born with a divine purpose or they wouldn't be here. This divine purpose is to show the greatest compassion to the greatest number, for it is in giving that we shall receive. We receive love by giving it. The more we give the more we get! So whatever it is we choose to do, it should in some way involve the act of compassion to those walking among us. It is these souls who have been chosen by the universe to be our companions in this sacred journey we call life.'

"I once asked Rama what he'd chosen to do on *his* journey. He tapped me on the head with a sandal he was weaving and said with a broad smile, 'Why, isn't it obvious? I've chosen to provide my fellow travelers with comfortable and fashionable footwear.'

"But this time, no amount of meditation could help me wash away the terrible anger boiling inside me. I often found myself wandering aimlessly through the crowded streets after work. There was a cold void left where my dear friend had once been. Almost every young man's face triggered an angry and fearful suspicion in me. *Is he the type who could murder a saint like Rama?* I'd ask myself.

"Then, as if things couldn't get any worse, I found out my most promising young student was in the hospital and in critical condition. She was a beautiful young woman with a brilliant mind. She always had a smile on her face and had an insatiable appetite for knowledge. She came from a poor upbringing, but everyone in her village knew from the beginning that she was something special, their pride and joy. Having scored high on her exams and finishing at the top of her class, the girl had been given a scholarship at my university.

"I remember the first day she walked into my classroom, like a frightened little deer, yet she was so excited for the opportunity to learn. Her big brown eyes took in her surroundings as if she were in heaven. It wasn't long before I realized that this young lady was nothing less than a prodigy. I would learn just as much about the mystery of quantum physics from her as she would from me.

"I was informed that she'd been a victim of an acid attack. I'd never heard of the term before, and after some research, I was horrified. It seems this type of crime takes place all around the world, although it's more concentrated in South Asia. The victims in almost all cases are women. The crimes often occur as revenge against a woman who rejects a proposal of marriage or a sexual advance. In this case, the young student refused to have sex with a particular man, so he threw sulfuric acid on her face while she was sleeping.

"I felt sick at the thought of the physical pain she must've endured. Besides being physically disfigured, I knew she'd also suffer social, psychological, and financial difficulties for the rest of her life. I was very upset over it and decided to show my support by visiting her in the hospital.

"I was turned away by one of the doctors caring for her. He told me she was in very bad shape and her chances for survival were grim. He also told me her family wanted only immediate family members to visit her. I returned home with an overwhelming feeling of helplessness. Two months later, a friend of the girl came to me and told me my prodigy wished to visit with me. I was given a time I could come and see her. I was overjoyed and looked forward to our meeting.

"She was still being treated at the hospital but was in stable condition. I found her room and walked in with fresh flowers. I'm ashamed to say that when I saw her, I became physically ill. This could not possibly be the same beautiful, bright student I knew. The trembling piece of humanity before me showed little resemblance to a human being. Her face, scalp, and neck looked as if someone had taken a blowtorch to the skin and melted it off. Large patches of her hair were missing. She was permanently blind in both eyes and had no nose or lips. My stomach convulsed uncontrollably.

"Oh God, how I tried my best to be strong for her, to reassure her everything would be okay, that soon she'd be back at university, still able to fulfill all of her hopes and dreams. My lips moved, but my voice failed me. I couldn't do it; I couldn't lie to her. What could I possibly do or say in such a situation? I just stood by her side, holding her fragile hand, crying with her. I cried like I'd never cried before. It felt as if a colossal dam had finally collapsed, releasing the pent-up emotions of a lifetime. It was as if I were being held deep under water, drowning in this deception called life—and I didn't care if I ever resurfaced again."

Kiwi began crying. Chills ran down her spine as she thought of how eerily similar the young girl's childhood was to hers—her village upbringing, her academic achievements, her hopes and dreams for the future. She, too, was probably once called the "Chosen One" by her family and village elders.

Lawrence was visibly upset. His eyes held tears as he continued.

"For months I was in an extremely low, depressive state. How was it that human beings, a class to which I belonged, were capable of such savagery inflicted upon one another? I began to give up hope for humanity, which I knew meant I was giving up on myself. Now more than ever, I needed Rama.

"Then, one summer evening, I was sitting on the side of a country road. It was where Rama used to collect his wild straw to make his sandals. The enormous sphere of orange fire was slipping below the horizon. The sound of children's playful laughter from a distant village rode on the soft breeze. The nectar and pollen from the wildflowers gave off a pungently sweet smell.

"I closed my eyes, focused on my breathing, and slipped into a peaceful meditative state. When I opened my eyes, a thin dark figure was walking toward me with the blazing sun at his back. I immediately recognized the bright and cheerful smile, but how could this be? I started to get up and run to my teacher, but he waved his hand for me to sit back down. When he arrived, he sat down next to me. His entire body seemed to radiate with light. We looked at each other with a sense of joy that cannot be described. He spoke, but his lips weren't moving. It seemed we were communicating only through our thoughts—or perhaps through our souls. I began to tell him of all my suffering, sorrows, and hatred, but then his thoughts overcame mine.

"'My dear Lawrence. I'm so glad to see you. I've traveled a long way to tell you of a story. Once there lived two great men. The men were well known throughout the land for their noble and valiant deeds in helping the weak and poor and for standing up for peace and against injustice. One man loved the good in his life, attracting to himself peace, harmony, and desirable circumstances. The other man hated the bad in his life, attracting to himself hatred, disharmony, and evils of every kind. One man made use of the constructive forces of the universe, while the other made use of the destructive forces of the universe. Each man reaped exactly what he sowed. So you see, my friend, we're not to hate even the bad, for when we entertain such negative thoughts, we attract into our lives evil, fear, greed, hatred, and countless other destructive forces. We must remain alert and be vigilant at all times. We must consciously guard our subconscious mind from all negative thoughts. When we find ourselves entertaining negative thoughts of any kind, we must immediately counter those thoughts with positive ones.

"'At first, this will be difficult. But if we are persistent, we will eventually see our circumstances change. Positive people and positive things will come into our lives—negative ones will leave. This is an infallible law of the universe. Always remember, our thoughts are one of the most powerful forces in nature. They are the creators of our reality. Of all the creatures on this planet, we have been blessed. We've been given the freedom to choose what we wish to think, but we must always remember that our thoughts are subject to the immutable laws of the universe. One such law is that like attracts like. The feelings or actions of hate we give to another cannot help but return to us tenfold. The feelings or actions of love we give to another cannot help but return to us tenfold.'

"Rama put his hand on my shoulder and continued. 'When you feel anger or hate, it would do you well to meditate on the words of a great man by the name of Martin Luther King, Jr., "Darkness cannot drive out darkness; only light can do that. Hate cannot drive out hate; only love can do that."'

"We sat in silence on the dirt road until it became dark. I looked up at the stars. When I looked back, he was suddenly gone. I don't even remember walking home that night.

"I woke the next morning with the sobering realization that my time was running out. How could I be so blind? Here I was, wasting my precious life away in search of my divine purpose, when all along Rama had been trying to show me that we must *act out* our divine purpose, which is to show the greatest compassion to the greatest number.

"I felt a strong desire to move to America and an unexplainable urge to visit—of all places—Las Vegas. I remembered that Rama had told me never to ignore the pull of the universe. So off to 'Sin City' I went."

The box of Kleenex on Lawrence's desk was empty, and in Kiwi's lap was a mountain of soggy tissues. Lawrence got up and brought her a fresh box.

"I'm sorry, sweetie. I can only imagine what you might be thinking about me by now."

Kiwi shook her head. "There's nothing to be sorry about. I feel honored you'd even tell me such personal things about your life. I was very moved. And as you can see, I've made a mess. I'm sorry for using up all your tissues."

"I'm sorry for making you cry," Lawrence replied.

He walked back to the window. "There's so much more I want to tell you, Kiwi. I hope I haven't scared you off."

"No, not all," she said. "I'm fascinated by your life and would love to know more. I just have one question."

"Fire away."

"May I please use the bathroom?"

"Oh, of course. You can use the one in my office if you like. I'll have refreshments brought in here and, when you're ready, we'll continue, okay?"

"That sounds great, Lawrence," Kiwi said with a smile.

"Thatta girl," he replied with a wink.

CHAPTER 8

FINAL AUDITION

———•———

THE WATER FROM THE RUSTY pump was clean and rejuvenating. It had a taste that reminded Sara of how, as a child, she would set cups on the ground outside her window whenever it rained. She'd sneak peeks through her window at the cups every so often; when they were full, she'd run outside and gather them. She'd decided rainwater was from heaven, so it must be from God...which meant it was surely blessed like the holy water at her church.

She named her collection of rainwater "angel water" and kept it in a gallon container. She took small sips of it every day because it made her feel happy and somehow closer to God. She carefully rationed her angel water until the next rain came, then she drank what remained and poured some over her head. Then, she began the ritual again.

The girls were now nearing their third month at the old farmhouse. With all the overtime work, Montana had managed to save almost enough money to take them all the way to Montana, as opposed to set-tling somewhere in between for a few weeks to earn more money, like they'd initially planned.

For the first couple of weeks, Sara was a complete emotional wreck when Montana was away at work. She felt as if she was perpetually hang-ing from the edge of a cliff, and that there was nothing she could do about it. Her mind filled with images of Chopper storming into the farmhouse at any moment and killing her, then waiting in ambush for his other prey to return home so he could chop her to pieces.

It was the part about Montana that bothered Sara more than anything. She'd accepted her own death long ago, but not that of her best friend, the person who had saved her in so many ways, the person she loved.

Montana came home to find Sara locked in the bathroom. She knocked on the door. "Sara? What's the matter?" Sara finally opened the door, and it was clear to Montana that Sara had been crying. Sara told her about all the fears she'd been having while Montana was away at work. They sat in silence for a while. *What if someone with bad intentions does come to the house when I'm away? Does she know how to protect herself?* Montana thought. *Probably not…*

Montana grabbed Sara's hand. "Let's go. Were gonna teach you how to defend yourself." Montana led her to the back of the house. Outside, she revealed to Sara something she hadn't spoken about for years. "Believe it or not," she said, "I was once one of the top female kickboxers in the country."

Sara was astonished, "Wow! Why haven't you told me before?" she asked.

"I don't know, it's just something I try not to think about. I had high hopes. My goal was to win a world championship someday. But that all changed when I started getting recurring concussions. My family got scared, and eventually so did I. We decided to let the sport go and move on when I was sixteen. It was one of the hardest things I'd ever done."

"I'm sorry," Sara consoled.

"That's okay. Come on—let's go out to that big backyard of ours and learn how to fight."

Sara was nervous but also excited. Being outdoors in the sunshine and spending time with her best friend were dreams she'd almost given up hope for. "Before we start," Sara confessed, "I'm sure to be the most hopelessly uncoordinated person you'll ever meet, so don't laugh."

"Ah, how bad can it be?" Montana asked.

"I trip over air," Sara replied with a smile.

Montana began to laugh but caught herself. "You're gonna do great—I promise.

Sara learned the proper athletic stance and how to protect herself from strikes. Montana had to literally stand behind Sara and work her arms and legs as if she were a puppet. Both thought it was uproariously comical, and their bellies hurt from laughing so much.

Sara learned the basic punches—jab, cross, hook, and uppercut—as well as how to use her elbows and knees as weapons. The sun was beginning to set, and after two and a half hours the girls collapsed with exhaustion. Panting, Montana yelled, "What's our motto?"

Sara caught her breath and replied, "Fight hard! Whatever's worth keeping is worth fighting for!"

Lying side by side on the cool, soft grass, they stared up into the evening sky. The moon and stars were already visible, and the frogs down at the pond had commenced their nightly chitchat. The girls were silent, both lost in their own thoughts. Sara felt a sense of belonging that she'd forgotten existed. Montana felt a sense of joyful relief; she'd finally found that missing part of her that had eluded her all her life in the beautiful soul lying next to her...

Sara turned to Montana and smiled. "I know now that God hasn't cursed me for questioning the Bible; I know it because she brought me you..."

The next day Sara was miserably sore but insisted on learning more. She learned the basic kicks—front kick, side kick, and roundhouse kick.

Montana felt a sense of satisfaction she hadn't felt for a long time. *Finally*, she thought. *A good reason for all the blood, sweat, and tears I've put into this sport.* "Maybe I should be a kickboxing instructor," she commented.

"Absolutely you should—you're amazing!" Sara replied. "You really do have a special gift for this, Montana."

As time went by, Sara gained confidence and learned to cope with her anxiety better. She started venturing further out into the yard, then into the fields of giant sunflowers, honeybees, and dancing butterflies.

One day, while walking through a pasture, Sara saw the exact same red butterfly she and Montana had seen outside the window at the mansion. She couldn't wait to tell Montana about how the butterfly landed on her hand and let her look at it really close before flying away; about how she was convinced that it was the spirit of her mama, because on the butterfly's wings were Mama's blue eyes; and about how the red butterfly sang to her in her mind in a child's voice. The song it sung was Mama's favorite from the television show *The Mary Tyler Moore Show*: "Love Is All Around."

Montana came home from work and announced that she was going to take the next two days off. She'd been working long hours six days a week for three months and had asked her boss for a short break. Sara was overjoyed and rattled off all the special places around the farmhouse she'd discovered and couldn't wait to show her. Montana smiled and agreed to the grand tour, but only after she revealed her real reason for taking the time off.

She told Sara she'd noticed her extraordinary gift for singing since coming to the farmhouse and how proud of it she should be. Sara confessed that singing to herself had always been her way of coping with the never-ending disappointments and chaos in her life. She told Montana that her mother did it too, and mused that it must've been passed on to her. "Mama always used to tell me I had come into this world not with cries of terror like most babies but singing a song. So I sang every chance I got, usually softly to myself, because I decided early on that I wasn't very good at it. And I was okay with that because I knew that the only reason I sang was because it made me feel good, and I know it sounds silly, but I really believed that whatever song I happened to be singing had chosen *me* to sing through."

Montana couldn't believe her ears. She grabbed Sara's hands and leaned her face close to hers and looked deep into her eyes. "Sara, listen to me. I swear to you, your voice is the most beautiful sound I've ever heard. Listening to you sing gives me the strength to make it through one more day, it fills my heart with hope. Never again think that you're not very good at singing; you are absolutely great at singing."

Sara's cheeks flushed, and she averted her eyes from Montana's for a second but then looked back at her. "Thank you," she whispered.

Montana ran through her mind one more time how she would drop the bomb on Sara, how she would explain about an upcoming musical audition in a nearby city. She had thought it through and the risk of being caught weighed heavily on her, but the fact that the city holding the auditions was almost three hundred miles from the mansion of gargoyles helped ease her mind. She had decided that boosting Sara's confidence was worth the risk.

There was no easy way to drop it, so Montana braced herself and just did it. "Sara, there's a musical audition tomorrow, and it would mean the world to me if we go to it and you sing."

Sara's stomach plummeted, her muscles tightened, and her heart raced. She looked down at the floor and shook her head. "I'm really sorry, but there's no way I could do that; I can't sing in public."

Montana saw the paralyzing anxiety that washed over Sara. "It would be for just one time, Sara. I just want you to realize how truly special your voice is, and what a God-given talent you have. I think that the only way to prove it is to display it to people who can really appreciate it and give you an unbiased critique. Please, Sara, would you do this one thing for me? I wouldn't ask you if I didn't know for sure that you could do it."

Sara was silent as she pondered the unthinkable task being asked of her by the most important person in her life. She wanted so desperately to please Montana in any way she could. *But of all things,* she thought. *Why this?* Finally, she slowly lifted her chin and looked into Montana's eyes. "Okay."

Montana was ecstatic. "Yes!" She ran to Sara, hugging her and lifting her off the floor and spinning her 'round and 'round. "Thank you so much. I'm so proud of you, Sara. I just know you're gonna do great!"

Sara giggled as she was spun around. She was on cloud nine, and she didn't care to ever step off again.

Montana told Sara that the song she would sing was "Amazing Grace," by John Newton. Sara was excited and relieved to know that it was one of her favorites; she'd probably sung it a hundred times to herself.

Standing in front of an old dresser, Sara snuck peeks from the corner of her eye at Montana's reflection in the broken mirror. *Why does my heart flutter like a hummingbird's wings every time she's near?* she wondered. As she sang, she watched Montana, who was trying to look busy, dusting off the nightstand. After just the first verse, Montana couldn't help but turn and listen in absolute awe of Sara's voice.

Sara rehearsed the song only once, deciding that, having sung the song all her life, it would be good enough. The song had chosen *her* to sing it, and she was determined not to let it down.

She asked Montana if it would be okay to sing her another song, one she'd written the other day. Sara wanted so badly to tell Montana the song was really written for her. She thought Montana was the most beautiful woman in the world and felt something special for her, something she didn't have the words to describe. But for lack of courage, she ignored her heart and left that part out.

Montana excitedly agreed, hopped on the bed, and sat wide-eyed. Sara was still turned toward the dresser mirror, and she looked at the reflection of Montana's face. Somehow through the mirror it became bearable to look deep into her big brown eyes—to embrace her soul. She began to sing:

Sometimes I'm so scared. Oh, what is this world?
Why should I try? My voice often told
Just leave it all now, it says with a sigh
Don't bother to write; don't bother to cry
Out on the ledge, oh, please let me see
The birds and the flowers, the sun and the trees
But dark clouds above, they rain and they pour
Then came along you—for you my heart's sworn
I don't have much. I have nothing at all

But if I could, I'd give you the stars
My heart's on the ledge. I see you and see
The birds and the flowers, the sun and the trees
So please hear me, darling, when I haven't the words
It's because of you I'm still in this world.

Through watery eyes, the women stared at each other's reflections. Montana tried to thank Sara, but her voice faltered, failing her. She intercepted a falling tear with her finger, and then fled from the room.

The girls left early the next morning. The rehearsal wasn't until noon, so their plan was to enjoy the morning together and do some window-shopping. They discovered that each had an obsession for pistachio nuts. The actual nuts were a bit out of their budget, so they settled for a massive double-scoop serving of pistachio ice cream, which they both devoured down to the tip of the waffle cone. On the count of three, they popped the last bit into their mouths, savoring it for as long as possible.

They walked for hours, lost in each other's company. Sara opened her heart to Montana. She explained that Montana was the first person she'd allowed herself to get close to since her mother's death. For so many years, she'd trusted no one—particularly men. She confessed that, for the first time in her life, she felt completely naked. Even the innermost walls of her heart had crumbled and dissolved.

Montana was at a loss for words. She, too, felt something special for Sara; but at times, she found herself wondering whether she was just extremely lucky to have a person like Sara in her life, or whether she was somehow taking advantage of a beautiful young woman with the mind of a child, a child who gave her love blindly to anyone with the potential of giving love back.

Montana put her arm around Sara's shoulders and squeezed her tightly as they walked to the theater. She looked into Sara's big blue eyes and smiled. She couldn't quite put her finger on it, but she knew the girl by her side had been given an extraordinary gift, something so profound it transcended space and time, logic and reason. Sara seemed to radiate an aura of all that was good in the universe.

They arrived at the theater thirty minutes early and saw that other women were already making their way inside. Montana could see that Sara was extremely nervous. "Okie-dokie, girl," she said, soothing and assuring her with her confidence. "This is where we part and you go in there and kick some butt with that incredible voice of yours! I'll be waiting for you right here."

Sara's eyes grew big as she watched two more pretty girls enter the double doors. Montana cupped her hands around Sara's face and turned it to her.

"Hey, look at me. There's nothing to be nervous about. You're an absolutely amazing singer. They're gonna love you."

Sara's big blue eyes looked into the big brown eyes in front of her, desperately drawing from them any bit of courage she could find. When she tried to look down in despair, Montana lifted her chin and gave her a quick, affectionate kiss on the lips.

"I believe in you, Sara. I know you can do this."

Sara was taken aback by the unexpected kiss. Her ears felt hot, and her lips tingled. A feeling of excitement mixed with joy, wrapped around the absolute terror of being inexperienced in such matters, washed over her.

Should I return the kiss? she thought. *I so want to, but would that seem desperate? Should I play it off as no big deal, or would that send the message that I didn't like it—that I didn't just totally scream inside with joy?*

Montana saw the innocent confusion in Sara's eyes. "Okay, how about I go in and sit with you? I'll pretend I'm there to audition. They won't know the difference." Still in a state of euphoria, Sara nodded, and they walked through the doors together.

The auditorium was lavish and much bigger than what they'd imagined. The lighting was dim...except for the enormous spotlight bearing down on the microphone perched on its stand at the center of the stage. The three judges were already at their positions—a very tall man; a short, bald man; and a pretty silver-haired woman.

Montana had warned Sara that because she'd barely made the cutoff time for signing up, she would most likely be either the first or last to go. Montana could tell this only added to Sara's anxiety.

There were thirty-two girls trying out for the same leading role. Sara noticed the beautiful clothes the girls were wearing and looked down at her old, worn-out sweat pants and t-shirt she'd borrowed from the farmhouse. She also noticed the glamorous hairstyles and makeup they had on. She unconsciously pulled at her simple ponytail and touched her naked, makeup-free lips. One of her tennis shoes had a big hole in it. Montana noticed Sara trying to tuck her shoe under her seat, so she squeezed her hand in an effort to distract her. Their eyes met, and everything was okay again. Sara exhaled a sigh of relief when another girl's name was called out before hers, and Montana bit her lip in disappointment. She knew it would only make it that much harder for her to keep Sara calm until her turn.

Sara sat biting her nails as she watched girl after girl climb on stage and sing. Each time a girl finished singing, Sara and Montana would look at each other, and Montana would give a small frown and a slight shake of her head, as if to say that she wasn't impressed and that Sara could do better. Sara wanted to clap for the girls, but they'd been instructed not to clap or make any noise. Each girl was simply to go up on stage when her name was announced, wait for the music to begin, sing, and then exit the theater through the double doors in front. A listing of the top three candidates would be posted on the front doors at noon the following day, along with information concerning when the final audition would be. Of course, Montana and Sara had no intention to ever return to see it.

Two hours had passed, and only three girls remained. The judges seemed exhausted and eager to wrap things up. Half the girls who auditioned had been cut short and told, "Thank you, that will be all," then asked to leave the building. Sara felt sad for each girl not given the chance to sing her song in its entirety. The lump in her throat grew bigger and bigger with each obvious rejection.

Surely I'll be cut short, too, Sara thought. *Some of the girls who were cut short are a lot better than I am.*

Finally, it was Sara's turn to go next. She felt on the verge of a panic attack and squeezed Montana's hand until it was white. Her heart pounded so hard she was certain the judges could hear it. Her breath seemed to have abandoned her, leaving her to fend for herself. Montana's reassuring eyes helped just enough to keep Sara from storming toward the exit sign. They were both caught off guard when, after only one verse of her song, the girl currently on stage was asked to leave—not a good sign.

The fat, bald judge's whiney voice rang out, "Sara Campbell."

Sara froze. Montana tried to make Sara let go of her hand, but Sara's fingers were like steel coils.

"Excuse me...which one of you is Sara Campbell?" the tall judge yelled. His deep and commanding voice was enough to snap Sara out of her fear-stricken trance.

She unclasped Montana's hand and sprang straight to her feet. Montana nodded toward the stairs leading onto the stage, and Sara robotically moved toward them.

"Excuse me," the silver-haired judge said to Montana. "Are you here to audition? Because if you are, you're not on our list."

"Oh no, ma'am, I'm just here for a bit of moral support for my friend," Montana coolly replied.

"That's strictly forbidden here! You'll need to leave immediately, or your friend will be disqualified," snapped the bald judge.

Sara was now at the top of the stairs, evidently oblivious to the conversation. Biting her tongue at the rudeness of the bald judge, Montana apologized and exited through the side door. The blinding afternoon light flooded the auditorium for a few seconds before the hydraulic hinge on the door finally slammed it shut.

Sara nervously walked toward the center of the stage. *Be strong, Sara. You can do this, Sara,* she heard her mother's voice say.

She halted fifteen feet short of the microphone and turned to face the judges.

"What in bloody hell is this poor girl doing? Does she think this is some sort of amateur high school audition?" the bald judge complained.

"And why is she wearing pajamas to audition for the biggest musical in town?" replied the tall judge.

The silver-haired lady intervened. "I think she looks absolutely beautiful. I love how her hair's tied up in a ponytail like that. She radiates a certain wholesomeness, don't you think? Her physical features are perfect for the part she's trying for."

"I'll give you that much. She's definitely got the looks," said the tall judge.

"Who wants to wager a round of beers that when the girl opens her pretty little mouth, nobody will care how beautiful she is?" joked the bald judge.

After leaving the building, Montana ran to her car and got her camera she'd forgotten to bring with her. This definitely was a moment she wanted in her album. She ran back to the building where, luckily, the rear doors were unlocked, and she made her way backstage. She tiptoed to where the sound technician was sitting. When he saw her, she threw her hands together in a gesture of desperate prayer, silently begging him to let her stay. He'd seen her earlier sitting with Sara and nodded with a smile. He pointed to where she could stand out of the view of the judges to watch.

"Young lady, you're welcome to use the microphone there to your right if you'd like," said the silver-haired judge.

Sara didn't move or reply.

"My God, she's going to bloody sing without a mic," snickered the bald judge.

Sara didn't hear the silver-haired judge. All she could hear was the pumping of blood crashing against her eardrums. She could barely make out the judges sitting midway up the hundreds of seats climbing before her. She felt nausea boiling up from the pit of her stomach. She turned to flee but then froze. She spotted Montana standing backstage next to the sound technician, an encouraging smile on her face. She felt a surge of courage and turned back to face the judges. Montana reached over the sound technician's shoulder and pressed his finger that was hovering over the play button. The sound of the music shot through the powerful surround-sound speakers, and something unworldly took possession of Sara.

She was no longer alone in a world of disappointments and suffering. She was no longer just another helpless victim, but became a conduit through which love, the greatest power in the universe, flowed. She became one with all, and all became her. Fear, greed, and hatred vanished; only love remained. And love was all she needed. Suddenly it was as if Sara was transported to a different realm. She saw before her billions of glimmering stars, of which she was one. Every star seemed to pulsate in rhythm with the heartbeats of humanity. The girl, no longer timid, scared, and insecure, opened her mouth, and the universe poured out Sara's song:

Amazing Grace, how sweet the sound,
That saved a wretch like me,
I once was lost but now am found,
Was blind, but now, I see.

Her voice had the energy of a supernova, yet was masterfully controlled and elegant. It was intense, yet silky and smooth as liquid gold.

T'was Grace that taught...
my heart to fear.
And Grace, my fears relieved.
How precious did that Grace appear...
the hour I first believed.

She closed her eyes and the whole of her body became an instrument; from the tips of her fingers, to her swaying hips, to her tiny feet, she moved to the music in a subtle and hypnotizing manner.

Through many dangers, toils and snares...
I have already come.
Tis Grace has brought me safe thus far...and Grace will lead us home.

Her fluctuating pitch effortlessly traversed the musical scale; the sound of her voice resonated from every object. It was as if every atom in the building became her voice.

The Lord has promised good to me...
His word my hope secures.
He will my shield and portion be...
as long as life endures.

For a moment in time, separation was an illusion—all was one. It was as if the entire universe had conspired to create this one fleeting moment and amassed the power of all its stars and poured them into Sara's heart to explode through her vocal cords.

When we've been there ten thousand years...
bright shining as the sun.
We've no less days to sing God's praise...
than when we've first begun.

People outside the auditorium stopped in their tracks mesmerized by the angelic voice. It was the first time anyone had ever heard sound penetrate the thick walls.

Amazing Grace, how sweet the sound,
That saved a wretch like me....
I once was lost but now am found,
Was blind, but now, I see.

With the final notes, the fluid motions of Sara's body came to rest, and she opened her eyes. The auditorium fell silent. Sara stood staring fawn-eyed at the judges—and them at her. There wasn't a dry eye in the auditorium.

Then it occurred to Sara. *Darn! I'm supposed to promptly leave the auditorium after I sing, she thought. No wonder they're all staring at me that way. How stupid of me to forget!*

As she quickly moved to the stairs, she heard a pair of hands clapping. Sara was startled when the nerdy technician with big glasses ran out from the side of the stage; he seemed to have been crying. He raised his arms into the air and said, "I don't care what the rules are. Your performance was the best I've ever witnessed in my whole entire life!"

Montana wanted so badly to clap for her friend, too, but didn't dare risk hurting Sara's chances by breaking more rules.

Sara lowered her head and quickly walked around the nerdy man, making her way down the steps. Before she'd reached the bottom, another pair of hands joined in as the silver-haired judge clapped. Then the applause became louder as the tall judge stood and created a thundering applause. Finally, the bald judge wiggled out of his chair and slowly clapped his hands together.

Sara was a bit confused and didn't know how to respond. *Did they actually like my singing or is this some sort of bad joke?* She kept her head and eyes fixed on the large double doors marked *"Exit"* and quickly moved toward them.

Someone came out from the side aisle to intercept her. The silver-haired judge had her arms outstretched, and then embraced Sara as if she'd known her all her life. "I just knew you were going to be great, Sara. I'm so proud of you!"

Sara's eyes misted. The beautiful woman reminded her of Mama.

"Please, Sara," she asked. "May we visit with you for a while?"

Uh oh. What did I mess up this time? Sara thought.

She and the woman arrived at the center of the auditorium, where the other judges stood in shock. Suddenly, a flash of light went off on stage. Somebody standing next to the sound technician had just snapped a photo. Then she remembered Montana had been on stage watching. She waved excitedly, and Montana waved back and blew her a kiss.

"I see your friend is quite a determined cat," the woman teased.

Sara just smiled and nodded. Both men stood staring at her as if she was some sort of extraterrestrial being, an angel descended from heaven now standing before them. She noticed the name badges taped to their shirts. The short, bald judge had a small number three on his badge, and the tall judge had a number two on his. Sara discreetly looked out of the corner of her eye to the number one on the silver-haired judge's badge. She decided she must be the one in charge.

Finally, the tall judge reached out his hand, and Sara watched as her tiny hand disappeared into his.

"Sara, it's an honor and a pleasure to meet you," he said. "I have to tell you that what you did on that stage just now was...well...indescribable. I've never heard anything like it before. All I can say is, thank you so much. It was an absolute privilege."

Sara blushed and was at a loss for words. She simply smiled and bowed her head. The bald judge stuck out his stubby fingers, offering, "I've been doing this for thirty-nine years, traveling to every continent on this planet. I, too, must say you're the first and most likely the last person I'll ever witness with the gift of a *perfect* voice."

"Thanks," Sara finally managed to say.

The silver-haired judge reached down to hold Sara's hands. "My dear Sara. Something magical happened here today, something not of this world. At the risk of overwhelming you with much-deserved praise and admiration, I, too, will say I've been involved in every aspect of the theater—from where you're standing now to performing in major Broadway productions, from producing award-winning musicals to teaching at the Julliard School of the Arts. My darling, make no mistake about it— you are the 'Golden Child.' You're what people like us seek all of their lives but rarely find. You're the precious diamond that blesses humanity maybe once in a thousand years. Everyone here should thank their lucky stars to have been fortunate enough to witness your heavenly voice.

"But enough of my babbling. We have lots of work to do, child. We must share with humanity what you've been created to do, what the troubled minds and aching souls of this world desperately *need* for you to do—sing!"

CHAPTER 9

THE PRINCE AND THE BLONDE

———◆———

WHEN KIWI CAME OUT OF Lawrence's extravagant office bathroom, there was already a silver plate with pitchers of ice water and lemonade on the table, as well as pastries, coffee, and tea.

"Your bathroom is almost as big as the house I grew up in," she commented.

"I know—such a terrible waste of space, isn't it?" Lawrence joked. "But then again, you're a woman, so there's no such thing as a bathroom too big, right?"

They both laughed, and somehow, in that moment, after all the things Lawrence had shared with her about his past, Kiwi felt that in him she'd found a true friend for life—something her Me'me' had told her was one of the rarest things in the world.

They sat down. Kiwi was starving, so she did what true friends do without worry of judgment. She devoured the pastries like a hog. Lawrence gave a big grin, and then began again.

"Four months and sixteen days after moving to Las Vegas, I was at the Caesar's Palace casino. It was winter, and tourist traffic was slow. I was sitting at a private blackjack table, the ones usually occupied by celebrities or big-time players. The only reason I was there was because I'd always wanted to know what it felt like to be inside a lavish, glass-walled room. So I just walked in and sat down like I belonged—and the nice lady smiled and dealt me a hand. As if out of thin air, a large entourage swept into the room and walked straight to my table.

"An Arab man in an immaculate white suit with all the right accessories joined me. Suddenly, we were surrounded by bodyguards and casino security. I quickly found out that an heir to one of the largest oil companies on the planet was in the mood to gamble. Feeling a bit intimidated, I began to get up to leave, but the man politely insisted I stay and be his guest. It turns out our meeting that evening was to be the very reason you're here."

Kiwi's eyes grew big on top of a perplexed expression. "Is that so?" she heard herself say.

Lawrence nodded and continued. "A tall, incredibly attractive blonde woman in a luxurious silver evening gown sat down beside the Arab man. She seemed almost unreal, like a masterpiece painting or sculpture. She had silky platinum blonde hair down to the top of her shoulders. Her posture was impeccable. Her sensuous neck and elegant shoulders maintained a perfect alignment with the exquisite curvature of her back. Her crystal-clear blue eyes were sharp and penetrating as they surveyed her surroundings. On her head, above her right brow, sat a beautiful hair brooch. The mixed array of precious stones formed colorful flowers. And above the flowers was a magnificent red butterfly. It was clearly made from the finest rubies and other colorful stones.

"The man shooed away the two bodyguards standing within arm's reach and introduced himself and his attractive friend. He asked what my profession was, and I told him I was a professor and asked if he knew anyone in the market for an unemployed physicist with an interest in quantum mechanics. I also told him I'd just moved there from India.

"He pretended to be impressed, saying, 'That's nice. So tell me, Professor, what's your honest opinion on the nature of dreams?'

"Taken aback by the unusual question, I told him I was no expert in the phenomenon, but that I believed they were our subconscious mind—singular—trying to remind our conscious minds—plural—who was really in charge.

"Surprisingly, he seemed very interested in my failed attempt to evade the question. He looked over at the tall blonde woman, who raised an eyebrow and slightly nodded her head in what appeared to be approval. The billionaire got up and moved to the chair next to mine. His guards clearly become uneasy with the unexpected move. The blonde woman whispered something to the pit boss, who then whispered something to the card dealer. The dealer smiled and excused herself from the table. The casino security and pit boss backed away from the table to allow the three of us to speak more privately. The Arab man said something to the bodyguards, and they reluctantly backed further away.

"I didn't know what to make of all the repositioning of people, but the blonde woman smiled at me reassuringly.

"The man leaned close to me and whispered, 'I knew it! I knew I'd chosen this particular casino and this table for a reason. Out of the thousands of gambling tables in this city, I chose yours. It seems God has blessed me with the presence of a wise man!'

"Feeling a bit uneasy about the label, I smiled and shook my head. 'Sorry sir,' I said. 'But I'm afraid you've got the wrong chap. I'm just a simple man who seeks truth, wherever it may lead.' He slapped me on the back, and his jovial smile revealed two rows of gold teeth.

"'You and me both, my friend!' he said. Then he asked, 'Please tell me, Professor, exactly what do you mean when you say conscious and subconscious mind? Is one an imposter and the other our true self?'

"'Neither is our true self,' I replied. 'One is merely the watchman at the gate, while the other is the most powerful tool in the universe.'

"His smile was replaced by a look of bewilderment. 'Ah, this watchman at the gate, what is he watching?' he asked.

"I said, 'The conscious mind is the watchman at the gate of the great domain, and it's responsible for guarding the subconscious mind.'

"The man slowly nodded his head as if he were beginning to understand. 'What is this subconscious mind?' he asked. 'I mean, what does it do?'

"I smiled. 'It's a creator of the very reality you and I are experiencing at this exact moment.'

"The man's eyes widened and his bushy eyebrows rose high on his dark forehead. His mind seemed to be racing as he tried to process the words that just entered his brain. With a critical tone, the woman asked in a thick Scandinavian accent, 'What information does this subconscious mind use to create this reality?'

"'Our thoughts,' I replied. 'Every thought is an input, and what we experience as reality is the output.'

"The woman took a quiet sip from her piña colada, then said, 'If this is the case, how does *your* subconscious mind and *my* subconscious mind know which input data, or thoughts, to choose when creating this reality at this exact moment? After all, isn't it highly unlikely we're both thinking exactly the same thoughts?'

"I was impressed with the Scandinavian woman's obvious level of intelligence. 'It knows because there are an infinite number of conscious minds but only one subconscious mind,' I replied.

"The man and the woman whispered into each other's ears. 'How do you know this to be true?' he asked.

"'Like I said, I seek the truth, wherever it takes me,' I explained, 'and having had a very wise teacher also helped.' I laughed.

"The Scandinavian woman moved to the chair next to the man and asked me, 'You said you're a physicist. Does this have something to do with your theory?'

"'Partly so,' I said. 'I'm trained to use the process of inductive and deductive reasoning when analyzing data and before formulating any conclusions. Thus far, my knowledge of physics, what I observe in my physical world, and the ancient teachings of history's great minds have led me to this conclusion or, as some might call it, this fundamental law of the universe.'

"The man smiled. 'I know of this process. I've studied mathematics in some of the finest institutions for learning in the world—it is my passion. I find solace in numbers. They seem to make the only language that does not mislead or judge.'

"There was a sort of melancholy in the man's voice, and we immediately connected on a deeper level.

"The woman then asked, 'Is there a time lag between our thoughts, the input, and our reality, the output?'

"'Yes and no,' I said. 'It gets a bit tricky here. No, because it's happening at approximately one hundred and eighty-six thousand miles per second.'

"'The speed of light,' said the woman as the man nodded his head.

"'Yes,' I said, 'and this is why nothing on this particular plane of space-time can move faster than the speed of light. It would be like a racecar, made of mass, which is actually energy, or E=mc2, trying to beat a car next to it, also made of mass or energy, to the finish line. This is impossible because both of the cars, the track, the spectators in the stands, the city, the country, the continent, the planet, the entire universe are all made of and are part of the exact same substance—energy. Energy, my dear friends, is light, and light is consciousness. In other words, consciousness is not within us, *we're* within consciousness. Are you still with me?'

"The man ran his fingers through his gray beard, a thoughtful look on his face. 'Yes, yes,' he said. 'I believe so; please continue.' The woman's face was blank for a few seconds, as if mentally calculating the information just given her. Then her eyes lit up, and she asked me to continue as well.

"'Okay,' I said. 'And now the second part of my answer is yes, there is a time lag, because our thoughts, which are made of energy in the form of information sent from an infinite number of conscious minds to the one subconscious mind, are processed by this one subconscious mind. It takes the data and, without bias or prejudice, converts the input data into output data, which are then used to create what we perceive as reality. Time is a man-made construct. It doesn't exist in the subconscious mind, so sometimes the results of our individual or collective thoughts are instantaneous, and at other times it may take millions or billions of years. In essence, every thought, whether it is constructive or destructive, is like a command or request—some call it a prayer.'

"I watched them for a time, as they appeared to be deep in thought.

"'In other words,' I continued, 'our thoughts are the cause, and the realities we experience are the effects. The ignorant person tries to change the effects by working with effects and doesn't realize the only possible way to change the effects is to change the cause.'

"The woman slowly nodded her head. I placed a finger to my temple and said, 'The world within is the cause.' Then I held my hand out, palm up, and said, 'The world without is the effect. To change the effect,' I placed my finger back to my temple and said, 'we must first change the cause.' The woman smiled, but the man still seemed to be deep in thought.

"'The brains of men and women are physically structured to think in specific ways,' I explained. 'These specific thoughts lead to specific actions, which create specific realities that are in alignment with their origin, the original thoughts—input/output. The process is a closed-loop system that cycles over and over, like the mathematical process discovery by Benoit Mandelbrot called the Mandelbrot set, also known as "The Thumbprint of God."'

"'Human brains are instruments for the creation of our world, our reality. They must be in a constant state of progressive evolution, or they will, by nature, self-destruct and become extinct. This may sound cruel, but it's simply a law of the universe, just like gravity.

"'In other words, to change our world for the betterment of human-kind, we must first change our thoughts, our inner mental conversations about our world. Reality follows thought, not the other way around. Our inner conversations do not recede into the past, but rather advance into the future, because we're all participants and creators, not onlookers.'

"The man leaned close to my ear and asked, 'Are you suggesting, Professor, that this subconscious mind is God himself? If so, this is blasphemy!'

"'No, sir,' I promptly replied. 'I don't pretend to know of such incredibly profound things. In these matters, I claim absolute and utter ignorance. I'm merely one conscious mind in search of the truth, wherever it may take me. To be honest, I don't even know if this God everyone speaks of is a man or woman; as far as I know, it is neither, or it may be both.'

"My frankness seemed to defuse the situation a bit with the man. The woman, however, sipped her piña colada anxiously.

"'As I said earlier,' I continued, 'I believe the subconscious mind is simply a tool, an infinitely powerful "thought processor," if you will.'

"Not ready to drop the subject, the man challenged, 'Do you even believe in the existence of a God, the great creator of all?' The woman looked away and nervously set her drink on the table. I picked up my watered-down tequila sunrise and took a long sip.

"Calmly, I said, 'I believe there exists something unexplainable, indefinable, and incomprehensible by the current evolutionary stage of the human brain. This something, I'm almost certain, is omnipotent, omnipresent, and omniscient. It supersedes everything and is all in all. Thus far, the only conclusion I've come to is that this anomaly must be that which has throughout human existence proven to be the *only* thing capable of transcending both space and time.' The man and the woman's stares burned into me with anticipation. 'This...thing, I believe, is the most powerful force in the universe, and it is perfect. This thing, my friends, is *love*, and it is the only thing real—all else is mind.'

"The silence hanging over the table was palpable. The man and woman sat for a while, looking with new eyes at the reality around them.

"'This means,' I continued, 'that each of us is a co-creator of the reality we're all experiencing right now. In essence, our individual and collective thoughts are creative energy.'

"The woman looked over to the man and then back to me and asked, 'So you're saying that we, all of us, have the power to create reality itself?'

"'Of course, but also the power to destroy it,' I replied.

"'This power you speak of is like a double-edged sword,' the man interjected.

"'Exactly,' I replied. 'We are free to choose our thoughts, which are creative energy, either constructive or destructive energy. But we must understand that these thoughts are governed by and subject to an immutable law and always in accordance with the divine purpose of the universe.'

"'Yes, and thus it's said that with great power comes great responsibility,' the woman offered.

"'Thank you very much,' I concluded with a smile.

"I looked at my watch and was amazed to see that more than two hours had passed since our unlikely meeting had begun.

"'Please, Mr. Gold,' said the man, 'I must speak with you more, preferably in private next time. I am very interested in your opinion about the recurring dreams I've had since I was a boy. Is it possible for us to set up a meeting for, say, tomorrow evening? Of course I will pay you for your time and generosity. Just name the price, and I will pay half in advance.'

"The woman gave me a pleasant smile with a hopeful look on her face. I said, 'Sure, I would enjoy meeting with both of you again, but please, you don't need to pay me. I'm grateful to have such inquisitive and open minds in my company.'

"The man handed me his gold-inlaid business card and said, 'Shall we meet here again tomorrow at six p.m.? I am staying in the penthouse suite upstairs. I can have my chauffer at your disposal if you'd like.'

"'No, that won't be necessary,' I said. 'I'll be in the lobby around a quarter to six.'

"We all stood, shook hands, and departed. This was to be the first of many meetings and the start of a collaborative mission to act with the greatest compassion to the greatest number.

"Later that evening, I lay in my bed at home and allowed my mind to wander.

"I couldn't help but be intrigued by the attractive Scandinavian blonde in the bright silver evening gown. She had an extraordinarily sharp mind. I had tried not to stare, but she was one of the most beautiful women I'd ever seen. What fascinated me most were her mind and her graceful poise. She seemed to wield a substantial influence over the billionaire Arab.

"It was obvious she was a woman of power. Whenever one of his aides had whispered in the man's ear about something, he'd turned to her to seek advice. She would consider what he said briefly and then whisper a reply back to him. He had then relayed their decision on the matter back to his aides.

"In a world dominated by men, I wondered, how could one woman have so much influence over such a powerful man?

"This question stayed with me long into the night. I walked outside and sat on my back porch, staring up at the desert stars. I wondered, *What if men of great power, with the potential to affect the world in either a constructive or destructive way, could somehow be persuaded by the right woman at just the right time to make decisions that would have a positive impact on the world as opposed to a negative one?*

"*What if certain women with the attributes of a beautiful flower yet the minds of scholars and the patience of stars were given small windows of opportunity to plant the seeds of goodness, hope, and compassion in the minds of men of great power, capable of making substantial differences in the world, and possibly even causing a paradigm shift in the mentality of an entire nation?*

"These seeds of course are thoughts, and because thoughts are causes and conditions are the effect, the sole purpose of these women would be to guide and help generate the proper thoughts in these powerful men so as to achieve the desired conditions."

Lawrence now looked directly into Kiwi's big green eyes. "In other words," he said, "the events of that night at the casino became my passion and the brainchild of the social companionship service I've called The One Percent—the reason you are here."

Again they sat in silence.

"Wow." The word sounded distant, although it came from Kiwi's mouth.

The moment started to turn awkward, so she searched her mind for something else to talk about.

"The double rainbow in your dream...what do you think was the meaning of it?" she asked.

"That's funny," Lawrence answered. "I've never thought about it. What do you think it means?"

"Well, according to my grandmother, rainbows are to remind us that everything we're experiencing right now is a dream."

"Very interesting. The teachings of Buddha say the same thing," Lawrence offered.

"She said that if we're lucky enough to witness a double rainbow, then we'll be one step closer to enlightenment," Kiwi added.

Lawrence smiled. "Sounds like you had a very wise grandmother."

"Yeah, she was my favorite, and I called her Me'me'. We always seemed to be reading each other's minds. Both of us had a passion for butterflies. We'd spend countless hours butterfly-watching in the summer. Rarely did we miss the annual migration of the monarch butterflies. When I was a little girl, she told me that in her next life, she'd return as a butterfly and come find me, so I'd better be watching for her. I asked her how in the world I was supposed to know which butterfly she was. She replied in a matter-of-fact tone, 'Why, I'll be in all of them, of course!'"

Lawrence laughed out loud. "You weren't kidding about her passion for butterflies, were you?"

"Nope. In fact, we got matching tattoos of a red butterfly on the napes of our necks."

"Wow!" Lawrence exclaimed. "I'd never have guessed *you* had a tattoo. So what's the story behind it?"

"Well," Kiwi began, "I was so devastated after my mother passed away, I didn't leave my house for an entire month. Then, one morning, Me'me' walked into my bedroom, made me get dressed, and practically dragged me to her car. We drove for more than an hour and pulled into the parking lot of a tattoo parlor. She told me that my mother spoke to her the night before and said that this was what we had to do. I really thought it was a big joke and wanted to go home right away. But Me'me' was different that day. She wasn't the free-spirited, always laughing, lighthearted woman I knew. For some unexplainable reason, she was dead serious about getting matching red butterfly tattoos. I remember being excited and scared to death at the same time. The thought of having vibrating needles pierce my skin wasn't my idea of 'a day out with Granny.'

"Me'me' called me a chicken and got up on the table first, handing the man her crude sketch of the butterfly. I remember being speechless at that moment. I stared in awe at the drawing Me'me' had made; it was the exact red butterfly that had landed on me that summer day when I was five!"

"The big Native American tattoo artist got a kick out of seeing a granny and her granddaughter getting matching tats. Then, when he heard the story behind it—that it was a vision from the Great Spirits that my Me'me' received the night before—he took extra special care to make the tats perfect and insisted it was free of charge. The tattoos turned out amazing, and we absolutely loved them. The tattoo artist told us our red butterfly was the most fascinating and original he'd ever seen. He said he felt something indescribable while he was doing them, something powerfully spiritual.

"Afterward in the car, Me'me' said to me, 'See, now it's official. Your Me'me' and your mother will always be looking over your back.' We laughed and cried. Then she hugged me and whispered, 'It also means we will always be there whenever you need us.'"

Lawrence stretched his neck curiously to the side. "Well, are you going show me, or do I have to beg?"

Kiwi turned to the side and lifted her hair up.

Lawrence stared at the tattoo in silence. *Where've I seen this before?* he wondered. "Wow, that truly is amazing," he heard himself say.

Then a serious look came over his face, and he raised his index finger. "Maybe your sweet old granny knew something of the power of loving mothers, beautiful granddaughters, and red butterflies that man has yet to discover."

They both laughed uproariously.

Kiwi intercepted a falling tear. "Yes, she certainly was a special spirit. I wish she was still with us."

"Oh, I'm so sorry," Lawrence consoled.

"Thank you. She lived a full life and departed on her own terms, just like she always said she would. She'd developed Alzheimer's disease when I was in high school. I was devastated and spent most of my free time looking after her. The disease progressed very quickly. One night she came into my room, sat on my bed, and hummed a French lullaby she knew was my favorite. I fell asleep. The next morning, she was nowhere to be seen. They found her body two miles away. She was lying peacefully in a frozen field that in the springtime is overflowing with wildflowers – and butterflies."

Lawrence's eyes filled with tears.

Kiwi was moved by Lawrence's emotional response and tried to lighten the mood. "So, whenever you see a butterfly, please say 'hi' for me."

Again, they laughed together.

Kiwi felt a whole world closer to Lawrence, closer than she had been to any other man before—in some ways, even closer than to her father. She could tell that neither of them was romantically attracted to the other; they just connected in the way true friends connect, honestly and unconditionally. Somehow she knew, too, that Lawrence would always have her back, and that she would have his.

After a short silence, she asked Lawrence, "So what were your other meetings with the Arab man and Scandinavian woman like?"

"Much more personal," he replied. "I learned deep, dark secrets about the brave man he'd kept bottled up all his life."

"Well, if it's too personal, that's okay. You don't have to tell me. I'm sure it was told to you in confidence."

"Actually, he asked me to speak freely about the terrible things he'd witnessed to as many people as I felt was necessary. He said that if more people in the world became aware of these things, maybe there would finally be change. He said it was his way of honoring the lives of his mother and sister. The only thing he requested was that I not divulge his family name or country. He said that, for now, doing so would probably do more harm than good."

Kiwi didn't know how to reply, so she just nodded her head respectfully to Lawrence.

He stood and walked to the window. "It's the first time I've shared the Arab prince's story with anyone."

Kiwi's eyes widened. "Oh. So he's a real prince?"

"Yes, a very wise and brave prince. The following day, in our second meeting, I was told about the prince's privileged upbringing. He lived a lavish lifestyle in a certain Arab country. His father was a powerful man who held a high position in the family hierarchy. The prince himself was the first son in his immediate family. Beginning at a very young age, his father insisted that he learn 'his duties' as a prince. The prince traveled with his father to many different countries on business trips.

"One day, when he was nine years old, they were visiting a neighboring country. That was the day he witnessed his first 'honor killing.' In his words, he said, 'This was the day my childhood died.' The nine-year-old boy stood with his father as they witnessed three teenage girls being buried alive.

"The crime, the prince was told, was that the girls refused to marry the men their families had arranged for them. Two of the girls were to marry men thirty or forty years older than they were. The other was to marry her first cousin. In essence, they were treated as property and given away as nothing more than gifts, usually to ensure the family status or the purity of the bloodline."

Kiwi's heart sank as she sat in shock from what she just heard. Her lips quivered. "But how can this happen? What is this 'honor killing'?"

Lawrence took a deep, slow breath. "Honor killings are acts of vengeance, usually murder, committed by male family members against female family members who are believed to have brought dishonor upon the family. A woman can be targeted by individuals within her family for a variety of reasons, including refusing to enter into an arranged marriage, being the victim of a sexual assault, seeking a divorce—even from an abusive husband—or for committing adultery. The mere perception that a woman has behaved in a way that dishonors her family is sufficient to trigger an attack on her life. Methods of killing include stoning, stabbing, beating, burning, beheading, hanging, throat slashing, lethal acid attacks, shooting, and strangulation. The murders are sometimes performed in public to warn other women in the community of possible consequences of engaging in what is seen as illicit behavior. Often, minor boys are selected by the family to act as the killers so they can benefit from the most favorable legal outcomes. Boys in the family are often asked to control and monitor closely the behavior of their sisters or other females in the family to ensure the females don't do anything to tarnish the 'honor' and 'reputation' of the family. The boys are often asked to carry out the murder; if they refuse, they may face serious repercussions from the family and community for failing to perform their 'duty.' The regime of honor is unforgiving: women on whom suspicion has fallen are not given an opportunity to defend themselves, and family members have no socially acceptable alternative but to remove the stain on their honor by attacking the woman. Different variations of these honor killings, these atrocities, against women have been going on for thousands of years all around the world in almost every society, in every country. It's not isolated to only certain countries, cultures, or religions."

Tears rolled down Kiwi's face as she wondered if these honor killings had ever taken place in her own tribe.

Lawrence handed her a box of tissues. "I'm sorry, Kiwi. I know this is very disturbing. May I finish the prince's story? It's very important for you to know."

She nodded and Lawrence continued. "The second time the prince witnessed an honor killing was while visiting his uncle. A pregnant woman was buried up to her neck in the town square and then stoned to death for marrying the man she loved. This woman was accused by her family of marrying without their consent. First, the terrified woman's family members lined up to take their turn in casting the stones; then, one by one, the people in her village did as was expected of them by their 'wise elders.' So in keeping with ancient traditions, these so-called human beings picked up small fragments of the earth's outer crust and propelled it toward the face and skull of their fellow human being, until there was no longer any sign of life.

"The prince said that while he was witnessing the brutal crime being committed in front of him, he had some sort of vision or flash of insight. He saw his older sister's face on the pregnant woman right before the first stone opened her forehead. He said he was so overcome with fear and grief that he pulled his hand away from his uncle and fled the scene.

"He ran and hid under an ox cart. He describes the moment as 'surreal and forever etched in his mind.' He was lying on his stomach with his hands over his ears when a beautiful red butterfly landed next to the wooden wheel in front of him. He stared into the gentle green eyes of the butterfly, and it stared back. He said the butterfly somehow took his pain and drew it away from him and into itself, as a mother would do for her child. Then it told him something and flew away. He never was able to recall what the butterfly said."

Kiwi found herself rubbing the nape of her neck.

"After the public stoning, his uncle found him hidden under the cart and pulled him out. When his uncle noticed he'd been crying, he slapped him on the back of the head and scolded him. 'Why are you crying, foolish child? It is the will of God!'

"'It was in that exact moment,' the prince confessed, 'that I began to have doubt…not in the will of God, but in the will of men.'

"Over and over the young prince either witnessed or heard of these honor killings taking place all around him, two or three a month. A seventeen-year-old girl of a certain faith was stoned to death in front of two thousand men for wanting to convert to another religion. A mother and her two daughters were beaten and strangled to death by ten male relatives for allegedly having illicit affairs with men. Their bodies were thrown into the river. A sixteen-year-old girl was killed by her father for having a boyfriend of a different faith. A man suspected of being gay was thrown out a ten-story window to the delight of cheering spectators below.

"The prince said he was especially sickened to hear of stories, aside from the honor killings, where entire villages were raided by certain radical religious groups, their women and children taken away, and all the men of the village slaughtered. These radical groups would divide the women and children among themselves to use as they pleased, buying and trading them like cattle. According to one radical group, their religion allowed a man to have sexual intercourse with a child when she reached the age of nine years; in this way, these so-called men could somehow rationalize and justify the raping of children."

The room fell silent. It was only after about five minutes that Kiwi noticed that both Lawrence and she had been staring blankly out the window, as if the murdered souls of the people the prince spoke of were out there somewhere, staring back at them. *What would they say? How would I respond?* she wondered.

Lawrence cleared his throat and continued. "The prince told another story about a friend who knew a family whose nine-year-old son was kidnapped by extremist rebels from a rivaling country. The boy was burned alive, which they recorded on video. The video was sent to the leaders of the friend's country. These rebels proudly claimed that this act was in retaliation for the kidnapping and murder of two teenage boys from their country months earlier by extremist rebels from the friend's country. These crimes of hatred disguised as acts of patriotism and honor have been exchanged between the two countries for as long as anyone can remember. Why? Because of differences in their personal beliefs, differences in their thoughts about what they think God should be and what God wants, differences in their thoughts about how the world should be and what people should want.

"These so-called soldiers of God actually believe their all-loving God spoke to them, telling them to bring peace to their people through hate and destruction. This God supposedly told them they must poison the hearts of their children with hate, then strap bombs to their little bodies and send them into a crowd full of their enemies. They believe their all-loving, all-forgiving God commanded them to have no compassion, no mercy for the enemy, and to seek unrelenting vengeance at all costs, for only in doing this could they guarantee themselves a place in the house of their God. And if they refused to do the work of their God, they risked being judged by their God as not worthy of heaven, destined to suffer in the fires of hell—just like the innocent boy they'd just set on fire in the name of their all-loving and merciful God.

"The thought never occurred to them that maybe the hell they feared so much was not something they might experience after this life, but instead was the one they themselves had so bravely, obediently, and blindly created for others in this life, in the name of their all-loving and merciful God.

"On and on these murders would take place, and it seemed to him that people had become desensitized, accepting these actions as a normal way of life instead of a horrific and unjustified way of death. Needless to say, the young prince became disillusioned with the world in which he lived. He felt a sickness in his heart. The faces of the slain women would not leave his mind. He became fearful—not for himself, but for his beloved mother, sister, and other female family members.

"Then one day, his worst nightmare came true. His older sister, a princess, had been sentenced to death. She was affectionately called Farashatan by everyone, which is Arabic for butterfly, and was only eighteen years old."

Again, Kiwi unconsciously rubbed the nape of her neck.

"The princess was attending a university in a neighboring country when she fell in love with a man her own age. He happened to be from the same country as she. They began an affair, writing love letters and meeting only in public places such as the local mall. When the two returned home to their county later that summer, they were immediately arrested and accused of adultery. Although the princess was promised by her family to another man many years her senior, the two had never actually married. Her boyfriend, not being of royal blood, was kept in a filthy prison cell and routinely beaten. The princess was locked up in the royal palace. The prince was sixteen years old at the time and was allowed to see his sister only once. He was ordered by his father and grandfather to condemn his sister and belittle her for her foolish actions and for bringing shame to the family name.

"When he walked into the room, he saw the fear in his beloved sister's eyes, and he fell apart. He ran to her and hugged her, trying to console her as best he could. He whispered to her that he would not allow her execution to take place, that he would figure out a way to stop it. His father grabbed him by the back of the neck and threw him out of the room. The young prince was scolded by his father and ridiculed by his grandfather for 'being weak and behaving like a woman.' He was forbidden from ever seeing his sister again.

"The prince said that after that incident—and for the first time in his life—he lost all respect for his father. Before that, his father was his hero and could do no wrong. But in that moment, as his father was dragging him away from his crying sister, their eyes met, and both knew each had lost the other forever.

"It was during this time that his mother had nervous breakdowns almost every day, and the prince spent most of his time by her side. She had no voice as far as his grandfather was concerned. She was even scolded for 'failing to teach her daughter better.' Over a two-week period, the 'wise elders of the royal family' debated as to what to do with the 'insolent and shameless princess.' It was decided that the princess's lover would be executed by beheading in the public square. The princess, being of royal blood, would be given a lesser sentence, but only if she admitted to her crime of adultery. The princess, however, refused to confess to something that wasn't true. She knew if she did, it would mean certain death for the man she loved. The princess did admit to holding his hand at the mall and having kissed him one time when they said their good-byes before parting for the summer.

"The princess thought that because it was impossible for them to find evidence of sexual contact, there was a small chance they would set the man she loved free. What she didn't know was that the decision had already been made by the royal family to execute the young man, regardless of whether she confessed or not. After all, he was just a commoner. In attempt to save his lover, the young man told his captives that it was his fault; that he had tricked the princess into meeting him at the mall and forced a kiss on her the night before they departed. His captors knew he was lying and beat him all the more. Meanwhile, the prince knew his sister's time was running out. He had to think of something quickly.

"His plan was to sneak into the room, disguise her as a man, and then sneak her out of the palace. Then, he would drop her off at the airport, where she would board a plane and fly out of the country.

"Because of certain loyal servants in the palace who conveniently turned a blind eye, they were able to sneak out of the palace. Everything went as planned all the way to the airport. He told his sister he loved her and not to worry. He, too, would leave the country as soon as possible.

"The princess sat anxiously as the Boeing 747 taxied its way toward the runway. Suddenly, the airplane turned around and then stopped. Two airport security men boarded the plane and arrested the princess. Someone had recognized her.

"The prince begged mercy for his sister's life, but to no avail. In fact, his grandfather had him locked away in another royal palace hundreds of miles away from his sister. Being a male and only sixteen years old, the prince was given a pardon for his disobedience.

"Three days later, the princess and her lover were taken to a public square. The young man was forced to watch the woman he loved be executed by gunfire to the back of her head before he was beheaded by sword. Soon after, the prince's mother mysteriously vanished and was never seen again.

"Love letters secretly safeguarded by the princess's female friends surfaced years later. They told of the lovers' promises of celibacy to each other until after they were properly married. The young lovers swore to each other that, no matter what happened, they would be true to each other to the end and beyond.

"After confiding to me his darkest secrets, the prince looked at me with mournful eyes and asked, 'please doctor, tell me, how is it that human beings are capable inflicting such horrific suffering upon one another? Are we no more than animals?'

"I walked to my shelf and pulled out a book. 'Are either of you aware of the experiment conducted by Dr. Stanley Milgram called 'Obedience to

Authority'? I asked. The prince shook his head. The Scandinavian woman turned her back and looked out the window. She slowly nodded her head. 'Yes', she said in a solemn voice. 'I'm fully aware of the cause of the extermination of my entire family'.

"The Prince and I looked at each another and he shrugged his shoulders. We stared at the woman for a moment and then I continued. Dr. Milgram was an American social psychologist. He is of Jewish faith and had asked himself the same question; how normal everyday people like you and I, in relatively a short period of time, can become accomplices to the systematic persecution and murder of approximately six million children, women, and men. He decided to do a controversial study on human nature. I will read to you Dr. Milgram's summarization of the experiment, 'The Perils of Obedience.'

Writing: The legal and philosophic aspects of obedience are of enormous importance, but they say very little about how most people behave in concrete situations. I set up a simple experiment at Yale University to test how much pain an ordinary citizen would inflict on another person simply because he was ordered to by an experimental scientist. Stark authority was pitted against the subjects' [participants'] strongest moral imperatives against hurting others, and, with the subjects' [participants'] ears ringing with the screams of the victims, authority won more often than not. The extreme willingness of adults to go to almost any lengths on the command of an authority constitutes the chief finding of the study and the fact most urgently demanding explanation.

Ordinary people, simply doing their jobs, and without any particular hostility on their part, can become agents in a terrible destructive process. Moreover, even when the destructive effects of their work become patently clear, and they are asked to carry out actions incompatible with fundamental standards of morality, relatively few people have the resources needed to resist authority.

"'You must understand', I continued. 'It's the combination of the primitive human brain and ignorance that is the demise of humanity. We have little direct effect on the former but we can each do our part about the latter. When we take action to shed light on ignorance, we stimulate and activate dormant neurons in the brain. This causes windows in the mind to open and we begin to see the world with new eyes—and hope.'

"The room fell silent for a while and then the prince finally spoke. 'It haunts me to this day that it was only after the murder of my own sister and disappearance of my mother that I realized the absurdity of an absolute monarchy, the idea that a person, by the mere act of being born with specific DNA, is not required to *earn* the respect, power, and monumental responsibility that goes with leading the people of a nation— that this so-called 'royalty' is an utterly appalling concept and is flawed in every way.

"When the prince was done unleashing years of pent-up rage and sorrow, it was clear to the Scandinavian woman and me why he had recurring nightmares. It was as if he knew the reason all along but needed to force himself to revisit the skeletons of his past.

"Together, the woman and I came up with the only way the prince could ever forgive himself, which was by serving others. Using his great fortune, the Arab prince and the Scandinavian woman set up many charities throughout his country. These organizations educate girls and counsel abused women. They provide a safe haven for those in need and teach them work skills so that, eventually, they can go out and be a functional part of society. In honor of his mother and sister he calls his centers 'House of Butterflies.' The effort has been a great success and model for future humanitarian organizations throughout the world. In fact, because of their courage and selfless efforts, the Arab prince and Scandinavian woman became laureates for the Nobel Peace Prize. Mysteriously though, when the day came to accept the prize the Scandinavian woman had vanished without a trace.

"The prince's paralyzing nightmares went away. It was as if his sister and mother were finally at peace. He told me what he had finally discovered: 'Compassion is not just a way to know God—it's the *only* way.'"

Lawrence stood, and Kiwi sat cross-legged on the floor next to the window. It was dim inside and night had fallen outside. The soft hum of the air conditioner was as soothing as a mother's lullaby. They stared up at the stars, and in those moments somehow they knew their destinies would move in the same direction and forever be linked.

CHAPTER 10

ETERNAL LOVE

———————

THE MEN WATCHED SARA AND Montana from a distance. The niece of one of Chopper's men happened to be auditioning for the same part as Sara, in the same city and at the exact same time. The scar-faced man and his partner made the three-hundred-mile drive because he'd promised his mother weeks ago he would take his niece to the audition. As he dropped his niece in front of the theater, he couldn't believe his eyes. Standing before them in front of the large double doors was Chopper's missing girl. He immediately recognized Sara's face. How could he forget? He was one of the men who abducted her and drove her to Chopper's mansion years ago.

After the girls entered the building, the scar-faced man called Chopper to tell him of his good fortune. He was given orders to capture both girls at all costs. If they succeeded, he and his partner would share the five-thousand-dollar bounty. If they failed, he was advised never to return. He was also told that Chopper himself, along with several of his men, would be departing for their location soon.

The scar-faced man's niece was one of the first girls to be rejected. He had his partner take her to the bus station and buy her a ticket home while he stood guard outside.

The men sat in the car, waiting for their prize to come out. Two hours had passed, and they started getting worried that the girls somehow managed to escape. Chopper would kill them if so.

They watched as the pretty, short-haired brunette that had been with Sara earlier burst out from the side door of the auditorium. She seemed a bit upset about something. Then she walked quickly to her car, climbed in, and searched through her glove box. She came out with a camera in hand and jogged back to the building. The anxious men were relieved to know the girls were still inside and wondered why she reentered the building through the back door.

The men discussed their plan to abduct the girls and after much debate finally came to an agreement. It was not yet three in the afternoon, which meant they'd most likely have to do it in broad daylight. This made them a bit nervous. They considered tailing the girls in their car until dark, but that was too risky. What if they noticed someone stalking them and drove straight to the police station? They knew this was a one-shot, one-kill type of situation for them, and they couldn't afford the slightest slip-up. There was only one thing to do to ensure their success.

The girls were giddy and excited as they walked out the front doors of the auditorium. The scar-faced man stepped out of the car to follow them on foot to the parking lot just around the block. He managed not to be detected and watched from the corner of the building as the girls made their way to a lone car in the back of the lot.

Montana slid the key into her door to unlock it. In the back of her mind, she felt something wasn't right. She climbed in and pressed the automatic unlock button. Sara stood smiling next to the passenger door, and when she heard the *click*, she opened the door and climbed in. The girls closed their doors, and Montana put her keys into the ignition. Just as she was about to start the car, a large man sprung up from the backseat and wrapped his tree-trunk arm around Sara's throat. Sara's scream was immediately cut short when her airway was clamped shut.

Montana also let out a scream but stopped right away when she saw the barrel of a .45 caliber pistol up against Sara's temple.

"Scream again, and I'll blow her damn head off!" the man said. "Stay in the car, and don't start the engine."

Montana connected the dots. In a hurry, she'd forgotten to lock her door when she retrieved the camera. When she'd inserted her key and turned it, she didn't feel the usual resistance. That was what made her feel uneasy about something.

Montana's mind was racing as she watched a scar-faced man approach her car.

Oh God, what do I do? How are we going to get out of this? Please don't let them hurt Sara. It's all my fault!

Sara stared in shock at Montana, barely able to breathe. *Please God, don't let them hurt Montana; it's all my fault,* she thought.

The scar-faced man entered the car directly behind Montana and put his pistol to the side of her neck. His partner repositioned his gun toward the back of Sara's head just above his arm, which was still wrapped tightly around her neck.

"Nice of you girls to give us total strangers a ride," the man with the scar said. "I've always liked these big-ass town cars, especially when they have such dark tinted windows. Keeps the cops from seeing what's going on inside, know what I mean?"

Sara immediately recognized the voice. An image of the man's jagged scar across his face filled her mind, and she instinctively struggled to free herself, to no avail.

"Please, let her go. I'll do anything you want, I promise," Montana pleaded to the men.

Sara shook her head in protest and tried to say no.

"Shut your mouth, both of you! Do exactly as I say, or I'll paint the windshield with your pretty little brains!" snapped the scar-faced man. "If you'll be good, ain't no one gonna get hurt, ya hear?"

Montana looked into Sara's terrified eyes and reluctantly nodded her head.

The scar-faced man ordered Montana to drive down a lonely stretch of highway. During the drive, they weren't allowed to talk but were able to hold each other's hand. Montana's mind searched for ways to get out of their horrible predicament. She thought about veering off the road and crashing into a ditch. Maybe it would buy them enough time to get out of the car and run…but where would they hide? The landscape was barren and flat for miles all around. She thought about slamming on the emergency brake, yelling to Sara to run, and then fighting off the men for as long as she could. But the thought of Sara being shot to death was too much to bear.

If it had been only one man with a gun, she would've taken the chance. It seemed the only thing they could do was to appreciate what remaining time they had together and hope for a miracle.

The scar-faced man noticed that the girls had matching tattoos on their wrists. "What're ya'll, the frick'n butterfly twins or something?" he laughed. His partner also noticed the tattoo's and felt a pang in his heart. It reminded him of a beloved little sister he once had whom he affectionately called Lil' Butterfly.

Sara held tightly to Montana's hand and prayed harder than she'd ever prayed before. She blamed herself for not wearing her rosary or bringing her Bible. *If only I'd remembered to, maybe this wouldn't be happening.*

Sara looked down at her hand clasped on top of Montana's. She pressed her wrist tightly down so that their butterflies touched. More than ever, she was glad they'd gotten the tattoos. Then she realized, *I didn't tell Montana about how I saw the same red butterfly in the pasture, and now it's too late.* Tears streamed down her face. *No!* she decided. *It's not too late.* She turned to Montana and quickly said in a low voice, "I saw our red butterfly the other day. It came to me out in the pasture and sang to me." Montana had a perplexed expression on her face. Sara looked down at their entwined wrists and lifted her arm slightly to reveal her tattoo.

Montana tried to keep the tears from escaping; she didn't want to show their captors any signs of weakness. A single drop escaped down her cheek and vanished into the unknown. She looked at Sara and tried to give a reassuring smile.

Sara felt the old familiar drowning feeling creep over her—the helpless feeling of being trapped at the bottom of a deep dark well as the cold water rose slowly, mercilessly, into her lungs. She felt the heaviness of her heart moan with sorrow as it silently pounded on the walls of her mind for a way out. Far away in the distance she heard a voice. The voice seemed to be moving toward her. She realized it was her own voice and that she was humming a favorite song by "The Smiths". She closed her eyes and did the only thing she knew to make her world bearable:

(First verse...)

The men were taken aback. The scar-faced man began to speak his disapproval but stopped short. They looked curiously at each other then turned back to Sara. The sound of her angelic voice was like a warm glowing fire in the dark cold night.

(Second verse...)

Somehow in that moment the men felt transported to a different space and time—a kinder, more hopeful place somewhere in their distant memory.

(Third verse...)

Both men recalled their childhoods, a time of innocence and carefree summers; when the sun seemed somehow brighter, bathing them in laughter.

(Fourth verse...)

Through teary eyes, Montana stared at the unforgiving road stretched out before her. Her heart begged her mind for a solution, a way to save the only thing she knew to be pure and wholesome and good.

(Fifth verse…)

For the first time in her life, Montana felt a complete and utter sense of helplessness. And for the first time, Montana's burning desire for life began to dim. Her mind spoke of hopelessness, of inevitable doom, of the capitulation to their cataclysmic end.

There Is A Light That Never Goes Out,
There Is A Light That Never Goes Out,
There Is A Light That NEVER Goes Out…

No! Montana heard her heart scream. *Pull yourself together, Montana; this ain't no time for self-pity. Fight! Fight like you've never fought before. Fight for Sara, dammit!*

There was a silent moment of reverence, as if the passing of time were a requirement for the witnesses to appreciate what had just occurred and then to let it go, set it free, and return to their obscure and arbitrary lives.

Montana lifted Sara's hand to her lips and kissed it.

The scar-faced man smacked his pistol against the side of her head. "Don't you be kiss'n on Chopper's girl!" he scolded.

Sara unconsciously threw her elbow hard at the man's face. "No!" she screamed.

The man caught her arm.

"Whoa there, princess! You're a wild one, ain't ya?" The scar-faced man laughed. He knew that, no matter what, he couldn't do anything to hurt Chopper's girl. If he did and Chopper found out, he'd literally have his nuts chopped off. "Don't worry, you're precious cargo, baby. We ain't gonna hurt *you*," he told her. "But your girlfriend here better watch it 'cause she don't mean shit to us."

A large purple welt swelled up on Montana's temple. She squeezed Sara's hand. "It's okay, Sara. I'm all right, really."

Sara's chest was heaving wildly. She was astonished at her reaction. She'd never tried to hurt anything before in her entire life.

"Hey, take it easy bro," the big man behind Sara said. "We don't need anything bad to happen to the girl—know what I mean?"

"Shut up, fool," the scar-faced man snapped. "I'm the captain of this ship. You just follow orders and keep your trap shut!"

After about an hour of driving, the man behind Montana pointed to an abandoned gas station in the middle of nowhere. "Pull in there and park it."

Montana inconspicuously scanned the area for any signs of people who could help. The only movement was the mirage of a shimmering puddle on the hot road ahead. A black spot emerged from the middle of the puddle. Gradually the spot got bigger and bigger in sync with the rapid acceleration of the women's hearts. A shiny black limousine carrying three men pulled up next to them. A menacing man with dark glasses stepped out and walked toward their car. The silver-mirrored window on the passenger side of the limousine rolled halfway down, exposing the face of the girls' worst nightmare.

Chopper's blood boiled as he glared at Sara's unveiled face. *How dare she defy me and expose herself to the lustful eyes of other men,* he thought. *That shameless whore will pay!*

Sara and Montana clutched each other in a desperate embrace. Tears fell as cries of sorrow and regret rang out. They knew they would never see each other again.

"I'm so sorry!"

"It's all my fault!"

"No, it's my fault!"

"Please forgive me!"

"I love you!"

"I love you, too!"

Montana pressed her mouth to Sara's ear and whispered, "You're gonna have to fight, Sara. Don't ever give up."

The driver-side door flung open; a large hand reached in and grabbed Montana by her hair and violently snatched her out of Sara's arms. Sara tried to follow Montana out through the driver door but was pulled back into her seat.

Montana's survival instincts took over. All the years of mixed-martial arts training became muscle memory. As soon as her legs cleared the vehicle she looked down behind her to spot her target. When the man's shin was within striking distance, she mule-kicked it hard. The infuriated man hobbled on one leg in excruciating pain. She immediately threw her right arm above her head so she didn't get caught in a fatal choke hold from behind. When the man pulled her in for the choke attempt, as she anticipated, she fired her left elbow into his lower ribs with devastating force. The man let out a grunt as one of his fractured ribs punctured his spleen. Montana felt the man's knees buckle and his grip loosen. She lowered her body and twisted away from his hold. The man dropped to his knees, clutching his side. Montana kicked the back of his head hard, sending his sunglasses sailing through the air. His eyes rolled back and he crumbled face-first to the ground.

Chopper watched with amusement from his car. "Damn, that pretty bitch can fight! He turned to the bodyguard in the back seat. "Looks like you're gonna have to go rescue your sorry-ass partner out there. But wait a minute; I want to see if my boys in that car got any balls."

Montana was free; she could've ran but didn't. Sara struggled to break loose from the vise hold on her. She managed to get her door open and one leg out. The powerful man snatched her up and pulled her over the seat as if she were a rag doll.

Montana glared at the men in the limo. She knew they were just watching the show for now. "Let her go; you can have me!" she yelled to them.

The skinny, scar-faced man watched nervously through the dark windows. He didn't want to go face Montana, but he knew he wouldn't be able to restrain Sara; physical strength was not his forte. He also knew that Chopper was watching, and that cowardice in the face of battle was *not* a forgivable act. Hesitantly, he opened his door and stepped out. The girl was nowhere in sight. *Oh shit, she got away!* he thought. *Chopper's gonna kill me.* He tried to look tough and strutted to the back of the car, keeping his head and eyes cautiously fixed on Chopper and his men. The impact of Montana's violent roundhouse kick to the temple could be heard from the limo—the skinny man was unconscious before he hit the ground.

Montana jumped over the fallen man and rushed through the opened door at Sara's captor. The shot from his gun blew her back out of the car in an instant. Horrified screams rang out. Sara violently punched and bit the massive arm coiled around her. The big man instinctively knew his only purpose for the moment was to keep Sara safe inside the car until the situation outside was under control.

Montana stared up at the vast blue sky. *Ah, Big Sky country,* she thought. *I'll finally get to see it.* Then the buzzing alarm in her head ceased—everything became silent. Her body was numb; there was no pain. Two men appeared in her range of vision. The limo driver and the other bodyguard stared down at her with pistols in hand. Montana faintly heard one say, "It's just a shoulder shot. She'll live—for now." Suddenly she became aware again of her surroundings and the situation. A surge of panic electrified her brain. *Where's Sara? I have to get to Sara, God help me!* She struggled to get up. The men reached down and grabbed her arms. The pain came back like a punch in the face. She was sure someone had stuck a hot iron into her shoulder, and she screamed out in pain. As she was being dragged off, she heard Sara yelling her name. "I'm here, Sara!" she answered. "I'll wait for you! I'll wait for you, Sara!"

CHAPTER 11

WHAT HAPPENS IN VEGAS

———————•———————

THE ROOM BECAME A BLIZZARD of confetti as the young, intoxicated client went up on stage to receive his award. The walls echoed with loud clapping and cheering. The short pharmaceutical CEO had the face and body of a sixteen-year-old, yet he was the mastermind behind the newest and most promising breakthrough cancer drug in the world.

Kiwi couldn't help but think about her mother and what the price would be when this miracle drug hit the market.

Finally, this was her chance to sneak off and use the restroom. She quickly made her way through the crowd toward the ladies' room. She knew she'd broken protocol by not making sure her bodyguard knew where she was going, but she'd been holding it for two hours and felt like her bladder was going to burst any second.

When she came out of the ladies' room, somebody grabbed her by the shoulders from behind. The door beside her opened, and she was shoved hard into the adjoining room.

The towering man pushed her with such force that she was slammed onto the floor. Before she could even let out a scream, the man was on top of her, his large hand pressed tightly over her mouth. She immediately recognized him as one of the VIPs who was part of the guest entourage. He had a sadistic smile on his face.

"Don't make a sound, little lady, and nobody gets hurt," he said. "We're just gonna have a bit of fun then return to the party. How's that sound? It's your job after all, isn't it?"

Terrified, Kiwi shook her head, begging him to stop. The evil smile left his face. With incredible strength he lifted her straight to her feet while he held one hand over her mouth and the other clamped to the back of her head. Her entire body was suspended off the floor as the man carried her to a utility closet on the other side of the room.

Panic shot through her as she struggled to stick her left leg out to keep the door from being shut. She knew that if the door closed, it would be over for her. The heavy wooden door slammed hard against her shin. She heard the giant fist smash into the side of her ear before she felt it. A numbing ringing filled her head. Everything went dark with the click of the door latch. Their bodies collided violently into the shelves. Cleaning materials scattered and fell to the floor. Kiwi's head slammed hard into a shelf, and she could feel something warm trickle down the back of her neck. She felt woozy as her arms and legs went limp.

She could feel his lustful panting against her neck. It reeked of cigar smoke and overpriced champagne. His thick fingers pressed her lips against her front teeth. She tasted blood in her mouth.

She closed her eyes and thought, *Is this how it ends? How my life story will be told? Is this what I deserve? What did I do that was so wrong? Will I never experience the joy of having children?* Suddenly a surge of incredible energy shot through her mind and body. *No, I refuse. I will not accept this. This will not happen to me! Great Spirit, please help me!*

The man's massive body pinned Kiwi against the shelves as his cold hand made its way up her dress. His fingers slithered underneath her panties in search of her innocence. He pulled down his pants, and then it happened—something primal took over. *I will die before I give up!* she thought. She suddenly possessed an incredible amount of strength. She freed her right hand from under his arm and raised it high above her head. A low, growling sound made its way from the pit of her stomach up through her chest and throat then reverberated through the suffocating hand of her captor. Her freshly painted, cherry-red talons came down onto his right eye with an animal-like ferocity that could only be explained as a reflex motivated by the most basic instincts and deepest desire to survive.

Kiwi knew immediately that her middle fingernail had struck home. It effortlessly sliced open his tightly clenched eyelid, and her finger penetrated deeply to the back of his eyeball. He let out a loud grunt as she gripped his eye between her finger and thumb. With a grotesque *pop*, the talon on her thumb pierced his cornea, spewing thick liquid down her hand. She made a quick jerk and ripped the eyeball out of its socket. A horrifying scream escaped the man's mouth. His powerful hands abandoned their sinful tasks and immediately moved to the small fragile hand holding his destroyed eye.

Kiwi was free to scream for help now, but she didn't. There was no need to. She was no longer the prey.

She released her hold on his eye, and he slumped to the floor like a defeated jackal. As he was trying to carefully push the bloody tangled mess back into his head, she pushed him off her legs and found the doorknob. Light rushed in, and she ran to it.

In the main banquet room, the party was going full force. The noise was deafening. Kiwi's bodyguard immediately spotted her and pushed his way through the crowd. On his face was a look of relief followed by concern. Then, when he saw the blood dripping from her lips and her torn dress, it turned into a controlled rage.

"What happened? Where'd you go?" he asked.

Kiwi pointed to the door she'd just fled through.

"He tried to rape me. Please, I want to leave right now!" was all she could manage to say as everything became silent and surreal. The six-foot-eight bodyguard wrapped his enormous arms around her and led her to the back of the room. He spoke into his microphone. Kiwi's chaperone quickly arrived. He explained what he knew and handed Kiwi over to her.

"Wait, don't leave us—where're you going?" the chaperone asked.

"I'm going to kill him," said the bodyguard in a chilling, matter-of-fact tone.

The room was empty when the mammoth bodyguard entered. The closet door was ajar. Streaks of blood stained the doorknob. On the floor inside the closet was a golden cuff link. He picked it up. The cuff link was in the shape of a buffalo head with small turquoise stones set as eyes.

CHAPTER 12

SACRIFICIAL LAMB

———◆———

IT HAD BEEN ELEVEN DAYS since Sara had eaten. Her will to live was non-existent. Life was simply the insistent beating of her stubborn heart. *Why won't it just stop?* she wondered. She wanted so badly for it to stop. *It'd be so simple,* she thought. *Fill the tub, take one last bath, and slash my wrists. But I can't. Mama said it's a sin to take your own life, that you'll be burned in the fires of hell for eternity. Wasn't it written in the Bible?*

She watched as her cheekbones and ribs pushed to the surface of her skin a little more each day. Images of Montana's face followed her from her waking moments into sleep. The dreams were always different versions of the same thing: A baby is crying, but it's dark and Sara can't find it. The screaming grows louder. She sees her mama searching frantically for her. "I'm right here!" she yells, but her mama doesn't hear her. The door opens; the light is blinding. Mama steps into the doorway. Sara sees her silhouette and tries desperately to run to her but can't. Then she notices it's no longer Mama. It's Father Odiar. He laughs out loud and holds the crying child out to her.

Suddenly, light filled the room. Chopper walked in and placed a crying infant on Sara's bed. "If you die, she dies," he said.

He placed a bag with baby formula, bottles, and diapers on the floor, and then walked out. Sara watched as the baby kicked, screamed, and punched her little fists at the air.

So you, too, are a victim of life's cruel joke, she thought. Something warm, strange, and compelling began to fill her heart, a powerful desire, and an instinct to do what she didn't want to but couldn't stop. Against her will, the will to live kicked down her dark walls and forced its light back in—except this time, the light's purpose was not for selfish reasons but for that of another.

Her baby girl was growing fast. Two months had passed, and both of their cheeks were filling out. The child was the sweetest thing and the joy of Sara's life. She secretly named her baby Joy. The child had oriental eyes and thick black hair. Surprisingly, Chopper had been keeping the house stocked with plenty of food for them both. He hadn't spoken another word to Sara since the night he dropped the baby off. Fear began to hang over Sara like an ominous cloud, not for her, but for Joy. *Why is he doing this? How long will he allow us to be happy before he destroys our hopes and dreams?* She forced the thoughts from her head.

And then the day came when the storm showed itself. Chopper and a heavyset man Sara had never seen before entered the house. Chopper left the man downstairs and walked into her room. He explained to her that she was to become pregnant by means of a revolutionary breakthrough in artificial insemination, and the doctor downstairs was going to teach her how it was done. She shook her head as tears streamed down her face.

Chopper held out his hand, "Don't worry—you'll remain a virgin. There's no sexual contact involved in any way. The doctor will give you the required instruments, teach you how to use them, and tell you exactly when to do it." Then he added, "This isn't an option. You do exactly what I say, or your little oriental princess there dies. You have three months to get pregnant or bye-bye, baby. Do you understand?"

Sara looked down at Joy sleeping peacefully in her arms. There was no doubt in her mind he'd do exactly what he said. Her voice trembled as she asked, "Who'll be the father?"

"Don't worry about that, damn it! You just do what I say, and everything's gonna be okay."

She became pregnant after just one session. The doctor called it a miracle and said he'd never seen anything like it before. Chopper laughed and proclaimed it an immaculate conception.

Sara gave birth to her baby boy the following spring during a fierce thunderstorm. Chopper insisted the doctor deliver the child by caesarean section, whether or not Sara required it, and that with the exception of her stomach, all other parts of her body were to be thoroughly concealed from the doctor's sight. He stood in the corner of the room next to Joy's crib. As usual, he watched intently to make sure Sara wasn't saying anything to the doctor she wasn't supposed to.

Exhausted, she held her beautiful baby boy tightly to her chest as the two men exchanged pleasantries and Chopper handed the man a briefcase. They shook hands, and that was the last time she saw the doctor. Chopper left the room to escort him out of the house.

Sara looked deeply into her baby's eyes and knew, as only a mother could, that it wasn't Chopper's baby. His soft skin was of a light olive tone and his hair dark brown. He reminded her of the pictures in the encyclopedia of children from the Mediterranean. Chopper's complexion was a sickly, pale white, his hair dirty blond, and his eyes gunmetal gray. What was obvious was that her baby had her mother's nose and Sara's thin lips.

She felt a sigh of relief wrapped in an aching sadness. *Would my child be like me and never know his father?* she thought. *But then again, would I really want him to?* A shot of panic ran through her. *Does Chopper think this child is his? Surely he must know it isn't. Or does he?*

"Oh God," she sighed.

The door opened, and Chopper strutted in with pep in his step. "Congratulations on the birth of our first male child. Make no mistake—he's now the most important thing in your life. All of your energy and focus will be on this child alone. It's your job to make sure he grows up healthy and strong."

Chopper looked over at Joy's crib, and a sinking feeling fell over Sara.

"Did you know," Chopper said in a low, dark voice, "that at the early stages of embryo development, a human being is indistinguishable from a fish, or a rabbit, or a pig? We even have gills and a tail. But then something happens along the way and it's decided that we will be human. If we're lucky we'll be a male and of value, instead of a female. This is obviously because males have been chosen by God himself to be the superior of the species. Don't you agree?"

"Please," Sara pleaded. "I can take care of them both. It's no problem. I promise." She tried her best to sound convincing.

"Relax," Chopper said coldly. "Sex-selective infanticide has been going on since the beginning of man, it's going on now, and it'll continue forever." He walked over to the crib, picked Joy up by her feet, and walked out the door.

Sara screamed for him to stop. She begged him to have mercy. She desperately prayed to God to save her baby girl. She heard the water filling the bathtub next door. She tried in vain to get out of bed but her legs cramped up. The pain from the stitches was unbearable, and she nearly fell to the floor with child in hand. Her baby boy looked up at her in silence while her baby girl screamed in terror—and then the screaming stopped.

Sara was sure she wouldn't make it through the night. She willed herself to die so she could be with Joy again. She begged the man who took her daughter's life to take hers, too. But it wasn't to be, and every minute she spent with her new baby boy was a minute closer to sacrificing her life only for him. An unbearable aching feeling of guilt hung over her. *Just six hours ago,* she thought, *I was holding my baby girl in this exact same spot; her beautiful little eyes looking into mine, full of hope.*

She trusted me.

CHAPTER 13

RAINBOW IN THE STORM

———◆———

WHEN HE WALKED INTO THE room, it happened oh so soon...

The man swept into Kiwi's life the way a rainbow appears during a raging storm, courageously, beautifully, and fleetingly.

She was doing volunteer work at the local Salvation Army. She'd been feeling hopelessly depressed about her foolish decision to work in Las Vegas. How she'd ever believed that sort of work would be the answer to all her problems seemed ridiculously naïve to her now. *What did I think was going to happen?* she thought. *It was only a matter of time before some Neanderthal man did what came natural to him.*

Because of her recent experience, she felt compelled to do some research and was appalled when she discovered the rape and sexual assault statistics in just the United States alone. She found out that:

- An American is sexually assaulted every two minutes.
- There are on average 237,868 (age twelve or older) victims per year.
- Ninety percent of rape victims are women.
- Sixty percent of sexual assaults go unreported.
- Victims are twenty-six times more likely to abuse drugs and four times more likely to contemplate suicide.
- One in four college women has been sexually assaulted.

The statistics went on and on, to the point it became nauseating. Images of the man—the animal—attempting to take by force what was not rightfully his somehow made her feel dirty. She felt an overwhelming sense of guilt and shame. The question never left her mind: *Wasn't the incident really my fault? It doesn't make sense, but this is how I feel—why am I blaming myself more than I blame the perpetrator?*

All she knew was that she somehow felt like less of a person than she was before Vegas. On the surface, she knew she did absolutely nothing wrong—nothing self-degrading or demoralizing—yet deep down something powerful was brewing.

She thought about Lawrence's and the Arab prince's stories of women who had been brutally victimized. It seems she'd become just another part of the sad story. *Someday I'll help put an end to these senseless atrocities against women. I'll create change, by force if necessary. I'll achieve this by doing something unforgettable, something unstoppable. To this I swear!*

Kiwi began to withdraw from family and friends, which was immediately obvious to them. She felt terrible about it, which only added to her misery.

Each time someone asked to visit with her, she'd give the same lame excuse: "I'm sorry, I'm just tired." She had no desire to work at the coffee shop or the diner. With the extra money she had after paying off all her college expenses, she really didn't have to work at all. And even if she did, she didn't have the will or motivation to. She felt like an insignificant fish tossed about in a vast ocean, dying, slowly sinking deeper and deeper into the cold dark, watching the light of life once cherished fade into the distance.

The volunteer work was Kiwi's failed attempt to somehow make herself feel worthy again, to change herself back to the naïve, happy-go-lucky girl she was before Vegas. She just wanted a reason to smile again.

And then it happened. The picture-perfect, James Dean–type was walking toward the front door of the Salvation Army donation center. It happened to be her day of the week to work the front desk instead of unloading boxes in the back. She could see through the glass door that he had a large pile of blankets in his arms. It was obvious he'd bitten off more than he could chew because he could barely see in front of him. So, of course, she ran to his rescue.

He didn't see her because of the tower of blankets, and as she pulled the door open, he pushed. The tall, broad-shouldered man met no resistance and lunged forward, catching his toe on the edge of the doorframe and falling flat on his face. The skyscraper of blankets toppled to the floor and scattered everywhere. Kiwi was so embarrassed and apologized repeatedly as she helped him to his feet. He laughed so loudly and for so long she thought he had to be drunk or high on something. But no, it was just Connor's nature to laugh at himself and at life as if it were all just a grand play on stage.

His unconditional smile was like the giant sunflowers in Kiwi's mother's garden back home. She knew in an instant her life had changed forever.

They discovered they had attended the same university. He was a senior majoring in law with a 3.9 GPA *and* the captain of the football team. She had to pinch herself. He told her that from the moment he saw her green eyes on campus, he "knew"—and that he'd tried every which way to get her to notice him, but she was oblivious to his presence.

How in the world could anyone not notice this man? she thought. She also couldn't help but wonder, *Was it really just chance he happened to be donating brand-new blankets to the Salvation Army on this particular day?*

But she never asked.

Connor refused to leave the donation center until she accepted his offer to a movie and dinner. He sat cross-legged on the counter with his boyish grin. He announced to everyone that he was, "Officially on a hunger strike, and only the beautiful princess before me has the power to spare me my miserable existence by agreeing to go on a date with me."

Kiwi's cheeks flushed with embarrassment. She felt the eyes of everyone in the room trained on her in anticipation. She acted irritated and uninterested, but inside she was tripping all over herself like a little schoolgirl who had just been asked to her first dance by the crush of her life. Finally, in a faked annoyed tone, she agreed. "Okay, *one* date. Now would you please mind your manners and get off my counter?"

"Yee-haw!" Connor did a backflip off the counter, cowboy boots and all.

Everything did change. It was as if in a single moment the past chapter of Kiwi's life had been wiped clean and a brand new one had replaced it, a chapter to a story that couldn't have been written any better. Amazingly, everything around her seemed to have a sort of sparkle to it again, a pulsating life of its own, just like when she was a child.

For the next six months, they were inseparable. She went to his football games and sometimes did her homework in the stands while he practiced.

They went on long nature walks on Sundays, high up into the mountains. On one occasion Connor's Jeep got stuck, so they had to walk ten miles to the nearest phone. Out of nowhere Connor asked, "If we had children, what would you name them?" Kiwi cheeks turned rosy, and for a few seconds she was speechless. She tried to conceal the flood of joy she felt at the thought of having Connor's children, but it was no use; the glowing smile on her face gave her heart away.

"I decided a long time ago that I was going to have a girl named Whisper and a boy named River," she replied confidently.

"Then I promise you that you will!" Connor swept Kiwi off her feet, tossed her on his back, and ran down the hill with ease. He imagined himself an eagle sailing lightly on the breeze with a small white dove on his back. Kiwi held on tightly and let out shrieks of joy.

They made it back to campus well after dark and exhausted, but were still unwilling to leave each other's side. So, they sat together in the dorm common area until finally falling asleep, with Kiwi's head on Connor's shoulder.

There was something Kiwi noticed about Connor's friends. Most of them seemed to act coldly toward her. The girls in particular would laugh out loud behind their backs, with obvious intentions for her to hear them. Finally, she asked Connor if his friends disliked her because she was Native American. He seemed completely clueless about the animosity and prejudice conveyed by people on campus toward minorities.

He brushed it off, saying, "They're just jealous that I'm madly in love with the most beautiful woman in the world."

It was the first time the L-word was used, and Kiwi was a bit shocked and a bit scared. Connor acted as if to say he loved her was as natural to him as breathing. In a joking tone, but for her dead serious, she asked him what exactly his definition of love was.

He cupped her face in his big hands and looked straight into her soul. The playful smile left his face and was replaced with a seriousness she'd not seen before. He softly whispered, "You."

Kiwi fell so hopelessly deep. In an instant, she felt as if she were two people sharing one soul. He wiped her tears away with his thumbs and kissed her in a way from which she could never recover. She wanted so badly to tell him she loved him, too; but for some reason, she couldn't. It was as if she were terrified that the moment she did, she'd wake up and it would all be a dream.

One night after a big home game, they decided to share their time together with some of Connor's friends. After all, they did take first place in their conference, thanks to Connor's interception in the final two minutes of the game. It was karaoke night at a local pub, and most of the team and the all of cheerleaders would be there. Kiwi was a bit nervous at first—until the margaritas started setting in. Connor was the life of the party, as usual, but rarely left Kiwi's side. The looks she got from some of the girls were pretty vicious, but she was beyond caring. *Yep, Connor's my man and that's never going to change, so get over it,* she thought.

By late into the night everyone was pretty toasted, including Connor. Kiwi watched as he walked over to the karaoke machine and said something to a staff member. Then he climbed up onto the stage and sat on the stool behind the microphone. *Oh no,* Kiwi thought. *Is he actually going to try to sing?* The crowd whooped and hollered, cheering him on. Then the music started, and everyone fell silent. The song "Just the Two of us" by Bill Withers began to play. Connor looked straight at Kiwi, blew her a kiss, and began to sing.

(First verse…)

Connor had the full attention of everyone in the pub. Amazingly, his voice was not only intelligible, but sounded silky smooth.

(Second verse…)

Kiwi's heart melted on the spot, and her eyes filled with tears.
   Everything around her faded away, leaving the only thing that mattered.

(Third verse…)

Whistles and cat calls rang out from the table of cheerleaders, but Kiwi was completely oblivious of them.

(Fourth verse…)

Connor pointed to Kiwi and sang the final verse.

The crowd went nuts. Connor waved to Kiwi to come up on the stage. She was unsure at first and shook her head, but the crowd wouldn't stop cheering her on to go. One of Connor's friends handed her a shot of tequila. She saw her hand reach out and accept the glass and toss it back. The crowd roared as she made her way to the stage.
   Connor met her at the steps and helped her up. More applause came, and Kiwi hoped they didn't notice her bright red cheeks. They walked to the center of the stage and faced each other. Everyone went crazy as

they embraced and kissed. Kiwi was certain she was in some perfectly orchestrated dream.

The weeks and months shot by as they were hopelessly lost within their own universe. They went on picnics and played silly games. They made a solemn pinkie promise to eat by candlelight at least once a week, even if it was just burgers, Chinese, or veggie pizzas. They took long walks around the campus pond in the evenings. She told him about her upbringing on the rez, her family, and her aspirations of making a difference in the world through journalism.

"I always wondered what it would be like living on a reservation," said Connor. "I mean, what did you guys do for fun?"

"Well, there wasn't a whole lot to do if you didn't like the outdoors," Kiwi replied. "I loved the outdoors, but I also loved to go to the library and read. Once a week the library would have movie night, and most of the kids would show up."

"That's cool. What kind of movies did ya'll watch?" Connor asked.

"I enjoyed the classics like *Gone with the Wind* and *Casablanca*, but my favorite movie is *Roman Holiday* with Audrey Hepburn. I could probably still recite every line by Princess Ann and the most unlikely man she falls in love with. The boys on the rez always wanted to watch the old westerns with John Wayne. It seemed ironic to me that they always cheered for the cowboys during the bloody battle scenes against the Indians. I often wondered if it ever occurred to those boys that *we* were the Indians. The only boy who was never present for the John Wayne movies was my little brother Johnny-Bear. Mother always loved the name Johnny and decided that her first son would have that name. Johnny-Bear was always different from the others. He seemed to me to live in a separate realm from the rest of us. He had always been the envy of the other boys because of his athleticism; in fact, they called him "Baby Thorpe," after Jim Thorpe, the Native American from Oklahoma. Jim Thorpe was an Olympic gold medalist and professional athlete. He was considered by many to be the greatest athlete in the twentieth century.

Johnny-Bear was one of those people who excelled at almost anything he did with little effort. Football, baseball, basketball, track, or rodeo, it didn't matter, he would be the best the rez had to offer. He had always been handsome, and every girl I knew who was near his age wanted to be his girlfriend, and he made it his duty to spend time with as many of them as he could. But there was always a sense of melancholy about my brother. He loved poetry and literature. He loved nature and proclaimed himself a naturalist after his hero Henry David Thoreau. He and I had this peculiar ability to communicate without words when we were kids. We were each other's best friend. Unlike most of the other boys on the rez, Johnny-Bear felt it important to know about the Trail of Tears, the massacre at Wounded Knee, and the other tragedies that took place in Native American history."

Connor didn't know how to respond, so he said what his heart knew for certain. "I want you to know, Kiwi, that whenever I leave this world, you will be the only thing to me worth remembering." Then he kissed her gently, passionately, and for so long.

Connor told Kiwi about growing up on a big cattle ranch outside Fort Benton, Montana. This was when Kiwi found out about Connor's father, the Washington senator from Montana. He jokingly asked her not to hold it against him, and said that he usually didn't talk about his father for fear it might intimidate his friends.

The rumor was that Senator Austin Stevens was a popular and controversial elected official. He was known to be a "gunslinger" when it came to the voices of Montanans. What most didn't know was that he also catered to lobbyists for personal gain. This revelation struck a chord with Kiwi for obvious reasons, but she vowed not to let it cause her to prejudge the man before she even met him, although she had to admit that it scared her to think how this fact might affect her relationship with the man of her dreams.

Connor said he loved and respected his father, but didn't want to be like him. He said he'd acquired his physical features and athleticism from his dad, but that his best trait was his mother's generous heart. She'd died two years earlier from a tragic accident while hiking the Rocky Mountains with his dad. She'd lost her footing and fell off a five-hundred-foot cliff.

Connor confessed that his father was a sort of Dr. Jekyll and Mr. Hyde, and that both sides had an insatiable appetite. He told of his father's wish for him to become a politician, and said that he didn't have the courage to tell his dad politics would never be in his future. He said after watching the torment and loneliness his mother had to put up with for so many years, he had absolutely no desire to follow in his father's footsteps.

Senator Stevens spent the majority of his time living in Washington, DC, pursuing his dream to become the president of the United States someday. He occasionally flew home to his ranch, more so for political reasons than personal. After all, he had to maintain the "family man" image if he were to have a chance at the White House.

The school year flew by. Soon Connor would graduate, and Kiwi would advance to her junior year. Connor was out of town for five days visiting family and interviewing for Harvard Law School. The plan was for Kiwi to transfer to a college near Harvard so they could be together. Kiwi was nervous about moving so far away from her family, but couldn't bear the thought of not being with Connor. She hadn't even built up the nerve to tell her family yet and dreaded the thought of it.

On the first evening Connor was away, Kiwi was at the campus library studying for an upcoming final in political science. It occurred to her that she still didn't know what Connor's dad looked like. He'd showed her a photo of his mother, but gave her the excuse that he didn't carry pictures of his dad around because he preferred to keep the influence of his dad's public status out of his personal relationships.

She decided that because she was already in the research section of the library, she might as well look up the Montana senator. She opened the heavy book, flipped to the tab marked "Senators," and turned the page.

Kiwi stared in absolute horror at the photograph of Senator Austin Stevens for what seemed like an eternity. She became nauseous, ran to the restroom, and was sick.

She walked in a daze back to her dorm. She felt like she was in a nightmare and begged to wake up. *Please God, this can't be happening!* she kept repeating to herself. *Of all the people in this world, how? Why is this happening to me?"*

She locked her door and collapsed onto her bed in tears. Horrid flashbacks of her last night in Vegas replayed over and over in her head, and of her assailant, Connor's father, on top of her inside the banquet room closet.

Kiwi had missed school for two days. She lay in her dark room, sick in every way possible. The tears were endless and unforgiving. It seemed to her the fairytale life she imagined with Connor was only a hoax—a deplorable lie. *Why would a nobody like me deserve to have someone like him anyway?* she thought incessantly. *Of course something had to ruin it.*

Kiwi ran through her mind every possible way to save her relationship with Connor. *What should I do? How will Connor react if I tell him? Will he even believe me? Will he still love me or will he dump me? If he believes me, can he forgive his father? Should I confront his father and try to make amends before I tell Connor? What will the senator do? Am I strong enough to face him? It's the only way, my only chance. I have to be brave—our love is worth it. I'll do it tomorrow!*

The senator's secretary confirmed that he was in fact in state and would be working at the capitol building for next seven days before returning to Washington, DC.

Kiwi entered the capitol building at 7:00 a.m. the following morning—right at opening time. The sleepy capitol police officers sprang to their feet with interest as she approached the X-ray machine. She gave them a nervous smile, and they tripped all over themselves to be the first to scan her with the metal detector wand. "What brings a girl like you to an old dingy building like this so early?" one of the men asked.

"Oh, actually I'm here to see Senator Stevens," Kiwi heard herself reply.

"You're in luck," said the other man. "He arrived about an hour ago."

"Okay, thank you." Kiwi grabbed her purse from the X-ray machine and proceeded toward the hall.

Her knees were weak and her shoulders shook as she walked down the dim hallway. The concrete walls and marble floors seemed to amplify the sound of her pounding heart for all to hear. *Do this for Connor. Do this for Connor. Do this for Connor,* Kiwi commanded her speeding mind.

Kiwi spotted the door marked Senator Austin Stevens and quickened her pace. She knew if she stopped in front of the door there was a good change she'd change her mind and flee from the building.

The door swung open and a blast of warm air enveloped her. The secretary looked up with a smile. "Well, hello there, darling. Come on in out of that cold hallway. What can I help you with?" The pretty woman with horn-rimmed glasses appeared to be in her mid-fifties.

Kiwi managed a smile. "Yes ma'am, I'd like to see Senator Stevens, please."

"Okay, but I'm not sure you're on the agenda for today. Did you have an appointment, dear?"

"Well, no, ma'am. I'm sorry, it was kinda…last minute," Kiwi replied nervously.

The woman looked at Kiwi questioningly but decided she liked her. "Well, it's still early, so let's see if we can't just squeeze you in." She picked up the phone and dialed the senator. "What's your name, sweetie?"

"Kiwi."

"Senator, there's a lovely young woman by the name of Kiwi here to visit with you. No, she doesn't have an appointment. She said it was last minute. She's a real darling; couldn't we just squeeze her in? Okay, I'll send her in right away." The woman pointed down the hall. "Last door on your left, sweetheart."

Kiwi nodded her head. "Thank you," she squeaked.

The moment felt dreamlike as she saw herself walk down the long hallway. Everything seemed to go silent. She saw her hand reach out for the senator's doorknob and turn it.

The senator, sitting behind his large desk in his large high-backed chair, was turned away from the door. Pungent cigar smoke swirled into the air as he sat staring out his window.

Kiwi closed the door. When she turned back around the one-eyed beast was facing her. She stood petrified.

The pleased expression on the senator's face at the magnificently beautiful specimen before him quickly turned sour when his memory jolted him back to the moments inside the banquet room closet—when his right eyeball was ripped out of his skull by the woman standing before him. *This can't be happening*, he thought. *How'd she find me? I'm ruined! Stay calm—there's no need for panic just yet. Find out what she wants. Maybe we can make a deal.*

"Please sit down, Ms. Kiwi, is it?"

"Yes." Kiwi moved to the chair directly in front of the senator's desk and sat down. The room seemed to spin slowly in a clockwise direction.

"Well now, how can this old senator be of service to you today?"

"Do you remember me?" Kiwi heard her shaky voice ask.

"No, I don't believe I've ever met someone as lovely as yourself before. Believe me, I'd remember. Is there a reason why you think we've met?"

"You tried to rape me in Las Vegas." Kiwi's voice suddenly sounded incredibly loud to her.

The senator's face grew dark and cold. He slowly put out his cigar and pulled his chair closer to his desk. He leaned forward and whispered, "What do you want?"

Kiwi turned her gaze toward the floor. She couldn't bear looking at the frightening black eye patch any longer. "I'm your son's girlfriend, and I love him with all my heart. We've been seeing each other for almost seven months now. He doesn't know about the work I did in Vegas or what happened between you and me. I only found out two days ago who you were.

"Please, all I'm asking is that we put everything that happened behind us—that we forgive and forget. I'm asking that you never tell Connor about us and not to interfere with our relationship. Please, sir, this is very hard for me, but I'm willing to forgive you for the sake of the love between Connor and me. I can't imagine my life without him. A part of his soul lives inside mine."

The senator replied in a mocking tone disguised as curiosity, "Oh, is the soul bit some sort of Indian superstition?"

There was a moment of silence. Kiwi turned her eyes back to the floor. She felt small and insignificant in the presence of the imposing man. "It's my people's way of expressing that the love one has for another is written in the stars, that our souls are intertwined—it is eternal."

The senator's vile laughter shook the walls.

A desperate feeling of hopelessness began to envelope Kiwi, but she savagely fought it back. "Please, Mr. Stevens, will you do this for me? I'm begging you."

The senator stared at the fragile girl sitting before him and brought his fingertips together in front of his lips.

Finally, he broke the tense silence. "I'm sorry to say, Ms. Kiwi, but you must have me mistaken for someone else."

Kiwi's heart sank as her eyes overflowed with tears. *What am I doing here? I should run to the security desk and tell them everything, that our great senator from Montana is a monster, that he tried to rape me. But then who in the world would believe an Indian girl from the rez?*

The senator stood up and brought her a box of tissues. With a sense of satisfaction he strode back and stood behind his desk. "But, what I'm willing to do for such a lovely lady as yourself is to forget that you ever came in here. I'll also give you my word that I'll have no memory of ever having met you. I promise I will not interfere with your relationship with my son. This so-called eternal *love* from the stars you claim between you and him, as far as I will be concerned, will be a 'match made in heaven,' as they say." A crooked smile snaked across the senator's face. "Do we have ourselves a deal?"

Kiwi was stunned. She couldn't believe what she was hearing. *He promised to do exactly what I asked. But yet he denies what he did to me. Is this some sort of game? Should I believe him? What choice do I really have?*

"Well, is it a deal or not?" the senator repeated sternly.

"Yes, yes, thank you so much, sir. I promise you won't regret it. We love each other so much." Kiwi stood up to shake the senator's hand but he turned his back to her.

Looking out his window, he lit his cigar and blew a dark cloud into the air. "Do me a favor, Ms. Kiwi, and never, under any circumstances, come back here again. That'll be all."

CHAPTER 14

ANGEL FOR AN ANGEL

———◆———

THE THOUGHT OF NAMING HER baby boy terrified Sara. It had been a month, and she still hadn't officially given him a name yet. The closest she'd come was to tell herself that if she could—if she weren't so scared he'd be ripped from her arms the minute she named him—she would call him "Falcon." Her reasoning was that the first thing she saw out her window the morning after his birth was a beautiful falcon perched on a tree. She'd never seen the bird before that day, and it seemed it had decided to make a home in the tree outside her window ever since. Sara decided the bird must be her little boy's guardian angel.

Sara knew the dangers of sleeping in bed with a newborn, but she couldn't bear the thought of him being outside arm's reach. She had terrible visions of her baby being stolen from her in the night. She was on pins and needles every second Chopper was in the house. She'd hold Falcon tight to her chest, and she rarely went out of her room. Chopper visited her occasionally to look at the boy as if he were inspecting cattle to ensure he was getting a fair trade. Upon seeing that his investment met with his approval, he'd let out a grunt and walk away. It was moments like this Sara wondered if Chopper knew who the child's father was.

What Sara didn't know was that her baby was worth a million dollars to Chopper. The boy wasn't like the other children he bought and sold. This child was truly something special and monumental in scale, and considered to be no less than a miracle baby. He was labeled by some as humanity's savior, and by others, its cataclysm. Falcon was a result of a top-secret scientific experiment using a radical form of genetic engineering. It consisted of a hybrid of DNA extraction, chromosome fusion, stem cell transplantation, and hyper-in-vitro fertilization.

The project was code-named GR 1.618, also known as "the Golden Ratio." It was the brainchild of three Nobel laureates in the fields of physics, chemistry, and medicine and was founded by one of the wealthiest people on the planet. Experiments were conducted over a ten-year period within a fortresslike laboratory located two thousand feet below the earth's surface, somewhere in North America.

If the theory was correct and the experiment successful, within Falcon was the DNA of some of the world's most brilliant minds, greatest leaders, famed artists, finest athletes, and…most notorious men in history. The parameters of the experiment required specific and unique characteristics in the host. After two years of extensive searching, the team finally found the perfect match—Sara; *she* was their Chosen One.

Sara's mind desperately searched for ways to escape. She had to get her baby out of danger, even if it meant losing her life. But how? Since her attempted escape with Montana, Chopper no longer allowed anyone on the property, not even the gardeners and landscapers, and especially not a cleaning maid for inside. He even had at least one guard parked in a car outside the front gate at all times.

Sara spent her days playing with, singing to, and reading to her baby, always hoping and praying God would show her a way to save her child. Then, one summer night, it seemed her prayers had been heard.

A dark man sat low in the tow truck down the road. He watched as the gate guard drove off to his Friday night poker game. From many weeks of conducting surveillance on the mansion, he knew he had about a twenty-minute window before the next guard arrived.

A rock bounced off the steel bars on Sara's window. She recoiled and instinctively ran into the hallway with her baby. Chopper wasn't home and had been gone for two days. Sara overheard him say on the phone he'd be leaving town for a few days. Another pinging sound echoed off her window, and she decided to take a peek.

She spotted the dark figure crouched behind shrubs below. He waved his hand then held up a sign that read, "*Get ready. Escape NOW.*"

Sara's heart pounded hard against her chest. *Is this really happening? Or is this a trick? Maybe Chopper's testing me; maybe he's not out of town at all. Oh God, what should I do?*

She looked back down at the man; he waved his hand again, a bit more urgently now. Then he flipped the sign over. Written on the back was: "*I'm Audition Judge #2.*" Sara was perplexed for a moment but then let out a sigh of joy. She knew this wasn't a trick.

She waved back to him, and he held up another sign: "*Go to front door.*"

"Oh, my God. Okay, keep it together, Sara," she muttered. "Get the baby bag. That's all you'll need. Oh—and, of course, don't forget Falcon. Oh, thank you, God!" Sara put as much baby formula and bottled water as she could into the bag with some diapers and then looked out the window one last time. The man was gone.

The tall, thin man scaled the wall with ease, climbed into the large tow truck, and looked down at his watch: 12:05 a.m. *I have fifteen minutes,* he thought.

Soon after the prodigy child with an angel's voice and her friend, Montana, had left the audition, something in his gut knew something was amiss. Growing up in the crime-ridden East Side of New York, he'd learned early on how to spot signs of a deception. It was obvious to him the girls seemed to be trying to hide something. For starters, the address they gave had no apartment number or phone number. Most people who tried out for a part made sure they could be reached, even if they had to give a work, friend's, or parent's phone number. Second, there was Sara's appearance. Although she was stunningly beautiful, most people tried to dress in something more than sweatpants and an old t-shirt when auditioning for such a big part. It seemed the decision to try out was a hasty or perhaps desperate one. And third, they seemed overanxious somehow. Even after they knew Sara was going to win the part, they appeared to constantly be looking over their shoulders, as if the boogeyman himself was going to march through the doors and snatch them away.

When the girls didn't show up the following day, he knew someone or something was interfering with their ability to pursue their dreams and perhaps even to live a normal life. He just had a sick feeling in the pit of his stomach that he couldn't shake.

As an African American who had attended a predominately white college to study criminal justice, he had learned to have thick skin, as well as assimilate the techniques and resources used to investigate crimes.

Something deep inside him twisted and turned, prodded and pushed him to dedicate the rest of his life, if need be, to solving this mystery. Thankfully, the savings he'd accumulated over his career in show business afforded him the opportunity to pursue his new obsession. So for more than a year, through many hours of interviews and combing the streets filled with millions of people, and with only a hand-drawn sketch of Sara and Montana, he was led to the infamous "Chopper the Terrible."

Research into the man's background revealed he was a well-known drug lord in New York with ties to the Colombian mafia and various other drug cartels. He seemed to be a sort of jack-of-all-trades, having his hands in other sectors such as prostitution and human trafficking. Police records showed his real name wasn't Chopper. The nickname had been given to him by those who feared him most. Word on the streets was that Chopper took pleasure in dismembering his victims slowly, while they were still alive, with a custom chrome-plated hatchet he carried with him at all times. Anyone who crossed him, or people he simply didn't like, had a way of showing up in multiple dumpsters throughout the city.

After learning the background of Sara's captor, the audition judge had no doubt she was in terrible danger, and that he, too, was at risk of losing his life, should he be discovered.

He knew the option of notifying the police was out of the question. He had nothing on Chopper except suspicions, and if Chopper realized someone knew about Sara, it would most likely be the end for her.

The judge spent weeks watching the mansion through his binoculars. He was fortunate enough to stumble onto an old tree stand used by deer hunters about a quarter of a mile from the mansion. It was high up and hidden in thick foliage.

On several occasions, he'd caught brief glimpses of Sara standing by her window. Sometimes she would be holding an infant. Over time, he learned the habits and patterns of Chopper and his thugs. Finally, all of his work had taken him to this very moment. Come hell or high water, there was no way he was going to fail in freeing Sara and her child.

Sara heard the squealing of tires in the distance followed by a thunderous crash. She pulled Falcon to her chest and ran into the kitchen. Something told her that being near the front doors was not the safest place at the moment. She heard the screeching of tires coming to an abrupt stop just outside the front doors, then chains being dragged, something clanging on the iron bars, more tires squealing, and then a loud explosion as the cage was torn free from the door frame.

Falcon began crying, and Sara was scared to death.

Then a voice called out, "Are you there, Sara?"

She ran to the window and called out, "Yes! Please help us!"

"Get away from the front doors! I'm going to ram them with the truck!"

Sara ran back into the kitchen and put her hands over her baby's ears. Suddenly, gunshots rang out. A bullet shattered the window, then more gunshots.

Oh my God! We've been caught. Chopper's going to kill us all!

She looked around for a safe place to put Falcon and then ran into the walk-in pantry and put him into a wicker bread basket, which she pushed into the far corner. She ran to the living room and crawled across the glass-strewn floor to a window and peeked out. The judge was kneeling behind the fender of the truck with a pistol in his hands. He was shooting back at the gate guard, who was standing behind a tree about thirty yards away. The shooting stopped. The guard ran out of ammunition and ran back toward his car. She saw the judge quickly climb into his tow truck, and smoke began rolling from the rear tires as he launched the truck in reverse straight toward the front doors.

Sara barely made it to the kitchen when another explosion went off and the heavy double doors shattered into a million pieces. She grabbed Falcon and rushed toward the massive hole in the wall. She ran right into the judge's long arms and saw blood was running profusely down his neck.

"Hurry!" he yelled. "Get in from this side and stay low!"

The judge climbed in and slammed his foot on the accelerator. It was then Sara realized she'd forgotten the baby bag.

Just as they pulled through what was left of the front gate, bullets shattered the passenger-side window. The guard had made it back to his car and reloaded. Fortunately, Sara had done what the judge told her and was crouched near the floorboard with Falcon tucked in her lap. They made a hard left and sped toward the highway. It wasn't long before the guard closed in behind them. Even at full throttle, the heavy tow truck was no match for the lighter Chevy Camaro SS.

The guard started to pull up next to them on Sara's side with his gun drawn. He knew he had to keep them from getting onto the highway at all costs. The judge thought about waiting until the car was right next to them and then ramming it, but it was too risky. Sara and the child might be shot. He slammed on his brakes, and the Camaro flew by. He made a hard right and drove toward his old stomping grounds, an area of town considered the most dangerous place in New York.

The bold move bought them a little bit of time. The guard had to cross over the center median to the other side of the two-lane road and make his way back to where they'd turned off. His car bottomed out on the median, spun out, and nearly got stuck.

"Get ready, Sara, plans have changed. I'm going to drop you off before he catches up. If you do exactly what I tell you, the two of you will have a chance."

Sara saw the judge's shirt was now completely soaked with blood and his face looked pale. "Oh my God, you're bleeding bad," she said.

"I'm all right. Just run and hide when I tell you to, okay?"

Sara looked down at her baby wrapped tightly inside the white blanket and then back at the dying man. "Okay."

The judge seemed to spot the building he was looking for and pulled up to it. "Go to apartment 316. Tell him Joe sent you. He's not expecting you, but he's my friend and he'll help you. Now hurry, Sara, go!"

Sara grabbed the judge's bloody hand as her eyes welled up with tears.

"Thank you Joe," she said. Suddenly she saw his entire body glow with the purest white light, as if an angel had reached out and touched him.

Somehow, the judge managed a smile. "It has been an honor and a pleasure to know you." The words sounded familiar in Sara's ears.

Just as she made it out of the truck, shots shattered the window on the driver's side, and the judge slumped over his steering wheel. The horn blared out. Sara clutched her crying baby and ran as fast as she could to the apartment complex.

The guard got out of his car, walked up to the judge, and shot him point-blank in the side of the head. The horn fell silent. Sara had almost made it to the second floor when the second shot was fired, startling her and causing her to trip on the last step. She fell forward, slamming her face violently into the brick wall. Somehow she managed to stay on her feet. She felt the molars inside her mouth shatter, but there was no pain. She heard loud ringing and saw multicolored dots floating all around. Something heavy was pulling her into blackness, but she willed herself to stay conscious.

As she spat her bloody teeth out, a terrible panic shot through her. *Falcon's not crying—he's silent!* She looked down at the small bundle in her arms and saw a blotch of blood where the child's head would be.

Is that my blood or his? Oh God, no! No! Don't die on me! Please don't you die on me now, Falcon! God, please, don't take my baby from me!

In tears, Sara reluctantly forced her shaking hand to uncover her son's face. She gasped at what she saw looking back at her, or was he looking through her? No, the child was looking *into* her! His face seemed to glow with a soft, luminescent white light. His tender smile spoke of forgiveness and unconditional love, something she hadn't had since Mama and Montana. His eyes were the purest, most brilliant sky blue. They pierced straight into her heart, into her soul. It was exactly what she'd always imagined it'd be like to look into the face of an angel. Maybe he *was* an angel, her guardian angel.

Sara's legs shook uncontrollably. She slowly slumped to the concrete floor. Her tattered white dress was covered with large red blotches. She cradled her baby tightly to her chest, rocking him gently back and forth. Endless rivers of tears were unleashed, leaving trails down her soiled face. For so many months now she wouldn't cry. She couldn't cry. She'd realized there was no point, that this cruel world had no point, so she vowed to never waste another tear. But now, sitting there in the dark, garbage-strewn hallway, Sara recognized for the first time something truly good, someone with a pure soul, somebody who didn't expect from her what she couldn't give. This was a soul who only wanted what she wanted, to love and be loved.

Suddenly there was so much to cry about, so much to cry for. She couldn't stop crying. She didn't want to stop crying. It was the least she could do for her baby boy.

Sara began feeling nauseated and lightheaded. Again, she felt on the brink of unconsciousness. See saw a bright red glow. The red faded out and an image came into view. *It's you,* she mused. The red butterfly flapped its wings frantically, moving up and down and in and out in circles.

Oh, Falcon! I have to save Falcon. I have to let people know his name and where he belongs—in case I don't make it.

She wiped the blood from her lips and wrote crude letters on her baby's blanket, *FALCON 316.* It was then that it struck her like a bolt from the sky: *John 3:16, Mama's favorite bible verse.*

"For God so loved the world that he gave his one and only Son, that whoever believes in him shall not perish but have eternal life."

With renewed strength, Sara forced herself to her feet. All she knew was that this was her second chance, maybe her only chance, to do what was right. She had never been so sure of anything in her entire life. She would be the goodness life had to offer. She would be the goodness in which her son would believe. She would be the courage for both of them.

Sara saw the guard walking from the apartment complex across the street toward her with pistol in hand. She knew the only thing that mattered was to get her child to the next floor, to apartment 316.

"Stop!" the guard yelled. She quickly turned the corner onto the third floor. "316...316...316," she whispered over and over. She could hear the man's footsteps running up the stairs. She spotted the door marked 316 and ran to it. She knocked just loud enough for the occupant to hear but not so loud as to give away where she was to leave her only son.

She heard the guard's footsteps right below her. "Please answer. Please answer," she begged. When she heard clattering from the door chain, she quickly kissed her baby, set him down, and ran straight toward the guard just around the corner. Sara heard Montana's voice, "Fight hard! Whatever is worth keeping is worth fighting for." This time she would not be a coward. She would have the courage to face the evil men who threatened her family. This time, she would at least die with a clear conscience.

The door opened, and a man with wide shoulders and an athletic build came into view. He wore a black robe with a large red dragon embroidered on the front. His thick black hair was long and slicked back into a ponytail. His facial features were sharp and hard as steel, yet his eyes were soft and of Asian descent.

The man knelt down on both knees in front of the small bundle before him. Oddly, he didn't look around to see who'd made the delivery. It was as if somehow he knew the situation at hand and embraced his destiny. He bowed low to the child, carefully picked him up, and walked back into his apartment.

CHAPTER 15

A TALE OF TWO SWORDS

———◆———

"BEFORE EMBARKING ON A JOURNEY for revenge, dig two graves." This was the Chinese proverb Ukko had meditated on ever since he'd been warned by neighbors that Chopper the Terrible was on his way to reclaim the infant child who had been left on his doorstep six days ago.

"This man's not the child's family," they told him. "He's a cold-blooded killer. You have to leave right away, or you both will be cut to pieces!"

Ukko sat, lotus-style and shirtless, in front of the two swords. The large crisscrossed samurai swords tattooed on his shoulders and back looked like battle wings and were a portrayal of the swords laid out before him. The tattoo of the swords' handles wrapped slightly around the tops of his shoulders, partially visible from the front. Each blade came down diagonally across his back, appearing to pierce through the flesh below his shoulder blades. The ends of the swords wrapped around his upper hips toward his outer thighs. The katana ran over his left shoulder and had blood running along the length of the blade. Etched in the katana's blade below the swordsmith's stamp was a tiger. The wakizashi was over his right shoulder under the katana. Etched in its blade, below the same swordsmith's stamp, was a butterfly. There was no blood on the wakizashi; the metal was shiny and pure.

Wrapped around his left forearm was a fearsome dragon, representing his grandfather. On his right forearm was a tiger standing on its hind legs in battle, representing his father. Across his chest were three butterflies. In the middle of his sternum was a bright blue butterfly called Miyama-shijimi, meaning "depth of the mountains," and below it were red Japanese characters spelling the name of his mother, *Mitsu,* or "light." On his left pectoral muscle, over his heart, was a bright yellow butterfly called Ki-cho, meaning "yellow butterfly," and below it were red Japanese characters spelling the name of his fiancée, *Aiko,* "love child." On his right pectoral muscle was a peculiar bright red butterfly. It had no scientific name, because it had not yet been discovered in this world. It was the butterfly with many eyes he had encountered during his attempt to commit seppuku. Below it were red Japanese characters spelling the name of his little sister, *Chouko,* "butterfly child."

The swords' somber spirits had been entombed inside their black-lacquered scabbards since the night he had killed the Russian agent. The gold-inlaid tiger, standing upright on its hind legs as it wrapped around the scabbard of the long sword, looked menacing and vigilant as ever. Its razor-sharp claws and ruby eyes seemed to follow his every move. Above the tiger and under many layers of thick lacquer, a single falcon's feather could be seen. On the scabbard of the short sword, the three gold-inlaid cherry trees with their falling blossoms continued to whisper the valiant and sad story of the lonely life of a samurai. Above the trees and under thick layers of lacquer, there was a single red butterfly that had once lived hundreds of years ago.

The swords seemed to radiate a turbulent energy, as if they were not at peace, somehow disgruntled with their premature retirement. They seemed to long once more to be of service, to be sacrificed once again to a noble cause. As Ukko looked down at the swords, the same familiar and aching questions resurfaced in his mind. *Are you a blessing or a curse? Are you the swords of light, or the swords of darkness?* He closed his eyes and recalled the ancient story his grandfather had passed down to him many years ago. It wasn't until later that he realized it was really the story of his life, a tale of two paths.

He heard his grandfather's deep, calm voice as he recounted the story, "A Tale of Two Swords."

Hundreds of years ago, there lived a Zen Buddhist monk in the most beautiful of mountains. This monk was revered in all the land for his sword-making ability, but even more so for his wisdom in "The Way." To this day, he is still considered to have been the greatest swordsmith in the world.

Legend recounts that this reclusive swordsmith was more spirit than man. Standing only three and a half feet tall, he had a hump on his back and walked with a pronounced limp. He was called by some "the mystic mountain troll," and by others "the goblin of the caves." But to most he was known as the "Mountain Monk." He wore a dark kimono with a large hood to hide his face. The mountain cave he lived in also served as a shrine. Inside the cave sat a nine-foot Buddha carved in the side of the wall. Only two apprentices were allowed to assist the swordsmith in the making of his famed swords. The apprentices were also monks and sworn to secrecy in order to keep the sword-making techniques exclusive to the monastery.

The mysterious monk made only four pairs of swords each year, one for every season. A pair consisted of one katana, a long sword believed by the monk to be the male spirit, and one wakizashi, a short sword believed to be the female spirit. Together the katana and wakizashi were equal halves of the whole. One complemented the other like the Yin and Yang, day and night, sun and moon. Without one, the other would be out of balance and could not exist harmoniously. The bearer of the swords would have to utilize the swords as a pair. They could never be separated or mismatched with other swords.

The katana was the primary sword used in battles—the workhorse. The wakizashi was the backup sword for the katana and was sometimes used to commit seppuku. At times, both katana and wakizashi were used simultaneously in battle, one in each hand. This was extremely rare, because it required a warrior who was extraordinarily skilled and spiritually balanced to the highest degree.

The swords were made from the finest materials money could buy. The Mountain Monk was the only swordsmith to discover how to fuse three different grades of steel—soft, medium, and hard—into one blade. This technique was unheard of in its time, and it allowed a sword to hold its razor-sharp edge while remaining flexible so as not to shatter under extreme stress.

At the end of the year, the four pairs of swords were put through three arduous tests. It's said the odds of any sword making it through even one of the tests were dismal, let alone all three tests. Each year, swordsmiths throughout the land offered their best swords in hopes of gaining the prestige of passing just one of the Mountain Monk's three tests.

The first test was a substitute for the infamous "body-cutting test" in which live human subjects were used. The strength, sharpness, and durability of the swords were tested on criminals of the state who had been sentenced to death. Back in ancient times, this was standard procedure in most of Japan and served to be a powerful deterrent for would-be criminals. The criminals were piled on top of one other or lined up standing toe to heel. The executioner would raise the sword high above his head and slash it in a downward or sideways motion at the criminals' midsections. An official of the state would then record the number of bodies the blade completely severed. Ratings of one through five bodies were given. Very few blades ever received the rating of five.

Being a Buddhist monk and an advocate for the sanctity of all life, the Mountain Monk did not use human bodies or animals for the cutting test. Instead, he used large stalks of bamboo wrapped in straw matting. The bamboo was cured so as to mimic the hardness of bone and the straw soaked in water to simulate flesh. For the katana, the bamboo was three inches in diameter and wrapped with twelve inches of wet straw matting, totaling fifteen inches. Cutting through them was no easy feat, as these rolls were actually harder to sever than any human body. For the wakizashi, the bamboo and straw matting were half the diameter required for the katana but with twice as many rolls. Swords made by the Mountain Monk were required to sever six of these rolls completely in one continuous motion, whereas swords made by other swordsmiths were only required to sever four. If this requirement was met, the swords would advance to the second test.

No other swords but those of the Mountain Monk ever achieved a six-body rating using his rolls of bamboo and straw matting. In fact, very few other swords ever achieved even a rating of four. During one cutting test, the official recorder excitedly suggested that, for entertainment's sake, eight human bodies be used for the Mountain Monk's swords. The old monk declined.

When asked why, his reply was, "It does not matter. After the first life has been extinguished, the wielder of the sword will no longer be in control."

The recorder was perplexed by the answer. It was only later, after many years of bloody wars and conflicts within the country, that he realized the meaning behind the Mountain Monk's answer.

The second was called the fire-and-ice test. It was a test of endurance, perseverance, and spiritual birth. This test would weed out all swords not made by the Mountain Monk, and even many swords made by him would fail.

The test required the katana, the male spirit, to be submersed in the freezing waters at the base of the mountain waterfall. Because this test was conducted during the coldest part of winter, the water would immediately freeze around the blade, thus holding the katana upright. At the same time, the companion wakizashi, the female spirit, was placed directly on top of the red-hot embers of a bonfire. The bonfire was constructed on the riverbank of the waterfall, near the frozen katana. Both katana and wakizashi had to remain in this state for exactly 365 minutes; this represented the number of days in a calendar year. After the required time in ice and fire, the katana and wakizashi would be joined together. The blade of the katana would be placed directly on top that of the blade of the wakizashi and bound tightly with a thick vine. The two swords would remain this way for exactly nine minutes, representing the number of months required for the gestation of a child inside a woman's womb. After the required time, the swords would be separated and thoroughly examined for any signs of weakness in the integrity of the metals. If even one flaw, minor fracture, or the slightest warping was detected in either of the swords, both swords would fail. Even if one sword from the pair showed no visible flaw, the monk knew that the spirit within this sword would forever be unbalanced without its equal half. It was usually after this grueling test that most, if not all, of the swords failed. In over thirty years, the old monk had never witnessed more than one pair of swords per year pass both the first and second tests—and all of them were his.

The third and final test was the purity-of-spirit test. According to the Mountain Monk, this was by far the most grueling test any sword or human being could ever face, for it was conducted by the universe itself.

In this test, the old monk would set up camp near the mountain waterfall and go into deep meditation. He would remain in this state until the universe revealed to him the nature of the spirits within the swords. If they were found to be worthy, they received the blessing. If not, they were returned to the monastery and respectfully laid to rest in the clay furnace in which they were born.

The very few swords that passed all three tests were given to the emperor of Japan as a gift to do with them as he deemed fit.

It was in the thirty-third year that something unexpected occurred, something some say forever tarnished the history of Japan and that, years later, pulled her from the ashes of shame and raised her to majestic glory once more.

After thoroughly inspecting the swords for the sixth time, the Mountain Monk sat back in astonishment. For the first time, two pairs of his swords passed the fire-and-ice tests in the same year.

Could this really be true? he asked himself. *Or is the universe now testing me?*

Before him lay two katanas and two wakizashis, each born and bonded in spirit by fire and ice—and now this bond would be tested in ways unimaginable. Both pairs were identical in every way, except for the mark below the Mountain Monk's stamp at the base of the blades. This special mark was the name given to each sword by the swordsmith and distinguished the swords as belonging to a specific pair. Each name was unique and inspired by what the old monk saw in nature.

The monk knew what he must do. He had planned for this scenario many years ago, but having never witnessed more than one pair of swords survive the second test, he'd given up the idea of ever needing to implement it.

That is, until then.

The mountain breeze was bitter cold as it wisped across the waterfall then down through the trees and into the tents set up near the river. The Mountain Monk sat lotus-style in his tent, the two pairs of swords before him. The flickering candlelight cast eerie shadows against the walls of the tent. The two apprentices sat in a tent they shared just a few feet away, watching attentively through their door. It was nearing the end of the sixth day since their master began the third test. The longest time the purity-of-spirit test had ever taken was three days. Their rations had dwindled down to only a half a cup of rice and one small jar of pickled vegetables. Their master refused to eat; his only sustenance was hot tea.

About three hours before dawn on the seventh day, the Mountain Monk scurried out of his tent with both pairs of swords in hand. The apprentices were startled and scrambled out of their tent to attend to their master's wishes. The old man sat cross-legged at the edge of the river. He laid one pair of swords to his left and the other to his right. The swords were in their scabbards, and the moonlight reflected off the black lacquer. The apprentices were perplexed as they watched the old man gaze up at the moon, then down at the reflection of the moon in the slow-moving river, then back up again. This went on for nearly two hours.

The Mountain Monk shot straight to his feet and looked up. A comet was blazing across the dark sky from east to west. The old monk looked down at the reflection of the comet on the surface of the river and saw the ball of light dance across the ripples against the current in the opposite direction the comet was moving in the sky.

The old monk snatched up the swords and ran to his tent. He gave orders to his apprentices to leave everything and take only three canteens of water. They were to return to the monastery immediately. The young monks were unnerved by his panic.

It was nearly daylight when the three monks were halfway down the mountain. The old monk insisted on carrying all the swords and had them in a bag over his shoulders. The young monks could tell the weight of the bag was taking its toll on the old man, but he refused their help.

While taking a water break, they herd rustling sounds in the forest. It became evident someone had been following them. A bandit jumped out from the trees—then another and another. The monks were now surrounded by three menacing men. The bandits' unsheathed swords made their intentions clear. The old monk backed himself up against the wall of the mountain in an attempt to hide the bag. One of the bandits, bearing a grotesque scar across his face, ordered the old monk to hand over the swords. The two apprentices stepped between the bandit and their master.

In what seemed a blur, moonlight bounced off the polished steel of the scar-faced bandit's sword and moved in a high arc through the air, then downward, meeting its mark.

One of the apprentices fell. The impact of his knees against the ground caused his head to detach from his neck and fall to the muddy earth. Terrified, the other apprentice ran to his master, grabbed the bag from behind the old man, and pulled out a long sword.

"No! You mustn't!" the Mountain Monk commanded. "You cannot fight darkness with darkness!"

But it was too late. The apprentice had already unsheathed the katana and stood at the ready. Although the young monk had never used a sword in battle, he had received basic swordsmanship training from his father as a boy. He knew he would be no match for the expertise he'd just witnessed. But for the sake of his master, he must at least die with honor.

The scar-faced bandit laughed. "So you want to test the fruit of your labor in battle, do you, boy?"

"No! Please stop, sir!" the old monk pleaded. "You know not what you do! The sword you now face knows no mercy; it has come from the fires of hell itself and must be destroyed!"

"Shut up, you old fool! You'll do no such thing. I'll live like a king after I sell your famous swords to the highest bidder!"

The scar-faced bandit lunged toward the shaking apprentice for a deathblow to the abdomen. The young apprentice stood petrified and braced himself for the afterlife, but something unexpected happened— something supernatural. The bandit's strike was expertly blocked by the boy's sword then followed by a vicious counter-strike.

The bandit was taken off guard and nearly lost his head. He stumbled backward a few steps and grabbed the hole on the side of his head where his ear had once been. The other two bandits looked on in bewilderment. The scar-faced bandit stared down at his bloody ear. Overcome with rage, he charged the apprentice with sword held high. Without even the slightest movement of his feet, and with blinding speed and accuracy, the apprentice split the bandit's face in two before the man even knew he'd been cut.

The bandit fell to his knees, his brains oozing from between his eyes. The other two bandits were in a state of complete confusion. The most skilled swordsman they knew had just been effortlessly cut down by a boy swordsmith.

"Come here now!" the old monk commanded. The boy, still in shock, cautiously walked back to his master, the sword held out on guard. "Put the sword back into its scabbard, and place it in the bag."

"But why, master? We must defend ourselves or we'll die!"

The old man placed his hand on top of the boy's head. "You've chosen the wrong sword, my son. We must have compassion. It's the only thing separating us from animals. Believe me, there are much worse fates in this life than dying."

The two monks looked deeply into each other's eyes. The bandits watched with curiosity. The tall one placed his sword back into its scabbard. The other, teeth as black as night, kept his sword at the ready, waiting for an opening.

The young monk reluctantly obeyed his master. Keeping his eyes on the bandits, he nervously sheathed the katana and then slowly placed it into the old man's bag.

With a scream, the rotten-toothed bandit charged the monks with his sword above his head. The apprentice scrambled to get back to the bag, but it was too late. The bandit's sword severed his right foot at the ankle, sending him face-first into the mud. The rotten-toothed bandit ran to the old monk and snatched the bag, but the old man's grip was like a vise.

"Please, son. You mustn't do this! Let me return to my monastery so I can destroy two of these swords, and I swear I will gladly give you the other two," the old monk pleaded.

The bandit, one hand on his sword and the other gripped tightly on the bag, scolded, "Why should I take only two swords when I can have four, old man?"

"Because the spirits of two of the swords in this bag are from the darkness. They'll unleash evils and destruction, the likes of which man has never witnessed!" the monk explained.

The rotten-toothed bandit looked anxiously at his partner. The tall bandit stepped forward. "Explain the purpose of your request, old man, and perhaps we'll honor it."

The Mountain Monk took a deep breath then exhaled. "Inside this bag are two pairs of swords, each with the ability to change the world in ways yet unfathomable by humankind. One pair contains the spirit of light. It is a beacon for justice by way of peace. It protects the weak and brings comfort to the suffering; it opens minds, creates friends, and finds cures to diseases. It knows only one path, the path of compassion.

"The other pair contains the spirit of darkness. It is the harbinger of evil. It seeks power for selfish purposes and preys on the weak. It knows no compassion and creates pain and suffering. It makes enemies of all and knows only one path, the path of destruction. It is the swords of darkness I must urgently destroy before they destroy us all."

The rotten-toothed bandit looked impatiently at his partner as if to signal they were wasting time talking to an insane man. Nearby, the apprentice began to moan as he desperately tried to staunch the blood flowing from his severed leg.

"Okay, old man. Tell us which swords are the evil ones, and I give you my word we will destroy them for you," said the tall bandit.

"No, this matter is of grave concern. I must perform this crucial task personally, in the exact manner required. I must ensure the swords are properly returned to the fires of hell from which they came. Please, sir, I beg of you!"

"How do we know you're not lying, that you're not just luring us into a trap back at your monastery? Perhaps you have the authorities waiting for us. They will have our heads on spikes!" the rotten-toothed bandit snapped in a paranoid tone.

"I give you the word of a faithful monk," said the old man.

"To hell with your word! I've had enough of this crazy talk. Let go of the bag or die, old man!" The black-toothed bandit yanked on the bag, sending the old man toppling forward, but the monk didn't let go of the bag. The angry bandit thrust his sword into the old monk's back, piercing his heart. He pulled one pair of swords out of the bag and tossed the bag with the remaining pair at his partner.

The tall bandit caught the bag, demanding, "Why the hell did you do that? We agreed the old man was not to be harmed!"

"Can't you see he's crazy? I'm not going to lose my head over such nonsense. Besides, our swords are now worth tenfold." The rotten-toothed bandit laughed.

The young apprentice began to weep, dragging himself to his master. Overcome with grief and remorse, the tall bandit pulled out his sword and charged the rotten-toothed bandit. The men fought ferociously. It was clear the dual was to be to the death.

Suddenly, the sound of women and children echoed through the woods. A large group ascended the mountainside in search of winter mushrooms. One of the children, a young boy, broke through the thick foliage and stood in fear. The bandits slowly backed away from each other and looked over at the trembling child. The rotten-toothed bandit felt behind his back to ensure that his two prizes, a long sword and a short sword, were still secured beneath his sash, and then escaped into the woods.

The tall bandit picked up the bag and ran to the dying apprentice. He removed his sash and tied a tourniquet around the young man's severed leg. He grabbed the canteen and lifted the young monk's head so he could drink water. The monk coughed and opened his eyes.

The men stared at each other—one in disbelief, the other with heavy heart and shame. The bandit looked over at the old monk lying in a large pool of blood then back to the apprentice.

The tall bandit lowered his head. "I am so sorry. Please forgive me. I've been a fool."

The young monk slowly shook his head.

A tear rolled from the bandit's eye.

A piercing scream bounced off the mountain walls as three women broke through the woods in search of the boy. The bandit looked down at the bag by his knees and then at the apprentice. He reached into the bag and pulled out the remaining swords to hand them to the apprentice.

"I've brought disgrace upon my family name," he said. "And I have stolen from you this day and from the Japanese people for an eternity. I am the least worthy of such greatness, and again, I beg your forgiveness."

The apprentice looked at the swords then slowly pushed them back to the bandit.

"I believe my master would think otherwise," he said.

The bandit was bewildered. Shaking his head, he bowed low into the mud. More screams rang out as several additional women pushed through the trees, viewing the scar-faced bandit's partially decapitated body.

"Please accept my master's swords and do honor by them. I will be all right, but you must go now," said the apprentice.

The bandit placed the swords in the bag and staggered to his feet. He looked over at the women gathered in a protective circle around the little boy. The bandit slowly turned and walked into the dense forest.

A few months later, one pair of the Mountain Monk's swords was sold to a sword dealer, who then sold the swords to a high-ranking official for an unprecedented price. The other pair of swords was never seen again.

As a result of the Mountain Monk's untimely death, a fortune had been made and lost over the centuries from counterfeits claiming to be "the universe's chosen swords of light." There was even a high demand for the swords of darkness.

Many men throughout history claimed to own the original swords, but none would ever agree to put the swords through the Mountain Monk's original tests. The excuses were always the same: "out of respect for the legendary swordsmith" or "for fear of his retribution in the form of a terrible curse."

So the legendary questions remained: Who was in possession of the universe's chosen one, the sword of light? And who was in possession of the demon's chosen one, the sword of darkness?

Considering the tale as he knelt before his swords, Ukko remained convinced the emperor of Japan or his commanding generals of the military when the bomb was dropped on Hiroshima and Nagasaki were the owners of the swords of darkness. How else could such blind arrogance, greed, and stupidity possess these men? How else could such horrible misfortune fall upon his beloved country? How else could he lose the three women he loved more than anything else in the world in one fell swoop?

They're no better than murdering bandits in the night stealing from others what's not rightfully theirs, he thought. *Then they mask it as patriotism and sell it as a necessary evil for the good of the nation, as if the heavens above would not know better and take swift action against them and those who blindly followed.*

Now, with the pair of swords laid out before him, Ukko contemplated the haunting question for the thousandth time: *Which am I—the sword of light?*

Or the sword of darkness?

CHAPTER 16

RETURN TO INNOCENCE

THE CLOCK READ 2:34 A.M., and Kiwi was wide awake. Thoughts of her meeting with the senator haunted her all night. *Connor will be back in town in two days,* she assured herself. *He'll make things better; everything will pick up right where it left off. Or will it?*

She had a sick feeling in the pit of her stomach. She knew a big part of the reason she felt so bad was due to guilt. She and Connor had promised never to keep secrets, to always be true to each other. Yet she'd never told him about her job in Vegas for fear he'd think badly of her. And then she'd asked his own father to hide the fact that he'd tried to rape her. Her life was a wreck, and she felt adrift. Her eyes hurt from crying so much. Nothing made sense. She didn't make sense. It was all she could do just to survive one more day. She decided that she couldn't take it any longer, and that she was going to tell Connor the truth—even if it meant losing him forever.

Kiwi sat at her desk and began writing the letter she would give him in case she lost her nerve and couldn't tell him face-to-face. She revealed everything.

When she was done writing, a mountain of tissues piled high in her trash can. Blotched ink spots on the paper told of her failed attempts to catch her tears in time. She sealed the letter in an envelope, wrote something on the front of it, and stuck it in her purse. She felt as if half the weight of a massive dam had been taken off her shoulders. She hoped that she would be relieved of the other half when she told Connor the truth.

Kiwi was still wide awake and decided that a walk down by the football stadium would do her some good. The air was cool and crisp and had the distinct smell of early spring in Montana. The walking trail across from the stadium circled around a duck pond and was landscaped with large boulders and lots of trees. The moon was nearly full and painted everything silver. After her second time around the one-and-a-half5-mile loop, she decided to take a break on the park bench before heading back to the dorms.

The ducks in front of her nestled at the edge of the water and, surprisingly, seemed oblivious to her intrusion upon their sleep. She recalled something her father told her one day while they were at her uncle's pond and heard his voice. "You see those ducks out there, Kiwi? We humans attach a name to a creature and think we know what it is, when in fact we know practically nothing about it—what its true essence is, why it's here, how it fits into the grand scheme of things. These same questions we cannot answer even for ourselves, yet we label others, study their actions, and believe we know them, so that we can judge them against others we've also labeled. Can you see the tragic flaw in this way of thinking, my daughter?"

The reflection of the moon dancing off the surface of the water was hypnotic. Kiwi began feeling sleepy.

The ducks scattered in panic as the bag slid over her head. A hand clamped tight over her mouth. She felt her entire body being lifted and pulled backward off of the bench. Someone else had her thrashing legs wrapped in his arms. Images of the senator flashed across her mind as she was being dragged away. He had that same sadistic grin on his face the day she went to his office to confront him about the unspeakable crime he'd committed against her in Vegas.

It was nearing sunrise. Through the dirty window of the box-shaped van, Kiwi could see the purplish glow on the horizon. Her captors failed to notice the silver dollar–sized hole in the burlap bag they put over her head. Her mind had been racing desperately for a long time and showed signs of fatigue. *Didn't Uncle have a van like this back on the rez?* she wondered. Her hands and feet had gone completely numb more than an hour ago. *So this is what it feels like to be hog-tied.* She thought about the show pig she had a lifetime ago. She wondered if he had been tied the same way before *he* was murdered.

Kiwi heard the men speaking as they drove through the night. The men argued a lot, mostly about the huge risk they'd taken by abducting her on school campus. The man in the passenger seat seemed extremely nervous and unsure. The man driving was obviously intoxicated and yelled terrible things at his partner. He threatened to do the same to him as they planned to do to her if he didn't shut up. The driver kept reaching back to touch Kiwi's leg, causing her to flinch in panic.

The nervous man kept repeating, "I don't know no more, Ba-Ba. Maybe this isn't such a good idea." He said something about how the big man hadn't paid them yet, and they could just stop now before it was too late.

"Yeah, and what, idiot, have the big man hire someone else to off us, too? No thank you!" the driver lashed back. "You just let me do the thinking round here, ya hear?"

The van swerved hard, and a loud *thud* came from the front of the vehicle. "Whoo-hoo! I got me one. Did you see the size of that doe? I think I mighta got Bambi, too! Them's extra points!" the driver yelled with pride.

Kiwi cried silently for the slain deer. It was because of people like him she'd vowed never to eat meat again since the slaughter of her beloved show pig. She recalled a quote by one of her favorite writers, George Bernard Shaw, "animals are my friends…and I don't eat my friends." Images of her friend being trucked away to the slaughterhouse flashed across her mind.

Her suspicions were confirmed as she lay there on the mildewed and carpeted floor of the van. The good senator of Montana, "the big man," had hired the hit men to get rid of the evidence—her. *Why did I take such a stupid chance and confront the senator?* Kiwi thought. *I should've known better. Any man capable of raping women, let alone a man with the power and influence of a senator obsessed with becoming the next president, couldn't allow such inconvenient setbacks to go public. Of course not; narcissists like him would stop at nothing to achieve their egotistical ambitions. Monsters like him are capable of anything, including cold-blooded murder.*

Oh God, why didn't I just leave—run as fast and as far away as possible? The senator would've never known, and this wouldn't be happening right now. But then, of course, my heart never lets me forget the reason—love.

The van hit a rut in the road, slamming Kiwi's head hard against the floor. It reminded her of the terrible roads back on the rez. Suddenly, it hit her: *What about Father and Johnny-Bear back home? Does the senator know about my family and where they live? Of course he does! He'll make sure to get rid of anyone I might've told about his crime. Oh God, what have I done? I've got to get out of this! I've got to somehow warn my family of the danger they're all in! But how?*

The van suddenly veered off the paved road and was now bouncing up and down along a gravel road. Kiwi tried to see what was outside the window, but the dust billowing up from the tires was too thick. It seemed they'd been traveling for at least two hours now, and her heart was beginning to pound out of control. Something told her they were near the destination—the end of her road.

After another fifteen minutes on the dusty road, the van came to a screeching stop.

"About damn time," the drunken man complained. "Riding on a shitty road like this, I wouldn't be surprised if our poor, darling princess back there isn't already dead. You all right back there, sweetheart?" The driver got out of the van and relieved himself.

Kiwi was overcome with panic and began kicking her legs and thrashing around inside the van. She tried desperately to scream for help, but the duct tape was sealed tightly over her mouth. The burlap bag suddenly flipped off her head, and light flooded in.

A chubby, round face with small, sorrowful blue eyes stared at her from the passenger's seat. He had her purse in his lap. She knew from her volunteer work with the school district Special Olympics that the man had some form of Down's syndrome. She shook her head, pleading for him to help her. The man swallowed hard and seemed to try to say something, and then his eyes glazed over with tears. For a second, Kiwi felt a glimmer of hope. But then the side door was flung open with a crash.

"Home sweet home, darling!" The drunken man climbed into the van and stood over her. "I see you managed to get rid of that old nasty 'tater sack. Don't matter. Least now you can see my partner's handsome fat face." He laughed.

"Shut da' hell up, Ba-Ba!" his partner yelled, clearly embarrassed.

The drunken man reached over and slapped his partner hard across the face. "Don't you get mouthy with me, you a-sorry sack a manure, or I'll cut your throat from ear to ear!"

The round-faced man recoiled and sat staring out the passenger-side window, quietly crying. The drunken man turned back to Kiwi. "Good help's hard to find nowadays. If I hadn't swore to his dead mama I'd look after the bastard, Lord knows I'd be better off."

Anger came over Kiwi as she watched someone so defenseless being bullied.

"Now, tell you what I'm willing to do outta the goodness of my heart," the man continued. "We both know how this ends for you, but I'm willin' to make it fast and painless so's you don't suffer. But in return, I need you to do a little somethin' for me."

Kiwi's heart sank.

"Now, it sure would be a cryin' shame for a girl like you, blessed by the good Lord with such a purdy face and body, to go to waste, wouldn't it?"

She heard the elders' voices whisper, *the curse of beauty.* Then panic shot through her. The thought of being raped before she was murdered shattered what little hope she had left. Thoughts of the incident in Vegas filled her mind, and she began crying uncontrollably.

"Now, now, darlin'. You ain't gotta be like that. I promise I'll be nice and gentleman-like," the man snickered. He closed the van door.

"Now, we can't rightly make sweet love with you all tied up like some swine, so I'm gonna free your feet, okay?"

After he cut the rope around Kiwi's feet, she began kicking at him violently. He caught her feet and slammed his knees hard into her stomach. Every ounce of breath exploded from her lungs. Gasping for air, she watched helplessly as he tore open her blouse and yanked down her pants.

"No! No! Stop, Ba-Ba! Stop it!" his partner shouted.

"You shut the hell up!" the monster ordered.

"Please Ba-Ba," the round-faced man cried. "She ain't hurt nobody. Let's let her go, and we kin go home and make popcorn and watch them dirty movies all day, like we always do. Okay?"

The monster's face turned red. He stood up and stormed toward his partner. "Goddamn it, that's it!" he howled. "I'm gonna beat the living shit out of you!"

Without thinking and still gasping for air, Kiwi somehow managed to raise her right leg and kick the monster in the back of his calf. He twisted sideways, tripped over his other leg, and smashed his forehead on the dashboard. The other man let out a load screech and escaped through his door. She heard his footsteps running away from the van.

The monster lay on his stomach between the front seats for a few seconds with his hand on his forehead. Then he got to his feet and clambered back toward her.

"What in the hell you go n' do that for? You some kinda retard lover or something? Well I hope you enjoyed it, 'cause now you gonna pay, bitch!"

Kiwi tried to raise her legs to protect herself, but they were like giant logs. She watched helplessly as his dirty fist smashed repeatedly against the left side of her face.

Something warm gushed from her nose as her lungs finally refilled with air. He stopped hitting and just stood over her, breathing hard.

"Okay, now let's just kiss n' make up, darlin', so we kin have us a little nookie time."

Kiwi stared hopelessly at the ceiling of the van as the monster standing over her took off his clothes. Her mind drifted to her childhood on the rez…her daddy swinging her 'round and 'round, her mother's sweet smile, the day her baby brother was born, Me'me' and her in a field full of flowers and butterflies. *The red butterfly. I see her—what's she whispering?*

Suddenly, something took over, something Kiwi could only describe as a warm, comforting, unfathomably powerful light, and she surrendered to it.

She looked down to see that she still had her clothes on. The monster standing over her was now down to his boxer shorts. Her arms were still tied behind her back, and she turned to her side and pushed against the floor to sit upright. There was a tranquil expression on her face.

"Ah, now, that's the spirit, darlin'. I knew you'd come 'round sooner or later. Now, let me take that awful tape off your pretty little mouth."

The man kneeled down to remove the tape. It'd been wrapped tightly around her head three times, and it felt like skin was being ripped off as he unraveled it.

Kiwi's expression remained the same and then the corners of her lips curled upward into a smile. She seemed to look straight through the monster before her.

The man's lust overcame him as he salivated over the glowing angel in front of him. He grabbed her head with both hands and plunged his mouth hard against hers.

As soon as Kiwi felt his serpent-like tongue deep inside her mouth, she bit down with a force so powerful that she heard the sickening sound of tearing flesh.

The monster let out a horrid groan and violently pulled away from her. Blood spewed from his mouth as he screamed in agony. She spat his bloody severed tongue into his face. In complete shock and with both hands over his mouth, he staggered backward and fell between the front seats. Kiwi stood up and made it to the side door. Turning her back to the door, she found the handle, and the door popped open. She climbed out and ran straight ahead as fast as she could.

The blinding light had impeded her vision for a few seconds before she realized in horror that she was running right into a dead end. She was on some sort of cliff, and before her was a raging waterfall. *I'm at the Great Falls in Montana…my class took a field trip here when I was in eighth grade.*

The cliff jutted out from the mountain like a spine and dropped off for hundreds of feet on three sides. Kiwi turned around to run back, but it was too late. Staggering toward her, blood spilling out of his mouth onto his boxers, the monster came. In his eyes was the fury of a rabid animal, and in his hand was a very large machete. He made groaning sounds as he quickly closed in. Kiwi searched desperately for escape, but there was none. She was too close to the tip of the cliff—the perfect trap. If she tried to run around the monster, she'd fall off the side. If she ran too close to him, she'd surely be cut down and hacked to pieces. The monster was walking slowly toward her now. He seemed to savor the final moments. There was no doubt he'd make her death as slow and painful as possible.

"Stop, Ba-Ba! Stop!" the round-faced man shouted. He was standing by the van about thirty feet away, waving his arms wildly. The monster didn't even acknowledge his partner. He had only one mission. Kiwi backed up little by little. Suddenly she stepped on a large rock and her ankle turned, sending a sharp pain up her leg. She fell to the ground just three feet from the edge. The spray of the water was cold against her body.

She watched in terror as a bloody smile slithered across the monster's face. He raised his machete high above his head and stepped forward. A shot rang out and dirt exploded into a cloud of dust just inches from the monster's foot. He stopped in his tracks, lowered his machete, and slowly turned toward the sound.

"Don't do it, Ba-Ba! I won't let you do it!" the round-faced man yelled. The large pistol in his hand bobbed up and down with his shaking hands.

The monster slowly raised his hand and pointed to his partner. Then he raised the machete near his throat and made a slashing motion.

The round-faced man began sobbing uncontrollably.

Kiwi was now on her feet just inches from the edge. She watched and prayed for the round-faced man's safety. Then she saw the monster turn back toward her. He let out a blood-curdling roar and charged.

As the monster was running toward his victim, he saw a white angel standing at the edge of the cliff. She was looking up to the heavens.

High above, Kiwi saw two eagles soaring together in a circle. *Forgive me, Great Spirit*, she prayed. *Please watch over Father, Johnny-Bear, and Connor.*

The monster slashed violently at Kiwi's neck just as she surrendered. He fell forward to the edge of the cliff and nearly went over. The monster cursed in rage as he watched his prey escape. A blast of updraft blew hard into his face, and he rolled onto his back. A patch of Kiwi's hair shot skyward. The man watched as each glimmering strand floated softly back to earth. *Did my blade meet its mark?* the monster wondered.

He clambered to his feet and staggered back toward the van, but someone was standing in his way, someone with a .357 Magnum revolver he'd removed from the glove box. Dangling in his other hand was a leather purse decorated with beads and turquoise stones in the shape of a butterfly. The monster snarled, and blood drooled down from the corners of his lips. He quickened his pace and walked directly toward his partner. With tears streaming down his face and a shaking hand, the round-faced man raised the pistol toward the monster—his brother. The monster raised his machete high and slashed down hard at the exact moment his skull exploded into the air, turning the spray of the waterfall crimson.

CHAPTER 17

WRATH OF CHOPPER

THE ROOM WAS LARGE AND had a pungent, nauseating order. The sound of water spewing from the ceiling onto the pitted cement floor seemed to be coming from every corner of the rectangular room. High in the ceiling sat dozens of birds' nests. Their droppings had painted the rafters white. Graffiti-covered boards blocked the light of day from entering through the broken windows.

Sara sat in a wooden chair in a dark, abandoned warehouse. Her teeth clattered as she shivered uncontrollably. She'd been stripped down to her undergarments, and her hands and feet were tied to the chair. Spread out underneath her was a large plastic drop cloth.

Chopper sat in a large Victorian-style chair six feet in front of her. It was the most terrifying object Sara had ever seen. It looked like something straight from the pit of hell—something the devil himself would lounge in with pride. From a distance, it appeared to be constructed of wood, brass, leather, and animal parts. The bulky frame looked to be made from a combination of exotic tusks, horns, antlers, and teeth, all jutting dangerously outward, ready to impale or slice open any who dared to come close. The seat cushion was made from the hides of tigers and zebras and lamb's wool. The legs were constructed from exotic woods wrapped in snake and alligator skin. At the bottom of each leg were mysterious, shiny spheres. Each was about the size of a bowling ball in different earth tones: green, blue, brown, and red. The bulging armrests appeared to be huge elephant tusks that created large arches on each

174

side of the chair. Protruding outward and upward from the armrests of the chair were smaller, sharp horns. Hundreds of razor-sharp teeth of some sort stuck out between the horns. It was evident that the crown jewel of the chair was what appeared to be a bleached white human skull mounted in the center of the high backed chair.

Oh God, please tell me that's not a real human skull, Sara thought. The monstrosity, along with its occupant, oozed a palatable evil energy.

On Chopper's lap sat a half-empty bottle of vodka; under the chair were other various bottles of liquor. Sara's heart sank when she noticed what he was wearing. Over the top of his usual black leather trench coat and pants was what appeared to be a butcher's apron. It had long sleeves and reached almost to his ankles. The light bulb suspended from the ceiling between them made the apron glow a ghostly white.

Chopper reached into his trench coat and pulled out his double-headed hatchet to inspect and admire. The light gleamed off the blade. Sara felt the room spinning all around her as she tried desperately not to vomit on herself. She felt her heart was going to pound straight through her chest. She wished it would explode, allowing her to die peacefully.

Smiling as if to deliberately expose his gold-capped canine teeth, Chopper offered, "Well, well, now. It seems you have a problem with obeying rules." His speech was a drunken slur and almost unintelligible.

Sara desperately shook her head, trying to say she was sorry. "Shut up, bitch!" he yelled. "Today could be a special day for you, kind of like your birthday except it's the other way round. Let's start with a lesson, shall we? A lesson in life."

He stood up and walked toward Sara, stopping directly in front of her. He took a long swig from the bottle. He looked up and pointed to the rafters. "You see all those damn raggedy pigeons nesting up there and shittin' all over my floor?" Sara looked up and saw the nervous birds staring down at them. She was reminded of the countless hours she'd spent looking at the beautiful birds outside her window.

"What if I told you that living among them worthless, flea-infested pigeons was another kind of bird, a big powerful bird called a tiger owl?"

Sara knew exactly what kind of owl he was talking about. She'd seen the bird outside her window in the evenings and had sketched it in her notebook. The *Encyclopedia Britannica* set in the mansion's library confirmed it was a great horned owl, also known as the tiger owl, native throughout the United States and Canada.

Chopper looked up proudly to the corner where the owl made its nest. "I named her Kali after the Hindu goddess of death. The reason I know it's a female is because I've watched her feed her babies before. Let me tell you, she's one badass bird! Yep, she's a natural-born killer, all right, of rats, bats, cats, and—yes sir—of pigeons, too! Except here's the damnedest thing, Sara. For some reason, she won't kill them helpless weak pigeons, even though they'd be an easy meal for her. Now, why you suppose that is? Why would nature sometimes allow predators and prey to live together in peace and harmony?"

Chopper turned and slowly staggered back toward his chair. "I don't claim to be no philosopher or nothing, but I can't help but wonder. Could it be a message from the big man above, a sign that maybe someday people like you and I could do the same?" He turned to face Sara.

A glimmer of hope flickered in her eyes. *Is there really a chance he won't kill me? That somehow Falcon and I could reunite and have a happy life together? Oh God, please let it be true*, she prayed.

"Hell no! It will never be that way!" He pointed again to the rafters. "You see, Sara, what's happening up there is a lie. A trick. A false hope."

Again Sara's heart sank. *I'll never see my child again.* She felt a deep sadness for the pigeons. She knew all too well of their predicament. *Maybe I, too, was a pigeon in a previous life*, she thought. *Or was I the tiger owl, and now the time has come to pay for my terrible deeds?*

Chopper made a slashing motion across his neck. "It's only a matter of time before Kali's gonna turn on those stupid little pigeons. She's gonna swoop in and kill everyone last one of them and feed their body parts to her killer babies, and then guess what? The cycle starts all over again."

Chopper looked at Sara with an evil grin. "You see, it ain't nothing personal, girl. It's just the way life works." He reached into his trench coat and pulled out a large chrome-plated pistol, pointing it at Sara's face. Her lips quivered, and she closed her eyes.

Thank you, God. At least this way will be quick.

Suddenly, he swung the gun upward toward the ceiling, and five shots rang out in rapid succession. The deafening sound felt like it pierced Sara's eardrums with an ice pick. Feathers rained down as the flutter of terror-stricken wings crisscrossed in the rafters above. With a thud, two lifeless pigeons dropped to the floor.

"Yes!" Laughing victoriously, Chopper raised his arms in a "V." Dozens of pigeons scattered, making their way to an exit at the other end of the building. A large pair of wings silently swooped down and flew directly toward the pigeons. Sara's heart sank again as she watched the inevitable massacre about to unfold. But the owl flew under the pigeons and glided right between Sara and Chopper. The bird's powerful wings pushed cool air against her face.

"That's it girl…go do your business!" Chopper roared.

The tiger owl circled around and headed back toward her nest, disappearing into blackness.

There was an awkward moment of silence. Chopper seemed to be pondering what he should say, what action he should take next. He took another swig from the bottle and slurred, "As you damn well know, I've always liked you best, Sara." Another pause, another drink. He inhaled then exhaled slowly. "Hell, I might as well go on and tell you my little secret."

Chopper looked away from Sara as if embarrassed about the confession he was about to make. "Actually, you could say I had special feelings for you. I worshipped you, only you didn't feel the same for me." He paused and took another drink. "From the moment I laid eyes on you, I felt something I know I've felt before but can't place where or when.

Somehow you give me something worth living for again. How you do it is a mystery to me and a curse. In your presence I feel clean again, somehow cleansed of the horrible sins I commit every day. Being near you for even a few minutes is like having gone to confession, like having an unbearable weight removed…like seeing the world in color again. The more time I spent near you, the more inspired I became to change my life, to be good again."

Chopper brought the bottle to his lips and tilted his head all the way back, finishing it off. "All I knew was that I couldn't lose you. You were like an addiction I couldn't live without."

Sara stared at the monster's back as he poured out his guts. Somehow the impossible happened, and she felt a tinge of compassion.

Of all the people in this world, he's the last I should forgive. He took everything from me. He took the two people I loved more than anything, yet I feel sorry for him. How can this be?

Chopper reached under his chair and picked up another bottle of liquor. With a bottle in each hand, he staggered a few feet away from Sara, then disappeared into blackness. There was a sound of bottles being placed on the floor, then something being uncased. He made a few snorting sounds before he continued. "But then every time I return to the world, the darkness takes over again. I become the person I hate, the person who holds me hostage, the person *you* hate, the monster you can never love." There was a moment of silence, and then Chopper screamed out in rage as a bottle smashed against the wall.

Sara began shaking uncontrollably again. She heard sounds of pills rattling in their containers and then falling to the floor. A few minutes passed, and finally the monster reappeared from the darkness.

Chopper staggered to his massive chair and dragged it toward Sara's, stopping just three feet away. He sat down and placed his hands on his knees. "Enough of the sentimental bullshit. Let's get down to business," he grumbled in a deep, low voice. "Now, had it not been for my incompetent gate guard not knowing you had the child with you the night you broke camp, we wouldn't be havin' this conversation, and I wouldn't be worried about losing a shitload of money on my investment right now. So I'm gonna ask you nicely, Sara. The boy... where did you take him? I want him back." Every muscle in Sara's body constricted, and she instinctively shook her head for what seemed like forever. She knew this moment would come and was fully prepared to protect her son to her last breath.

The monster's lips curled upward, revealing his gold canines as he reached into his trench coat. Sara closed her eyes and braced herself for the first blow from the hatchet, but then nothing happened. When she opened her eyes, she saw her soul mate. Chopper held out the Polaroid picture of Montana's battered face, taken the day after her capture.

Sara gasped in horror and began crying hysterically, "No, no, no, please God, no!"

The monster smiled with pleasure. "This little whore look familiar to you?"

"Is she okay? Please tell me she's okay," Sara's trembling voice begged.

"Well, that all depends on you, Miss Sara. Right now, she's safe and sound not too far from here."

Sara's heart suddenly filled with joy. She'd long ago assumed her best friend had been murdered. Now she was being told Montana was still alive. *Oh God, please let this be true*, she prayed.

Chopper put the photo back inside his coat. "I'll make you a deal. Tell me where the boy is, and I give you my word I'll return Montana to you unharmed, releasing both of you forever. The two of you can ride off into the sunset and live happily ever after. How's that sound?"

Sara was devastated. How could she possibly choose? Falcon and Montana were the only two people in the world she'd die for; now she was being forced to basically kill one for the other. She vomited, but nothing came out. *Oh God, I can't do this anymore*, she prayed. *Please take my life now.*

Chopper leaned forward. "What's there to think about, Sara? You can always have more children, and the two of you can even raise them together. Doesn't that sound just peachy?"

Sara imagined her and Montana happy and living on a horse ranch with small children running all around. But then she imagined Falcon somewhere far away being subjected to God knows what and wondering where his mother was and why she allowed this to happen to him. She broke down crying, shaking her head. "No, no, no. I can't tell you. I *won't* tell you—I will *never* tell you where my baby is!"

Chopper stood up. "Tell me, goddamn it!" He slapped her hard across the face, splitting her lip. Blood ran down Sara's chin as she continued to shake her head in refusal. "I was afraid this was going to happen. Have it your way, bitch." Chopper turned and walked away into the darkness. He returned with something in his hand. Sara watched as the monster made his way toward her. She noticed the mason jar clasped in his hands. The clear liquid inside splashed up and down as something inside spun in slow circles.

Before Chopper made it to his chair, Sara knew what it was and died inside. She closed her eyes tight and began to hyperventilate. Chopper sat down in his chair.

"So, you choose to be with a lesbian over a man, huh? Didn't you think I'd find out about you two kissing in front of that theater? I can't believe you allowed that whore to manipulate you into being gay. Don't you know that's a sin? That it's written in the Bible that God condemns all homosexuals and burns them in the fires of hell?"

Sara's eyes were still shut tight as images of Billy in Sunday school and Father Odiar flashed across her mind. Chopper slammed the heel of his boot onto the floor.

"Well, guess what? I saved God some trouble by doing his work and ridding the world of one of its sinners. I know God was proud when he saw me rip your gay lover's heart out!"

Sara had begun dry-heaving. She heard the sound of metal twisting against glass. The cold liquid splashed onto her legs followed by a *thud*. She opened her eyes and let out a harrowing scream. On her lap sat the heart of her soul mate. Wrapped around it was Montana's necklace, and protruding grotesquely out of the top was a crucifix.

Sara's eyes rolled back and she fainted.

Chopper knelt down inches from Sara's face and took another long gulp of liquor then tossed the bottle to the side. He pulled out his hatchet and held it up against Sara's cheek, nicking her with its razor edge. A drop of blood rolled off the side of the hatchet. Sara's body appeared lifeless.

"Oh no you don't, bitch! You ain't gettin' off that easy. I want your ass awake when I cut you up nice and slow." Chopper stood over Sara and began violently slapping her. Blood from the cuts on her face splattered everywhere. After several hard blows, Sara regained consciousness and opened her eyes.

What Chopper saw before him scared him so bad he staggered backward and stumbled over his chair. He dropped his hatchet to break his fall; the sound of metal scrapping against concrete slid away into the darkness. Sara looked directly into Chopper's eyes, into his soul. In her eyes was the same soft glow of peace, love, and forgiveness that was on her baby's face the night he was delivered to room 316.

Chopper was shocked and disoriented. He was not sure what to do. Deep down he knew someday he'd have to meet his maker, but he never imagined it'd be like this.

Sara sat there with blood dripping from her face and ears. The corners of her busted lips turned upward into a gentle smile. She radiated an aura of tranquility and unconditional love.

The maddening sound of his own thundering heartbeat consumed Chopper like a wildfire out of control.

His breathing became heavy and erratic, and the corners of his eyes and lips began to twitch. He wanted to run out of the room like a coward, but his feet wouldn't move. He was overwhelmed with a drowning sense of fear and shame. He wanted desperately to look away from Sara, but his head and eyes were stuck. An eternity seemed to pass.

Then suddenly, in a rage of madness, he lunged forward, smashing into her so hard they both toppled over backward with a loud crash. Two of the legs on the chair shattered and were thrown spinning across the floor.

He had Sara's throat clenched tight between his thick, meaty fingers, strangling her with what depleting strength he had left. Their eyes were locked, his pulsating with the fury of a rabid dog about to be put down and hers with the calm of an island sunset, a surrender to what was.

As the monster on top of her was busy doing his work, the blood vessels in Sara's eyes suddenly burst. Everything within her vision turned bright red, and everything became silent.

She noticed a large web in the corner of the ceiling. *How beautifully spun it is,* she thought to herself. A frightened butterfly struggled desperately from within as a hungry spider moved eagerly along its trap. Silvery dust from broken wings scattered then floated gracefully back to the stars.

With a final breath Sara exhaled to freedom. *At last, my darling Montana, at last...*

Chopper collapsed to the side of Sara's body, gasping for air. The guard posted outside pounded on the door. "You all right, Boss? You need me to come in or somethin'?"

Moaning and with the last of his energy, Chopper pushed himself up to his knees.

Suddenly, he watched in horror as out of nowhere a large pair of black talons silently swooped down and smashed into his face. He grabbed the great horned owl with both hands as she desperately flapped her wings to maintain a good hold on his skull. Chopper let out a blood-curdling scream as one of the talons hit home. A sickening *pop* echoed through the room as the razor-sharp talon punctured his left eye and sliced it in half. He ripped the bird from his face and slammed her to the floor. In a state of sheer hysteria, he began violently beating the great horned owl with his fists until there was no life.

Chopper dragged himself to his chair and pulled himself onto it. He tried to yell to the guard, but the words wouldn't come out. Finally, the guard rushed into the room. He looked at his boss slumped over in the chair with bloody hands over his face. He noticed the bloody pile of ruffled feathers on the floor. To the right of the bird was the twisted, mangled body of a girl sprawled out on the floor. She was still tied to what was left of the chair.

The guard was speechless. What he saw sitting before him was a hollow silhouette of a man he hardly recognized. "Chopper the Terrible," "Butcher of East Side," the man who claimed to have more power than God himself, looked like a defeated ghost. He looked like he'd aged twenty years. He had that ten-thousand-mile stare one saw in insane asylums. He seemed like someone who had gone on a long journey far away to a place he wasn't worthy of and now had come back a soulless lump of flesh and bones.

"You okay, Boss? What you need me to do?" stuttered the guard.

Unable to raise his head, Chopper struggled to speak. "Dumpster number nine," was all he could manage to croak out of his parched throat. His bodyguard knew this was code for sticking a hypodermic needle in the body to make it look like a drug overdose and tossing the carcass between the dumpsters on Ninth and Main, a location known to be infested with heroin and crack addicts.

Without hesitation, the bodyguard obeyed the command. When he bent down to pick up the girl's body, he was overwhelmed with grief and shame. He'd arrived at the warehouse just ten minutes before to relieve the other guard and had no idea the girl named Sara was being murdered inside. He happened to be one of the men who'd helped kidnapped her years ago and also helped in capturing her and Montana after their audition. But for months, he'd been plagued with sleepless nights and dreams of his deceased baby sister and Sara. Somehow he knew Sara was someone special, that she was everything good and pure like his sister. He couldn't explain it, but it was as if somehow Sara and his sister were connected in spirit.

A lifetime ago, when he was a young man, he had a baby sister with a heart of gold and a constant smile that gave people hope. It was that fateful night when stray bullets from a rival gang showered their home and pierced a hole in his beloved sister's heart that he'd lost all hope for goodness. It was the moment he had chosen to see only the dark in humanity.

The guard carefully lifted Sara's lifeless body into his massive arms. She felt like a small bird in his hands. Her skinny, fragile arms and legs dangled toward the floor. As much as he resisted, he couldn't help but look at her face. *How amazing this girl is to have such a peaceful look after such a horrifying death,* he thought. He gently placed his hand over her eyes to shut them forever. The guard suddenly realized Chopper was looking straight at him, and he had to be very careful not to show his emotions. He knew to be seen showing any sympathy for Chopper's victims could be hazardous to one's health.

Chopper did notice and took mental note. "Take her damned lover's heart there on the floor with you and get rid of it," Chopper ordered. "She cost me my damn eye." Somehow in his delusional mind he had seen the face of Montana on the Tiger Owl.

The guard stared at the cold chunk of flesh lying on the floor, the crucifix still attached. He pulled out a handkerchief and squatted down with Sara's tiny body still in his arms. He closed his eyes for a brief second as if saying a silent prayer, then gently picked up Montana's heart. Again, Chopper noticed the compassion and decided he must rid himself of such a dangerous man.

When the guard placed Sara's body in the van, he noticed the small red butterfly tattoo on her left wrist. Again he thought of his baby sister "Lill'l Butterfly." He tried to find something to put over her, but there was nothing clean. He placed Montana's heart on top of Sara's chest, took off his jacket, and laid it over them.

Suddenly, tears began to fall. "I'm so sorry, Sara," he whispered. "God knows I'm so sorry for what I've done to you. I ask for your forgiveness, but I know I'll never forgive myself."

By the time he climbed behind the wheel, his decision was made. He knew what he should do, what he must do. He decided that in honor of his baby sister, he could no longer live the shameful and destructive life he was living. Somehow, Sara broke through. She'd managed to open his heart when nobody else could. He heard about what Chopper had done to Sara's friend Montana, and again felt sick, knowing he'd assisted in their capture and in essence, their murder. So in honor of them, he decided he would leave for the state of Montana that night. He would give them a proper and respectful burial and lay them to rest in a beautiful, secluded spot far away from the pain and suffering they'd endured here.

He searched through the glove box and pulled out an atlas. He ran his fingers over the map and stopped at a random location. *This sounds like a nice place—Great Falls, Montana. It's the least I can do for two beautiful stars named "Sara" and "Montana."*

CHAPTER 18

MESSAGE FROM BEYOND

———◆———

KIWI WATCHED HER BODY SLICE through the air. The frilly sleeves on its blouse made a rippling sound as it flapped violently toward the earth. Above, two eagles riding an updraft gazed intently.

The first thing to go was her sense of touch. She could no longer feel the fast, cold air rushing across her face.

Next was sound; everything became utterly silent. The body barely made a splash as it vanished below the chaotic surface of the water.

The metallic taste of blood in her mouth disappeared, followed by the fishy smell of the water.

A tranquil feeling of peace enveloped her. She felt like a feather floating atop a summer breeze, and she exhaled a silent sigh.

But then, it suddenly dawned on her that the last string, a thing resembling a sliver of light, was about to be cut. This was the moment she was given a glimpse of the world within, a world that was the creator of what she perceived and experienced as her objective reality. This world was transmitted to her brain through tiny beams of light, like the kind she used to stare up at through the leaves of the trees when she was a child. Inside these slivers of light were continuous flows of information that created and controlled her sense perceptions: sight, sound, taste, smell, and touch. Without this information, her dream was over, and all that remained was consciousness—the essence of what she is, of what we all are.

Somehow she had a feeling an important decision would soon be made, a decision that would have a profound effect on something very important. *But how and why…and by whom?*

Through the murky water, she saw the blurry image of a man looking down at her from the edge of a cliff hundreds of feet above. He seemed angry for some reason. Then, from high above, she looked down to two men standing near the edge of the same cliff. To their left was a beautiful waterfall. The men faced each other. One of them was nearly naked and holding a big knife, while the other was holding her purse and a gun.

The tail from a large fish brushed the side her head. Suddenly, she realized the unthinkable—it was her! She was the one who was to make the most important decision in the history of humankind. She could either cling to this last string of light and pull herself back into her world—helping to change it forever—or she could let go and relinquish all ties with this world forever. At first, the choice was so obvious. Why would anyone want to give up the unearthly peace and tranquility she was immersed in just to return to more pain, suffering, and disappointment? She hastily and selfishly made her decision, but then something happened.

Something bright red landed on the surface of the choppy waters above. She watched as her pale hand reached out to it, and then the image of the object became crystal clear. Where had she seen this before? Her mind searched and then recalled the moments in her stored memory. She was a child in a sea of wildflowers and this thing, named a butterfly, landed on her lips.

Instantly, the emerald-green eyes of the red butterfly above the water united with hers…and its childish voice became hers…and it whispered into her mind, *This decision is yours to make right now, but it will be for everyone forever.* Then the butterfly flapped its wings and was gone.

The faces of her mother, children, and women she had known flashed before her. Then, at blinding speeds, the faces of other children and women she had never met but somehow knew flashed before her mind—hundreds, thousands, millions, and billions of them!

She grabbed the last sliver of light and inhaled. The cold, fishy-tasting water entered her lungs like a red-hot poker. She heard the roar of the rapids above and let out a gurgled scream. An undertow sucked her down deeper and pulled her sideways. *Let me go! I have to go back! I have to help!* her mind pleaded, and then everything went dark.

A calm voice faded in and out. "Twenty-eight, twenty-nine, thirty. Okay, now pinch nostrils, tilt head, and give two breaths—now repeat," the off-duty nurse said as her wide-eyed teenage daughter watched anxiously.

Kiwi sat shivering under a wool blanket as the car bounced down the gravel road toward the nurse's home. She begged the woman and her daughter not to say anything about her or the incident. She warned them that if they did, it might put their lives in danger. She didn't go into details, but it appeared that the woman and the girl understood and trusted her. She sat twisting her fingers through her partially chopped off hair as she racked her brain for how to deal with her predicament. A very powerful man wanted her dead, and it was obvious he was capable of anything, including harming her family. This meant contacting anyone from the reservation was out of the question. Connor came to mind, but she was terrified that if she told him it might cost him his life. There were no doubts now as to how far the senator would go to keep his crime a secret. There was only one thing to do—call the only other person she trusted.

Lawrence immediately flew from Las Vegas to Great Falls in his private jet. Within hours, they were high above the clouds, streaking toward his secluded cabin near Juno, Alaska.

Kiwi never told anyone about her strange experience under the water. *How could I?* she thought. *Who'd believe me? Even I'm not sure it really happened. Was it just a dream or some sort of weird, near-death experience? But then what about the strange red butterfly with green eyes…what was it she said?*

CHAPTER 19

UKKO VERSUS CHOPPER

———◆———

IT SEEMS NO MATTER WHERE I go, what I do, or how hard I try, I cannot escape the darkness of this world, Ukko thought.

Warily, he allowed his mind to drift back to a time and place he'd tried unsuccessfully to extinguish. It was years ago when he had turned his back on his country and fled Japan. Ukko swore to himself then that he would never again shed the blood of another man; he would choose to stay only in the light. He vowed to bury his blood-stained swords forever. But now it seemed the winds of change had come, bringing with them something new, something worthy, something with the light of hope—a child. He found himself excavating his closet in an attempt to reconnect himself with the only physical evidence left of his family's violent past. It had been easier to strip himself of his own past by discarding almost everything he had owned, particularly anything that had reminded him of his little sister, mother, and the love of his life, his fiancée. He would always blame himself for their deaths, for not being there to protect them on that horrific day in Nagasaki.

Before leaving Japan for America, Ukko couldn't bring himself to leave behind the coveted family heirloom handed down to him through many generations. He knew that no matter what tragedies he might face in his life, it was his duty to preserve the only remaining relic tying him to his family lineage. There was no escaping the fact that he was a samurai, or that samurai blood pulsated through his veins, as it did in the veins of his ancestors as far back as the twelfth century. There was no denying he was a descendant of the great samurai general Lord Kiso no Yoshinaka and Tomoe Gozen, the most famous female samurai warrior in the history of Japan. Legend had it that Tomoe Gozen was renowned for her beauty, physical strength, and martial arts skills. She was known by her foes to be a worthy adversary who would not hesitate to come to the defense of her family, friends, and their honor.

Lord Kiso no Yoshinaka had been so impressed by her skills with the bow, battle tactics, and extraordinary courage as a warrior that he had appointed her as his leading commander in the Genpei War.

Lord Kiso no Yoshinaka and his lover Tomoe Gozen had fought valiantly by each other's side to victory. But soon after, Lord Kiso no Yoshinaka had been fatally wounded. Though it was unclear what had become of Tomoe Gozen, the first and only woman samurai to lead an army into battle, some said she had become a Buddhist nun until her death at the ripe old age of ninety-one. Others said she had avenged Lord Kiso no Yoshinaka by killing his attackers, stealing back Yoshinaka's head so no one else could defile it, and then had walked out into the sea—head in hand—to drown.

So, for reasons of honor and respect for his ancestors, Ukko had brought the ancient samurai battle armor and, most important, the legendary swords worn by many generations of great samurai. The famous swords were more than six hundred years old. They had originally belonged to a great shogun, a supreme military leader.

Ukko removed the box from the closet and laid it on the floor. He sat down cross-legged and opened it. He moved slowly and deliberately, as if performing a ceremony.

With the battle gear laid out neatly before him, Ukko began to meditate on his teachings.

He had learned from his father, grandfather, and from other great teachers—and eventually from his own personal experience—that hate and fear were the greatest deceivers. They were the most cunning adversaries and, when left unchecked, became one's own worst enemy—destroyers of body, mind, and spirit. He knew that soon he would face a man who had not learned this and that, because of this fatal ignorance, Chopper the Terrible would inevitably be consumed in the fires of his own vengeance.

It was just after midnight when the visitors came. Chopper knew exactly where to go. He'd been informed by a resident living in the same complex where the child was located. He had been told a mysterious Japanese man working as a taxi driver had the child. He was told to go to apartment 316 and look for a yellow "happy face" sign on the window. Now he and four of his most vicious henchmen stood just down the hall from the front door.

Chopper had handpicked these particular men because of their reputation for being cold-blooded killers. They'd worked for him for a long time, and their loyalty was unquestionable, unlike the bodyguard who had been tasked to dispose of Sara's body but disappeared with it instead. He knew for a fact that between the four men, one had murdered a cop, one had murdered a political official, one had murdered a female judge, and one had murdered a child—and they all had done it simply because he'd given them orders to. He didn't want any hiccups with this one. A lot of money was at stake.

Chopper had made an offer to the police chief he couldn't refuse and, as a result, the cops patrolling this area would be conveniently unavailable. They were not to respond to any emergency calls in or around this apartment complex, no matter what, until the police chief himself personally gave them permission. The police chief was not to do so until Chopper called him personally to give him the all-clear sign.

Chopper was wearing his eel-skin cowboy hat and his black leather trench coat. On his face was a black patch over his left eye. After an emergency operation, he was told there was nothing the doctors could do; the eyeball was completely destroyed. He decided somebody would pay dearly for his loss.

Chopper stood near Ukko's apartment door, surrounded by his men. The yellow smiley face was visible in the eerie, dark hallway. The only light came from a street lamp a few hundred feet away. The stale air was perfectly still. The only sound was from barking dogs in a distant alley.

Chopper nodded his head. The politician slayer and the woman killer stepped forward. Both expertly stood to each side of the door in case they were greeted by a gun blast. The politician killer knocked loudly, but there was no answer. He knocked again, but still no answer.

"Try the damned doorknob," Chopper whispered impatiently.

Surprisingly, the doorknob turned with a slight squeak, and the door opened. The men were overwhelmed by a pungent odor of fermenting cabbage. "Damn! These asshole chinks and their kimchi," the woman killer protested. They looked at Chopper for the signal. He nodded, and they pulled out their handguns and stepped in.

The living room was an empty open space. A large oriental rug covered the green shag carpet. The only furniture was a simple wooden chair in front of a small rabbit-eared television set sitting atop a bamboo stand. Hanging on every wall were large, frameless sheets of white paper displaying Japanese calligraphy.

The woman killer split off to the left to clear the kitchen. Like the living room, the kitchen was almost bare. Drying on a dish towel next to the sink was a brown ceramic bowl, a ceramic teacup, and bamboo chopsticks. On the stove sat a metal teapot with steam still rising from the spout.

Tucked in the corner of the living room was some sort of shrine. Behind a small bowl of fresh fruit and rice cakes sat a statue of a jolly golden Buddha. One of the Buddha's hands was on his fat belly, and the other was raised, with the thumb and middle finger touching. *Is Buddha trying to warn us of our inevitable demise, or is he just giving us a reverse birdie?* the politician killer thought humorously to himself.

On the wall above the statue were two faded black-and-white photographs. One showed a beautiful young Asian woman dressed in a silk kimono that had large flowers on it. She sat stiffly upright with her small hands on her lap. Her face was expressionless, yet seemed to glow with a gentle kindness. The other photograph was of an Asian man in his mid-twenties sitting causally on a chair. He wore simple clothing and large baggy pants. His hands were clasped loosely in his lap. His dark hair was tied back in a knot and folded onto the top of his slightly turned head. A stern, confident expression was on his face. At the middle of his waistline, just above his hands, the hilts of two swords jutted outward.

In front of the fruit bowl was a simple green ceramic box containing sand. Sticking upward from the sand were five burning sticks. Thin white smoke from the jasmine incense spiraled softly into the air like departing spirits.

The men exchanged uneasy expressions. A curtain made from bamboo beads separated the hallway from the living room. A light from the hallway danced off the shiny lacquered beads, luring the killers in like moths to a hot lantern.

The men looked nervously at each other, and then the politician killer took the lead. The man gently separated the beads with one outstretched hand while holding his handgun close to his body with the other, just in case somebody was waiting on the other side. The hallway was empty and led only to the right. At the end of the hallway was a single bedroom to the right. The door was wide-open. The killers cautiously moved forward.

Outside, Chopper and his men listened attentively. Five minutes passed and nothing, not even a sound. Ten minutes passed and still nothing. "What the hell are those assholes doing in there?" Chopper complained.

Five more minutes passed. Chopper finally told one of the men to go in and find out what was taking so long. The cop killer nervously looked at his partner, and then stepped forward. He cautiously entered the apartment with gun drawn, ready for trouble. He called out the names of the first two men and began to methodically clear the apartment the way the police academy had trained him years ago. *Living room clear, kitchen clear,* he thought.

He entered the hallway and immediately sensed death approaching. The unmistakable odor of fresh blood was as thick as smoke from a burning tire.

The bedroom door was wide open. He could hear the cooing of an infant coming from inside the room. The cop killer desperately wanted to run from the apartment, but his pride wouldn't let him. The barrel of his Glock .45 trembled in synch with his racing heartbeat.

Go get backup! Go get backup! his police training screamed. *Hell no!* countered his stubborn pride.

He moved slowly along the wall nearest the opening to the room. At the edge of the doorway, he yelled out his partners' names again and was met with more eerie silence. *Damn!* The cop killer's heart desperately pumped oxygen to his brain. *Just breathe, nice and steady; don't linger in the fatal funnel of the doorway. Enter quickly and move along the path of least resistance. Scan from near wall to far wall; check under and behind furniture. Clear any adjoining rooms. Don't forget the ceiling. Double-tap all targets."* He stepped into the cold dark room.

The pale, severed heads sat side by side on the blood-soaked bed. The heads were facing the doorway as if to welcome their comrades properly, one with his blue tongue sticking out and the other with his terror-stricken eyes wide open. The walls looked like balloons full of red paint had exploded all over them.

"Shit!" the cop killer yelled out unconsciously. Muscle memory took over, and he began to clear the dark room from left to right. He moved along the wall toward the closed bathroom door.

He tripped and fell over the headless bodies. The shag carpet was like an overflowing sponge, and thick blood splashed up onto his face.

Petrified and disoriented, he stumbled to his feet and turned to run from the room.

The cop killer was halfway to the doorway when he faced the unfathomable beast just long enough to witness two swords intersect at lightning speed and extinguish his light. His severed head hit the floor with a *thud.* He'd failed to check the ceiling.

Another ten minutes passed, and Chopper began to feel edgy. "Damn! If you want to do something right around here, you gotta do it yourself!"

His last remaining hitman said nothing. He just stood there, a look of disbelief on his face. Residents of the apartment complex nervously peeked out their windows.

Chopper stepped in front of the doorway and yelled "Hey, Jap asshole! You messin' with the wrong son of a bitch here! All I want is the baby. Hand the little shit over, and all's forgiven. I'll go my way, and you can go yours. We got ourselves a deal?" There was no response. "Okay, dammit. Have it your way."

Chopper pointed his finger at the apartment and looked over to his last man. "Go in there and kill that Jap, and put him out of my misery, now! Just don't hurt the kid or I'll have your ass!"

The baby killer looked at Chopper like he'd just been asked to shoot himself in the head. He looked into the apartment and froze with fear.

"Get your candy ass in there!" Chopper yelled.

The man mumbled something under his breath, shook his head, and turned to run away. Chopper pulled out his Smith and Wesson .44 Magnum and cut the child killer down. The bullet entered the man's shoulder blade and left a gaping hole in his throat. He fell to the ground and began to crawl away. Chopper shot again, and the baby killer's buttocks exploded into a pile of hamburger meat.

The deafening sound of the .44 Magnum reverberated through the walls. Lights in the surrounding apartments immediately came on, and outlines of figures behind closed curtains could be seen on their telephones.

Chopper was furious and out of his mind. He could hear the baby crying from inside the apartment. "Okay, bitch! You wanna play? Then let's play."

He reached into his jacket. "You have exactly ten seconds to come out with the baby before I throw this here hand grenade into your shit-smelling rat hole. And if you think I'm bullshitting, take a look at what I have in my hand." Chopper pulled out an M-33, military-issued fragmentation grenade. His contacts at the local National Guard Armory served him well.

Chopper tucked his pistol in his pants and pulled the safety pin on the grenade. He slid the safety pin through the middle finger on his right hand. The grenade was not yet armed, because the spring-loaded spoon, which when activated ignited the internal fuse that then detonated the explosives inside the grenade within four to five seconds, was still pressed tight between Chopper's palm and the grenade body. "Okay, the ball's in your court now, asshole. Ten, nine, eight, seven, six . . . .."

People began running out of their apartments, some with small children in their arms.

Inside, Ukko knew his options were very limited. A hand grenade was not a contingency he'd planned for. The only window in the apartment was next to the front door. There was no time to escape through the ventilation system. The detonation of the grenade would surely harm the child. Deception was too risky. If this madman suspected that the bundle of towels in his arms was not actually the child, he would demand the baby's face be shown, at which point Chopper would most likely shoot him and possibly even throw the grenade. There was only one way—face the monster with the child in hand.

"Five, four..." Chopper positioned himself as if to toss the grenade into the apartment. "Three, two . . . .."

"Stop! Okay...I come out." Ukko conceded from behind the hallway.

Chopper smiled. "Come out nice and slow, and you better have that little bastard baby in your hands, or I'm throwing in the grenade."

Chopper stood in the doorway with the hand grenade in his left hand and his .44 Magnum and the safety pin in the other.

A dark, scaly hand slowly separated the curtain of beads, and a hideous figure stepped through into the living room.

Chopper was stunned. Standing before him was the most bizarre monstrosity he'd ever seen. It looked like some black mystical dragon from prehistoric times. It was covered head to toe in some type of armor made of leather, metal, and silk cords. On its head was a brass helmet with horn-like projectiles sticking up from the sides. An armored flap extended from the bottom of the helmet down the back of its neck.

On its face was a terrifying half mask. It was glossy black and covered the face from the cheekbones down to the chin. It had a wide snarling nose and an angry, downturned mouth with a breathing hole between its black lips. It wore a leather suit of some kind, and there were intertwining plates of overlapping armor running its entire length from the top of the neck down to the tip of the toes. Strapped to its back was a very long sword, and on its hip was a short sword. Its feet wore straw sandals.

Chopper didn't know whether to cringe in fear or laugh hysterically. He chose the latter. "Are you goddamned kidding me right now? What the hell are you supposed to be?" He laughed nervously as he tried to keep the handgun steady on his target.

Ukko walked slowly toward Chopper. The child tucked in his left arm started to cry. He held his right hand to his side, palm forward in plain sight for Chopper to see he wasn't carrying a weapon.

"Stop, you slant-eyed son of a bitch! Take one more step, and I'll blast your ass back to Chink-land!"

Ukko calmly stopped. His mind raced through progressions of probabilities. He would most likely be asked to lay the child down at his feet. If he did so, he would probably be shot immediately. If he didn't lay the child down he'd be taking a chance of the madman harming the child when he shot at him.

Then it occurred to Ukko that if this fool tossed the grenade now, he would lose the prize he came for—the child. The child was the key. Ukko slowly moved the baby to the center of his body.

"Put the baby down and step away!" Chopper yelled.

Ukko just stood there looking at Chopper.

"Put the damn kid on the floor, and step the hell away!"

Again, Ukko stood in place as if confused.

"What, you don't understand English, asshole? I said—"

Ukko held the baby in both hands and extended the child toward Chopper as if offering him to him. He began walking slowly toward Chopper.

Chopper was taken off guard and unsure of what to do. "Stop, bitch...I said stop!"

Ukko was thirty feet away. His attention was fully focused on Chopper's eyes. He continued walking slowly with the crying baby held at chest level.

Chopper's mind raced. He knew he had to make a decision quickly. *Is this Jap playing me for a dumbass, or does he really not know what I'm saying? I should blow his head off right now. But if I miss and hit the child, there goes one million dollars! Damn! Oh, shit, the asshole's too close. Just shoot!*

Ukko's mind was processing the information unfolding before him at lightning speed, yet everything was moving in slow motion. Chopper's right thumb moved to cock the hammer back on his gun. His eyes diverted from Ukko to the child. He had decided. He was going to fire the pistol...but at what?

Ukko's senses worked with laser precision. *The man's lips are moving; he is yelling at me to stop. I'm now fifteen feet away. The barrel of his gun is moving upward. My window of opportunity is opening right... . . . now!*

Ukko rolled forward, laying the baby on the floor, and was halfway through his combat roll when Chopper deliberately fired a round skyward into the balcony above. Fragments of cement and dust showered down on Chopper's head.

Just as Chopper realized he'd been deceived, it was too late. He was face to face with the black dragon. Both his hands were crushed shut by the vice-like grip of his adversary. The momentum of their colliding bodies sent both men slamming violently into the steel railing of the balcony. Chopper heard the sickening sound of his vertebrae shattering. His eel-skin hat popped off and spiraled like a Frisbee to the parking lot below. His legs were pinned to the railing, and his back was grotesquely folded backward. He felt more vertebrae give with a loud crack. The brass plate on the dragon's helmet smashed into his nose and mouth, shattering four front teeth and sending two of them down his throat.

An armored knee moved upward between his legs with such force Chopper knew with absolute certainty the prospect of fathering any more children was no longer an option.

Almost at the exact moment his testicles exploded into mush, his right elbow shattered as it slammed into the top of the railing, followed by a grotesque *pop* as his right wrist snapped completely backward, exposing bone and ligaments. Chopper's .44 Magnum hit the ground three stories below before he even knew what had happened.

His mind was reeling from the speed at which the last three seconds unfolded; it all seemed a blur. Chopper's back was screaming in pain. He couldn't feel his legs. The fingers in both hands went numb from the vises still gripping them.

The two men stood face to face so closely they felt each other's breath. There was a moment of silence as their eyes locked. One eye was full of vengeance, shock, and a mind-numbing pain so excruciating, its owner felt he was going to pass out. The other set was as clear and tranquil as a freshwater spring on a bright sunny morning.

Suddenly Chopper unleashed a scream of agonizing pain so loud and for so long that Ukko considered ending the man's misery right then and there. But there was a question he needed answered first.

Finally, Chopper became silent. His breathing was hard, and he was frothing at the mouth. Blood trickled from the corners of his lips. Chopper yelled for someone to call the cops. He began slipping in and out of consciousness.

A crowd had gathered at each end of the balcony and in the parking lot below. Chopper's gun lay untouched; nobody dared to pick it up. The man Chopper shot in the back lay in a pool of blood that was now dripping off the edge of the balcony. Several people ran for blocks, only to find two cops sitting in their cruiser eating hot dogs. They told the cops what was happening and was directed to stay away from the scene and was told that help was on the way.

It never came.

The baby in the apartment was crying even louder now. Ukko thought he had little time left before the police would arrive. He had to disarm the hand grenade, get the answer he needed from Chopper, and escape with the child.

Chopper was unconscious. Ukko saw the grenade's safety pin was no longer looped around Chopper's right middle finger. Ukko let go of Chopper's right hand, and it fell lifeless to his side.

He carefully grabbed the left hand, holding it with both of his hands. He had to be extremely careful not to allow the spring-loaded lever to release. If this happened, the striker would ignite the fuse.

Ukko knew that if the fuse ignited, he had four to five seconds before it detonated, sending lethal fragments of metal in every direction. Anyone within fifteen feet would be killed, and anyone within fifty feet would be severely injured.

He looked around at his feet for the pin, but it was too dark to see something so small. He would have to somehow remove the grenade from Chopper's hand without arming it, then use a makeshift pin to secure the arming lever to the grenade.

Ukko began carefully removing Chopper's fingers from the lever while diligently maintaining the correct amount of pressure with his own fingers.

"Screw you!" Chopper's one eye was now staring into Ukko's. He clamped the grenade securely in Chopper's hand with both of his hands again.

Chopper's words were slurred. "What now asshole? Go ahead, blow us all to hell." He was struggling to maintain consciousness.

"Where is the child's mother?" Ukko asked calmly.

Chopper's eyes lit up, and he smiled. "I cut that damn whore to pieces, nice and slow, just like I'm gonna do to you."

Ukko sensed an extraordinary level of evil seeping from every pore of the man before him. *This man has hurt many innocent people. After today, he will hurt no more.*

Ukko's left elbow exploded into Chopper's face. His head snapped back hard, sending an arc of blood from his nose over the side of the balcony. His eye patch popped off the side of his head, revealing a grotesque black scab surrounded by disfigured skin and stitches.

Ukko reached down with his left hand to remove his short sword while simultaneously slamming Chopper's left forearm onto the top of the railing and being careful to maintain a tight grip on the grenade-clenching fist.

The razor-sharp blade came down with a swift chop, severing the arm midway between the elbow and the wrist. A scream rang out from the crowd below.

It all happened so fast. Chopper didn't feel pain in his arm until Ukko held the severed limb in front of his face.

It took Chopper's mind a couple of seconds to register that the severed hand he was looking at was his. Horrified screams escaped his mouth as he turned to see pulsating streams of blood shooting from the stump below his elbow.

"You son of a bitch!" Chopper violently rocked his head back and forth. His bloody saliva was slinging everywhere. "I'm going to cut your ass to pieces!"

Ukko looked calmly into Chopper's wide, bulging eye. "You have caused much sorrow with this hand."

Chopper's lips curled into a snarl revealing his gold canine teeth. "Go to hell! What about your hands, huh? You're a liar. You are just like me...we're the same, you and I..."

The moment suddenly gave way to the impossible, the unthinkable. Somehow Chopper had managed to land a staggering blow to his adversary. His words penetrated deep into the fortress-like barrier surrounding Ukko's mind, striking him directly in the heart. Ukko was stunned. He was bewildered at the ease with which Chopper's thoughts entered his mind. It was as if the madman had the key that, until now, Ukko thought only he possessed.

Keep your wits about you, Ukko warned himself. *This is uncharted and dangerous territory.*

The men looked at each other with an intense indifference capable only of killers. The only sound was of their thundering heartbeats. The beating stopped; time stopped.

Ukko desperately searched for any sign of his soul within the black hollow eye of the man before him. *Is he right? Am I no better than he? Am I the sword of darkness?*

Suddenly, the walls of Ukko's mind collapsed. He was now vulnerable to every thought in the universe, like a television set tuned to every station all at the same time.

Images flashed across Ukko's mind. An avalanche of sights, sounds, smells, tastes, and touch sensations enveloped his brain, bombarding his neurons like scavenging vultures descending upon a kill. Then, like a runaway projector that began to slow down, the images on the screen became discernible.

He saw an old Buddhist monk and a seven-year-old boy. They were outside near a snow-capped mountain. The monk was blindfolded and had a bow and arrow in his hands. He took aim at a target a hundred yards away. His fingers moved; the arrow vanished with a twang. He stood quietly to listen. He slowly lowered his bow, removed his blindfold, and opened his eyes.

The boy sat patiently, attentive to his teacher's every move. The monk waved his hand. The boy sprang to his feet and ran like the wind toward the target.

The arrow had pierced the small pear dangling from a string tied to the limb of a pine tree. Six inches in front of the pear was a sheet of white paper also suspended by a string. The boy read the Japanese calligraphy on the rice paper: "*As within, so without.*" The boy then noticed the paper didn't have a puncture hole. He pulled the arrow out of the tree and ran back to his teacher with the pear and arrow in hand.

"You did it! You hit your target!" The boy shouted as he showed his teacher the pear with the arrow through its center.

"Ah, is that so?" the monk replied.

"But teacher, please tell me: how is it you hit the pear without damaging the paper in front of it? This cannot be possible!"

The teacher looked at him with an unexpected seriousness. "Do you doubt I've achieved this miraculous feat, child?"

The boy was confused at his master's reply. They sat silently for a while. "Oh! I get it now," the boy said. "It was a trick, a deception! This arrow was already in the pear before you shot yours. Is this true, teacher?"

Again the master gave him a hard look and offered, "Well now, that depends, doesn't it?"

The boy grew even more puzzled. "But on what does it depend, great teacher?"

His master looked at him with affection. "On *you*, little Ukko."

The monk pulled out a small bell from his robe. He struck it with a wooden stick three times, pausing three seconds between each strike. The pleasant sound echoed through the valley.

"Remember this," he said. "Everything in this world is always exactly what you are thinking it is at the exact moment you are thinking it. Good, bad, right, wrong, truth, lie, saint or sinner—each ever-unfolding moment is for you, the master of your reality, to perceive as *you* wish."

The old Buddhist monk laughed uproariously as Ukko sat perplexed.

Then the avalanche of vultures returned, tearing at the flesh of his mind. Ukko heard his own voice, except the voice seemed much older somehow.

Are you worthy of the existence that has been entrusted to you?
Or is the man before you correct?
Are you, too, just another monster disguised as a human being?
Do you not value the miracle of life?
If so, then why do you take the lives of others so callously, as he does?
Who gave you this right?
Is the life force within a butterfly less valuable than that of a human being?
Are they not the same life force?
Or is life force merely a form of energy, like that of electricity?
If so, what separates man from beast?

Is it the mind?

Or is the mind simply no more than a tool?

Is it the heart?

Or is the heart merely flesh?

Are we not more than energy, mind, and flesh?

If so, then what?

Are we not infinite souls on an arduous journey?

If so, what is the destination to be reached?

Why are we like aimless ships, adrift on stormy seas?

What is the point of all this madness?

He watched as his ten year old body followed his mother through the fish market. Suddenly a beggar, labeled by the locals as the village idiot, grabbed hold of his arm. For some reason he was not afraid. They look deep into each other's eyes and the man spoke. "There is a point in your life when intellect, regardless of popular opinion, must conquer animal instinct, bypassing all forms of dogma laid down as traps. Only in this way can you achieve the highest nobility; the fullest potential of a human being."

Finally, his nemesis took a stranglehold on him, and images of his recurring nightmare appeared.

The small room is full of cigar smoke. The seven-year-old German girl plays happily with her dolls. She notices him through the smoke, and he yells for her to run. She waves to him; he yells to her again. She drops her dolls and picks up a dagger, plunging it into her stomach. She smiles at him as the blood rolls down her angelic chin. He then notices her face. She is Chouko, his little sister! Everything turns red. He hears the voices of both girls screaming, screaming, frightful screaming.

The screaming child behind Ukko pulled him back into the raging river of time. *The child, yes! Children! We endure the suffering of this world for the children...for hope!*

The gathering mob below began chanting, "Finish him! Finish him! Finish him!"

Ukko's eyes locked on to Chopper's. "The moment of your death was chosen at the moment of your birth." He shoved Chopper's grenade-holding fist into his face. "This is for the child's mother," he said. Ukko loosened his grip. Chopper's cold fingers extended slightly. The lever popped free with a metallic *click*.

Four...

The blood left Chopper's face, and he was consumed with utter fear. He knew he was seconds away from meeting his maker. Chopper stared at the thing that would kill him, the thing held by his own hand. His lips moved, but no words came.

Three...

Ukko stuck the severed hand down Chopper's black leather pants. The cut end of the severed arm protruded out from the top of his pants behind the brass skull-shaped belt buckle.

Two...

He grabbed Chopper's legs and flipped him backward over the balcony railing.

One...

The horrified mob below scattered.

Chopper's body disintegrated before it hit the ground.

Three of Chopper's men had just arrived at the scene and ran to the largest part of his remains. One of the men pointed up to Ukko. "Kill him now!" he commanded. Two men pulled out their pistols and ran toward the stairwell. The third man grabbed what was left of Chopper's arms and dragged his upper torso across the parking lot, leaving trails of blood behind the exposed entrails.

Ukko turned and calmly walked into his apartment.

The twang from the strings of the seven-foot tiger-striped samurai bow cut the air at nearly the exact moment the first man rounded the corner. The arrow made a hissing sound followed by a thump as it penetrated between the third and fourth ribs, slicing cleanly through the heart. The second man slammed into the back of his partner and caught him in his arms.

One second after he noticed the arrow protruding from his partner's chest, he felt his trachea rip in half, his C5 vertebra shatter, and the arrowhead exit the back of his neck. He dropped his partner, clutched his throat, and watched in horror as the armored dragon, half exposed outside his doorway, slowly lowered his weapon.

Ukko walked quickly to the child and scooped him into his arms. He made his way to the closet and removed a duffel bag. He walked into the living room, centered himself in front of the shrine, and sat the child down. The five incense sticks were extinguished; their ashes lay solemn atop the sand. He bowed low to the photos of his grandparents, then picked up the golden Buddha and put it into the duffel bag, followed by the framed photos. He removed his battle armor and carefully placed it into the bag. Sirens blared in the distance. He threw the bow over one shoulder and the duffel bag over the other. Gently, he tucked the sleeping child inside his kimono.

I wonder how much it rains in Las Vegas, he pondered as the two souls vanished into the darkness.

CHAPTER 20

LOVERS' REUNION

———◆———

THE FLIGHT FROM MASSACHUSETTS WAS turbulent. It had hardly been eight hours since Connor found out about Kiwi's death. His eyes were swollen and bloodshot. He refused to cry. He just couldn't believe it; he wouldn't believe it. *Until I see with my own eyes that she's gone, she's still alive. She is alive—she has to be alive!* he thought relentlessly.

When Connor was notified by his best friend that Kiwi had been abducted the night before and was presumed to have been murdered, Connor's immediate reaction was complete and total denial. His survival instincts took over. He knew that if he were to entertain a single thought of the possibility that his Kiwi was gone forever—that his light, his only reason to live had been taken from him—he would simply lose the will to live.

He vowed that he would find her. He would dedicate his very existence to the task for however long it took.

The plane touched down in Montana at 2:35 a.m. to a nearly empty airport. He had told no one he was coming. Connor drove the rental car straight home to an empty house. His father was conveniently away on business at a time when he needed him most. Later that day he called his father at his DC office. "I'm so sorry, son," his father consoled. "I didn't know you even had a girlfriend. Why didn't you tell me?"

The senator told Connor he would fly home right away, but there was a small crisis going on there that required his presence. He said he was scheduled to be back in Montana in two days. "That's okay, Pop,"

Connor replied. "There's nothing you, or anyone, can do for me. I'm going to have to figure this out on my own. Thanks anyway." Connor hung up the phone.

He sat in the dark, cold house late into the night. He'd unplugged the ringing phones hours earlier. *What to do, where to start, how will I find Kiwi?* The thoughts played over and over in his mind. He'd read the newspaper and saw the news reports on TV. But something just didn't make sense to him. *Why Kiwi of all people?* A chill ran down his spine when he remembered what Kiwi had told him about her fear of what the elders of her tribe used to say—that she had "the curse of beauty." Connor violently pushed that thought out of his mind and began pacing the floor.

Then it dawned on him: one of the men who had admitted to abducting Kiwi was incarcerated not too far away. *I have to speak to him; he may know something nobody else does. I'll make him tell me where Kiwi is!*

Early the following morning, Connor pulled into the parking lot of the Montana State Penitentiary. He walked to the front desk and asked when visiting hours began. He was told that visiting hours weren't until later in the evening and that he had to schedule the visit ahead of time.

"I'm sorry, but you don't understand. I can't wait until this evening. I have to talk to him now," Connor snapped.

"Well, I'm sorry, but you're going to have to abide by our guidelines," the woman replied.

Just then a high-ranking supervisor happened to walk by and recognize the star football player. The man's son played on the same team as Connor. He also was aware of who Connor's father was. "Hey there, Connor, what brings you to these parts?" he asked.

Connor recognized the man from meeting him on several occasions after football games. He explained his situation about being Kiwi's boyfriend and asked the man for a favor.

The man spoke in private with the woman and it was arranged for Connor to visit the man right away.

In a matter of minutes, I'll face the murderer of the woman I love more than anything, Connor thought. *Please, Lord, give me patience and the strength to control myself.*

The short, round-faced man scooted across the floor as the clanging of his leg shackles echoed off the walls. Connor's adrenalin was pumping hard, and it took all his will not to lose control. He imagined his big, powerful hands squeezing tight around the man's neck and the sound of it snapping. The short man seemed to have a sense of serenity about him, as if life for him was nothing more than the slow, methodical unfolding of compartmentalized moments for which he was now entombed.

Connor was surprised how quickly he was disarmed of his anger. It was as if the man before him was not the monster he'd made him out to be, but rather a victim somehow.

He introduced himself to the man and explained his relationship to the woman the man had helped to abduct and allegedly murder. The man broke down in sobs. "I'm sorry, I'm sorry. I didn't kill her. Big brother, he killed her."

Connor could tell the man had some sort of learning disability. He had to ask his questions slowly and keep them as simple as possible. He asked him to tell him everything about the planning, abduction, and murder of his girlfriend.

The man told Connor that his brother called the man who hired them the "big man," but that he didn't know who the man was. He confessed to having helped in the abduction of Kiwi at the duck pond on campus. He said he wanted to save her but his brother beat him up.

Connor didn't want to ask the next question, but he knew he had to. He was barely able to choke it out. "Did you see your brother murder Kiwi?"

The man slowly nodded his head. "Yes, brother cut her throat with his big sword and pushed her off the cliff. After he did that I shot him to death, and now I'm paying for my sins." Again the man began sobbing.

The men sat in silence for a while.

Connor couldn't stand it any longer and finally demanded, "Didn't you do *anything* to help her at all?"

The man nodded. "I tried to shoot brother in the back before he got to her but I messed up and missed. Then I got scared and it was too late. I'm sorry; I'm scared of guns."

Connor saw the turmoil on the man's face and felt sorry for him. *At least he tried,* he thought. He wanted to thank the man, but his mind was in conflict with his heart. *He helped abduct her. But did he even know what he was doing? Either way Kiwi is gone now...*Connor sat there stunned. Even after what he had just been told, it still wouldn't register in his brain.

"But I saved her purse and hid it really good," the man said excitedly. It's inside a hollow log between two giant pine trees, right there where she was killed. One of the pine trees is bent over like an upside-down L."

A guard arrived and told them their time was up. Connor thanked the round-faced man for his honesty. It was obvious to him that, like his beloved Kiwi, this man was nothing more than a victim of evil men.

From the research he'd done, Connor knew the exact location of the murder. He filled his gas tank and began the ninety-minute drive. The gravity of the fact that the love of his life was gone began to cave down on him. Details of what the incarcerated man told him about Kiwi's abduction flooded his mind. *Was she in pain? Did she suffer? Why wasn't I there to protect her? I failed her.*

He was overcome with grief by the time he pulled up to the scene. He sat in his idling car, staring through his windshield at nothing. Finally, he spotted the twisted pine; before he knew it, he was running to it.

Just as the man said, there was a hollowed-out log between the two trees. Without concern for snakes or other poisonous critters, Connor shoved his hand inside and searched around, but felt nothing. He reached deeper until his entire arm was inside the log, but still nothing. His heart sank. It occurred to him that maybe the man put the purse inside the other end of the log, even though that side was buried in a thick thorn bush.

Of course! Connor realized. *He was probably hiding from his brother inside the bush.* He ran to the other side and fought his way through. He reached inside the log and immediately felt leather and beads. Connor pulled the purse out, and tears instantly welled in his eyes. Memories of Kiwi smiling and carrying her purse in one arm with her other wrapped around his waist flooded his mind. He made his way out of the bush and got back into his car. He sat for a while, trying to gather his emotions. Then he picked up the purse to look inside. The crumpled envelope was still sealed and he recognized Kiwi's handwriting. On the front was his name, and on the back was something familiar, something Kiwi affectionately drew on all her letters to him, a heart with "C + K" inside. Connor put his hands over his face and sobbed.

When he'd composed himself, he carefully opened the letter and pulled out the three pages inside. In her letter, Kiwi told everything. She explained her reasoning for taking the job in Vegas and exactly what it consisted of, and how she truly believed the job was honorable and would help make the world a better place. She told in detail about the incident at the banquet, how his father had tried to rape her in the closet. She said that had it not been for her gouging out his father's right eye, he would probably have succeeded.

She told of how, when her bodyguard went to search for his father, all he found was a cuff link in the shape of a buffalo head with turquoise eyes, the kind his father often wore. She told how she came about discovering the identity of her assailant and how scared she was of losing Connor because of it. She told how she'd decided to confront his father first before telling him in the hopes she and his father could somehow forgive and forget, so he would be spared the pain and suffering of knowing what his father did to her.

She explained how his father denied everything, but promised not to interfere in their relationship. She told how his father said he would pretend he had never met her before if Connor introduced her to him. She recounted how his father had treated her coldly and told her to never come to his office again. Then she explained that the reason for the letter was in case she couldn't find the courage to tell him face to face.

Kiwi ended her letter: "I miss you. I miss your touch. I miss your soft passionate kisses. I miss your hand always in mine. I miss feeling your soul—you will always be a part of mine. *I'm so sorry, my love, for not finding the words to say 'I love you' and not making the time to say 'I need you.' I wanted so badly to, but the words just came out all wrong. You were always like a dream to me. A dream I was so afraid would vanish the second I let my walls down. But now I tell you openly that you have my heart, so please don't hurt me. Nothing compares to you. You're everything to me.*

"*I love you so much, and I'll wait for you for as long as it takes. ~ C + K*"

Connor completely broke down. The dam collapsed, and every negative, painful emotion humanly possible poured out in a violent rage. He opened his door and became physically ill. He staggered from his car and fell to his knees. Pounding his fists on the ground until they were caked with blood and dirt, he looked toward the heavens and repeatedly yelled, "Oh God, no! Please! No! No!" Facedown in the dust, he cried so hard and for so long he fully expected to die right where he lay.

The secretary confirmed the senator was scheduled to be in his office first thing in the morning. "Oh, by the way, ma'am," Connor added, "did a girl by the name of Kiwi happen to come there to visit the senator recently?"

"Well yes, a few days ago," the secretary replied suspiciously. "Why? Who is this?"

Connor thanked her and hung up the pay phone. On the way home, he stopped to pick up a couple bottles of liquor.

It was just after dark when the senator pulled into his driveway. He noticed the red rental car with Connor's cowboy hat on the dashboard and the kitchen and porch lights on. *Why would Connor leave his truck at the airport and drive a rental? he thought.* His senses were on high alert.

"Hello, son…is that you?" the senator called out as he placed his hat on the coat rack. There was no reply. He noticed that none of the lights were turned on in any of the other rooms. He walked around the corner to turn on the living room lights.

"So, what *really* happened to your eye, Pop?"

The senator nearly jumped out of his shoes, and his heart shuddered. There was no question now as to the nature of his son's visit.

"Hello, Connor…you scared me. What a pleasant surprise," he managed to squeak out.

"Answer the goddamn question!" the thundering voice in the dark commanded him. The senator knew the masquerade was over. *The boy knows.* The silence between them grew, but only for a moment.

"What do you think happened to my eye, son?"

Connor laughed. "Well, let me take a wild guess. Could it happen to be the result of a woman's fingernail, a woman fighting for her life as you were lost in your sick, lustful desires and attempting to rape her?"

The senator laughed nervously. "Well, I'm not sure who your sources are in getting this information but—"

Connor shot up off the recliner. The kitchen light lit up his enraged face. "How about straight from the woman you tried to rape! The woman I happen to love? Is that a good enough source for you, you sick son of a bitch?"

The senator slowly sat down on the leather sofa. A look of shock and bewilderment was plastered across his face. *How can this be? I had the girl abducted and thrown off a cliff to fake her suicide. The retarded man, who turned himself in, admitted to the abduction and her murder. What the hell is going on?*

Connor walked over to his father and stood in front of him. He took a big swig from the liquor bottle and then pointed his finger at him. "You're a goddamned liar, a rapist, and a murderer. For so many years, you slowly killed Mother with your cruelty and neglect. Then you sexually assaulted my girlfriend, and when she confronted you about it, you had her murdered. Tell me, Father, did you murder Mother too? Huh? Did you push her off that cliff!"

The senator shook his head. "No, no, that's not true, son…"

"Shut your filthy mouth and let me finish!" Connor yelled.

The senator tried to get up but was immediately shoved back down.

"Give me one reason why I shouldn't just kill you right now! Surely I'm capable of murder, too, because—like they say—the apple doesn't fall far from the tree, right?"

The senator gritted his teeth and snarled, "Goddamn you. I did you a favor. That half-breed squaw of yours was nothing more than a worthless whore who deserved—"

Connor's fist came down hard across the senator's jaw. The sickening *crack* echoed off the walls as his jaw snapped out of its socket.

"That's for Kiwi."

A vicious blow caught the senator across the temple.

"That's for Mother."

The last punch shattered the senator's nose.

"And that's for me."

The senator curled up into a fetal position with his arms over his head, moaning.

"I'll give you one reason why I shouldn't kill you, Pop. Because, thank God, I took after Mother instead of the low-life, worthless piece of shit father you are." Connor tipped the bottle high and finished it off. "Rot in hell, Mr. Senator."

He dropped the empty bottle and walked out of the house.

The sky was red and orange with slivers of purple right above the horizon. Connor stood at the edge of the cliff, almost in the exact spot Kiwi had stood. The spray from the waterfall was cool and forgiving against his resolute and tranquil face.

He looked up at the two eagles riding the warm updraft high into the heavens. He folded Kiwi's letter, gave it a kiss, and tucked it deep into his pocket. "Please forgive me, my darling. I wasn't there for you when you needed me most. Please forgive me for what my father did to you. You did nothing wrong. I'll always love you with all my heart and I can't wait to hold you in my arms again - I remember only you..."

He jumped.

Connor's body was never found. The police announced that based on evidence and statements from Connor's father and friends, it most likely was a case of lover's suicide. The senator told police that his son seemed extremely depressed the night he came home to visit him. He said Connor had been drinking and told him he loved him before leaving the house on the night of his apparent suicide.

Recent reports of multiple maulings by a rogue grizzly bear in the Great Falls area sparked rumors that both Kiwi and Connor's bodies were devoured. Newspaper headlines read, "Did monster Grizzly eat Great Falls lovers?"

CHAPTER 21

COLLATERAL DAMAGE

———◆———

IN THE COVER OF DARKNESS, the ex-agents accepted the envelope containing their down payment. They knew the senator would be good for the other half upon completion of the mission. The men were what the US government considered bad apples and had been fired from the Secret Service years ago. They since had gone underground as hired assassins for various unscrupulous characters.

The senator had hired the men two days after the surprise visit from his son. He became paranoid, convinced Kiwi had told her family about his dirty deeds. His nomination and election as the next US president were so close he could smell them. Now that the prize was finally in sight, he couldn't afford to take any unnecessary chances.

He'd worked all his adult life to prepare for this opportunity. Over the years, he'd managed to stroke all the right people in just the right way. He'd turned millionaires into billionaires through his dealings with big company lobbyists. He'd worked aggressively to slow down or block bills and, at other times, to push certain bills through. It didn't matter if his actions resulted in a detriment to society, the hardships or deaths of thousands of people, or irreversible damage to the environment. As far as he was concerned, it was just collateral damage. Sometimes, he shook hands and kissed babies; at other times, he bullied and threatened incarceration for those who opposed him.

The reason he did it wasn't for the lucrative cash he made on the side, or the huge profits these corrupt companies would gain. It was for one reason only, the favors he would ask later of these giant companies in the form of campaign contributions.

Yes, he understood the game of power better than most and fully admitted the tactics he used were consistent with those used by brutal dictators and totalitarian regimes throughout history:

1. Suppress the rights of people to express their opinions.
2. Control the media outlets.
3. Lie, deny, and make counteraccusations.
4. Control the election process.
5. Neutralize and destroy the "enemy".
6. Become "the man" in charge.

He'd become a master at the game. He cleverly pulled the wool over the eyes of millions of average citizens. He made them believe he was an honest, hardworking, common person like them, that he was their best choice for commander in chief. In fact, he was convinced he would have already become president had it not been for women.

To him, women shouldn't have the right to vote. They were not capable of making such vital decisions. His theory was that God made women inferior to man for a purpose: to breed, cook, clean, and raise brave young men so they could go off to war and die for their country. He especially despised women in politics and firmly believed allowing them to hold office was a grave mistake. His reasoning was that women were too emotionally sensitive. They literally and figuratively didn't have the balls to take a stand against America's enemies, preferring to hold hands around the campfire, singing "Kumbaya" instead of going to war. If he had his way, America would return to its former days of glory with an all-male government.

The dog gave away the assassins long before they reached the house.

"What is it, Zena?" Johnny-Bear whispered. Zena was part timber wolf and part German shepherd, and although sixteen years old and nearly blind, her hearing, smell, and sixth sense were marvels to witness.

Johnny-Bear lay in his bed, listening intently as Zena growled in a low, whiney tone. "Shhh, Zena," he soothed.

Johnny-Bear quietly rolled out of bed and tiptoed to his father's room, with Zena close in tow.

Red Dreams was already sitting upright on his bed. "What does our old girl smell now?"

"I don't know, but she's pretty upset about it," replied Johnny-Bear.

"The strangest thing happened last night," said Red Dreams.

"What?"

Red Dreams stared out his window. "I had a dream. It was in the color red, just like your grandma's when she was pregnant with me."

"Wow, what was the dream about?" Johnny-Bear asked.

Suddenly, Zena went crazy. She barked and ran to the front door, growling and snapping her teeth. She'd never done that before.

Visibility favored the assassins. The moon wouldn't appear for a few more hours. Roughly five hundred feet from the front door, the men split up. One was to stay in place while the other conducted a perimeter check around the small house. They would then meet back at the original location.

Zena began pacing the hallway as if she knew something was amiss. Johnny-Bear looked out the back window while Red Dreams walked out onto the porch. It was too dark to make out any movement in the yard, so Red Dreams decided to walk out to the picket fence. He thought he heard rustling in the brush in front of him, but it could've been an animal. He heard Johnny-Bear step out onto the porch. "It's me," Red Dreams called. "I'm just checking the fence line."

"Okay, I'll just wait here," Johnny-Bear replied.

Five minutes passed. Zena suddenly bolted into the yard toward Red Dreams. Three consecutive *wisp* sounds sliced through the air, followed by two loud shots. Johnny-Bear knew the sound of his father's revolver and ran into the house to get the shotgun. As he rushed out the door, he heard Zena barking and then a loud yelp, followed by silence. As much as he wanted to run as fast as he could to the sound of the shots, Johnny-Bear knew he had to move with caution and stealth. It was clear they were being hunted.

As he got closer, he heard his father's labored breathing. He heard him trying to speak, but his voice was garbled. Johnny-Bear knew from the many hunting trips he's been on that he had to get to his father fast. His lungs were filling up with blood. He quickly low-crawled toward his father and then stopped. Fifteen feet away, he saw a man walk up to his father and extend a pistol to his head. In an instant, Johnny-Bear fired a shot, and the man was blown off his feet, landing belly-down on top of the picket fence.

The man began pushing himself off the fence. His bulletproof vest had done its job and taken most of the shotgun blast. Johnny-Bear rushed toward the man before he could swing his pistol around and fired another shot into the back of his head.

The boy crouched low next to his father to assess his wounds. His father was still alive, but there was too much damage. The greenish-yellow liquid from his liver was oozing from the gaping hole in his side, and the two holes in his chest went clean through his right lung.

Thirty feet away, a man called out, "Federal agents! Drop your weapons and put your hands up!"

Red Dreams grabbed Johnny-Bear's arm and shook his head, "No."

Johnny-Bear raised his shotgun and fired two shots toward the sound. He heard the man let out a groan and shout, "Oh shit, you son of a bitch, you shot me. You shot a federal agent!" Then he heard the man stagger away.

Johnny-Bear held his father's head off the ground and looked into his fading eyes. From the severity of the wounds, he knew his father had little time left.

Oh God, why? First Kiwi and now dad, Johnny-Bear thought. Only weeks ago they had been notified of Kiwi's abduction and presumed murder, and now men claiming to be federal agents were trying to kill them.

Red Dreams spat the blood out of his mouth. "Go to mountains... wait for Kiwi...she will come."

Johnny-Bear watched as his father's eyes rolled to the back of his head, and the Great Spirits swept him away.

CHAPTER 22

ANGEL'S SAMURAI

———————

KIWI FINALLY HIT THE WALL. She was tired of running from her past. It'd been two weeks since her miraculous resurrection from the River of Spirits. Lawrence stayed with her at his enormous Alaskan cottage but maintained his distance as she'd requested. He insisted she stay in the main cabin while he stayed in the detached guest house.

When Lawrence's connections in Montana delivered the news to him about the murder of Kiwi's father, the disappearance of her brother, and the suicide of Connor, he was torn between telling her right away and waiting until she was stable enough to handle the news. He decided to wait because there was nothing anybody could do about the events that had occurred. He thought that if she knew and rushed back to the reservation, the senator would know she was still alive and expend all his resources to exterminate her.

Lawrence ended up telling Kiwi a week later while they were on a nature walk. His intentions were to wait just a few more days because she seemed to be making a little progress. But as they were walking, something came over her, and she said, "I think something terrible has happened to my family back on the rez."

Lawrence stopped in his tracks, and the look on his face was all Kiwi needed to see.

"What? What happened to my family, Lawrence? Tell me!" she demanded.

That's when Lawrence told her everything he knew. He explained his reasoning for not telling her right away. She burst into tears and ran all the way back to the cabin.

Kiwi mourned for two weeks then abruptly stopped. She'd reached a conclusion about the way "life" works. One evening, she approached Lawrence and told him she needed to go back to Las Vegas.

Lawrence was dumbfounded. *"Why on earth would you want to go back there, of all places?" he asked. She* told him she wanted to meet the Angel's Samurai. She had seen on the news and read in the papers about the living legend, how Las Vegas was home to a maverick vigilante who went out at night fighting crime. The word on the streets was that somehow this one man was able to swiftly correct injustices committed against women and children where law enforcement could not or would not. They said he moved among the shadows, descending upon his unsuspecting victims—drug lords and human traffickers—like a fog in the night, removing the heads of those who abused women and children.

He supposedly conducted these missions using a combination of ancient and modern weapons such as swords and bows, as well as night-vision goggles and concussion grenades. Rumor had it the enigmatic man was funded by the government, which explained why the cops were unable or reluctant to stop him.

One tale especially stuck out in Kiwi's mind. Witnesses said the Angel's Samurai had rescued twelve women and nineteen children from a cult compound where they'd been held prisoner. The cult was evil and twisted, and its leader had proclaimed that sex with children was natural and righteous, as they were "The Children of God." The compound was hidden away, deep in the unforgiving backcountry of eastern Utah. The story was that the Angel's Samurai had parachuted into a location near the compound and, under the cover of darkness, breeched the triple-razor-wired perimeter undetected. Then he had systematically terminated every evil man but one. He had loaded rations, fuel, and most of the women and children onto the cult's shabby school bus. Four of the women had followed the bus in two beat-up pickup trucks for 150 miles. When they had reached the nearest telephone at an old gas station, everyone had begun weeping with joy. By the time the sheriffs had arrived, the mysterious assassin had already vanished without a trace. When the police and FBI arrived at the cult compound, all they had found were the slain bodies of eight evil men. The site had been thoroughly sterilized. Although the women spoke highly of a hero in a black mask, and of harrowing details of arrows protruding from necks, chests, and eye sockets, there was no evidence left behind except for one survivor.

The charismatic cult leader had been hog-tied and suspended twenty-five feet off the ground from the branch of a giant juniper tree at the center of the compound. He'd been castrated, and his eyes had been plucked out by the flock of turkey vultures still circling above.

Another story had been one especially heartbreaking to Kiwi. It was said that the Angel's Samurai had rescued many teenage girls from various human trafficking rings throughout California and Nevada. On one occasion he had staked out and conducted a raid on a location, killing most of the perpetrators and freeing almost all of the twelve- to fourteen-year-old girls from their sexual enslavement. Rumor had it that during this rescue, one girl had already committed suicide just before he had arrived. They said the tall mysterious hero in black clothing and mask personally carried her broken, twelve-year-old body out of the slum building, his head hung low.

It was said that he had been so distraught over the incident that he had spent many weeks tracking down the main human trafficking ringleader. He discovered that the man was to be at a particular high-end nightclub on New Year's Eve. The occasion was perfect, as it was also to be a masquerade party. The club surveillance cameras showed a tall dark assassin wearing an Armani suit with a black half-mask, coolly stalking his prey throughout the night. In order to get closer to the target, the assassin had mingled suavely with the crowd and had even danced with several attractive women. At the stroke of midnight, while the ringleader was celebrating on the dance floor, sandwiched between three of his prostitutes, a razor-sharp dagger slid quickly and efficiently between two of the dancing women. Within one second the blade penetrated the child trafficker's gut below the navel, parted everything in its path up to the sternum, and retracted. By the time the pudgy man's stomach and intestines spilled out onto the dance floor, the vigilante assassin from Vegas had disappeared into the chaotic maze of celebration.

Lawrence knew of the legend Kiwi spoke of. He'd also heard stories about the Angel's Samurai—how at one time the man had been known as the Satan's Samurai. He tried without success to talk her out of using violence to resolve problems. She told him that she was sorry, but that she couldn't bear it any longer and needed closure. She said that she couldn't explain it, but somehow she just knew Johnny-Bear was still alive, and the only way to save him was to remove the senator once and for all.

Lawrence was in a difficult position. Whether he supported Kiwi or not, he knew there was no stopping her. There was only one thing he could do.

Kiwi agreed to give Lawrence one week to see if any of his friends in positions of power could help locate the mysterious Angel's Samurai. It turned out that one of Lawrence's contacts at the White House had a friend in the CIA, who in turn had a friend in the DEA who was an undercover agent and who was told by an informant of the possible identity and location of the reclusive assassin.

Kiwi asked Lawrence if she could write a letter to the legendary vigilante and have one of his people deliver it to him. She felt that if she explained her situation and asked for his help, he might consider it. Lawrence agreed it might work and had the undercover agent deliver the letter to the assassin.

One week later, she received a response from the Angel's Samurai himself. Her hands shook as she read the letter. When she was finished, she jumped up and down hysterically. "He'll do it…he's agreed to meet me in Vegas!"

The old, inconspicuous station wagon pulled up to the dilapidated laundromat. The bodyguards Lawrence had hired were some of the best money could buy and already in place. He'd reluctantly agreed not to be present for fear his anxiousness about Kiwi's safety might interfere with their meeting. *After all, she would be in highly competent hands,* he thought. Instead, he settled for monitoring the situation via communications from a van nearby.

They were in the poorest part of Las Vegas, the drug-infested slums where even police officers dared not go unless accompanied by a SWAT team. It was here the Angel's Samurai had been living and working as a taxi driver. Of course, he also had a second job, a job at which he was very efficient.

Kiwi sat, nervous but resolute, on the fiberglass chair inside the laundromat. She had been intrigued when she discovered the location at which the legendary assassin had chosen to meet. The air smelled of mildewed tile mixed with fried chicken and curry. It seemed everywhere you looked there was peeling paint or something in disrepair. It reminded her of the shanty buildings on the main street back on the rez.

She felt a pang of guilt. For the past several months, she'd gotten used to being surrounded by the best of everything, yet here, mothers sat hungry watching their children eat what little they could provide while deadbeat fathers did time in prison.

She thought of Johnny-Bear. *Where is he? Is he feeling the merciless gnawing pain of hunger right now?* She knew if he were free in the mountains, the answer would be no. Father had taught him well how to live off the land. She heard Father's deep voice say, "Our warriors are great hunters and fishermen. Mother Earth always provides for those who are grateful and respectful."

Kiwi knew deep in her heart she would never forget where she came from. She heard her mother's soft voice say, "Within the darkest parts of humanity the universe is busy manifesting its finest creations, like magnificent lotus flowers springing up out of the sewer."

They were twenty minutes early, so she sat watching the regular people around her. The undercover guards posted both inside and outside carefully scrutinized every person within a hundred feet.

Kiwi saw the mothers, most with small children, doing what they probably saw their mothers and grandmothers do all their lives, scratching out a living from day to day. Their dreams of a better life had long faded with their childhoods. Their only purpose now, the only reason to get up in the morning to face the madness of this world, was straddled on their hips or running joyful and carefree around the washing machines.

She thought about the children in the room. Unbeknownst to them, they would become the new bearers of the torch of desperate hope, not just for themselves, but for all of their families. No pressure, only the ever-elusive thing called happiness was at stake—a happiness they made-believe would somehow magically appear the minute they escaped from the miserable existence they'd identified as their lives.

A small girl with big brown eyes and a runny nose sat near Kiwi. She looked to be six or seven. Her mother was mopping the floor nearby. It appeared the mother took the child to work with her. The girl watched with sad eyes as the other children played.

"Why aren't you playing with the other children?" Kiwi asked. "Is that your mother over there?"

The girl nodded and looked down at her little feet. Tears immediately welled in Kiwi's eyes as she noticed the deformed legs and tiny feet squeezed tightly inside the girl's white ballerina shoes.

The child obviously has some sort of disease, Kiwi thought. *Was the disease incurable, or was the child suffering because her mother couldn't afford to pay to have the disease treated?* Images of Kiwi's mother flashed across her mind, the beautiful woman lying on her deathbed, painfully coughing up her lungs. She remembered the agonizing hopelessness she felt as her mother slowly withered away, dying from a disease entirely treatable but whose treatment would cost a lot of money—something they had little of. She thought about her ambitions as a young college student to become a journalist. She had wanted, she recalled, to expose to the world the depravity of the greedy pharmaceutical companies and the crooked politicians who supported the outlandish prices the drug companies demanded for lifesaving drugs, while the poorest of the poor suffered and died unnecessarily.

Kiwi looked up at the beautiful splinters of light cascading through the cracked glass of the large window. *How ironic,* she thought, *that dreams have a way of fading little by little into obscurity each time we believe the voices around us or, even worse, the voices in our heads saying, We can't do it, or We're not good enough, until one day we "grow up," and suddenly those magical dreams once cherished become lies we've told ourselves—lies disguised as hope, but in actuality was the universe's sole purpose for our very existence. She remembered what her Me'me' had once told her, "There're two kinds of people in this world: the wishers and the doers. As soon as you decide which it is you are, the sooner you'll know what you are."*

In an instant, she saw her future in her mind's eye. The image was clearer than she'd ever seen it before. She saw herself as more than the journalist. She saw herself sitting at a large conference table, conducting meetings with the most powerful decision-makers in the world. She knew now how to gain their ear, how to influence and convince them to do what humanity needed them to do, what was just and right for the good of everyone. She would patiently guide them in a way so subtle, they would think it was their idea all along. Perhaps the universe was waiting for her to live out the necessary chapters of her life in order to get to this point, to gain the skills and experience necessary to accomplish such monumental tasks.

Yes, Kiwi decided. *I can be what I will to be! Now, If only this Angel's Samurai agrees to do a much-needed deed for society's meek and poor.*

The tall and strikingly handsome man walked confidently with an erect, youthful gait. He looked to be in his mid-thirties and had a powerful, athletic build. The muscles in his shoulders and chest rippled through his white t-shirt. He had on black jogging pants with two white stripes along the outer seams. On his feet were clean white tennis shoes with red Nike swoosh logos on the sides.

His stride was wide and long. His thick black hair was about mid shoulder length and tied behind his head. The black facial hair on his

squared jaws was peppered with gray. His nose was thin and well pro-
portioned. His lips had a stern tightness to them, revealing a barely
noticeable smile. His almond-shaped eyes effortlessly surveyed his surroundings, as if his subconscious mind were making mental notes to
itself. He had a large laundry bag over his shoulder, and his right arm
swung wide to his side as he walked.

"This is the guy," whispered the senior security guard through his
microphone. "Look at the joker. He walks as if he's got the world by the
balls, and he knows it. Search the bag in case he's hiding weapons."

Everyone in the laundromat seemed to notice the man enter the
double glass doors, including Kiwi. He didn't look at all like what she'd
expected. *Could this be the most feared assassin in the world?* she asked herself.
Suddenly it dawned on her that he was walking straight toward her! The
two guards posted inside stepped in front of him. He stopped and smiled
then slowly raised his arms. He had been aware of the guards' presence
long before they had noticed him. He allowed the men to do their job,
patting him down for weapons and searching through his laundry.

It was obvious to everyone watching that there must've been at least
forty pairs of white underwear in his bag.

Kiwi felt a little embarrassed for the living legend. She wanted to
tell the guards to stop, but restrained herself. The senior guard nodded
his head in approval, and the men stepped aside and posted themselves
nearby. The women and children looked on curiously. The attendant
seemed to know the man and sat nervously behind her desk.

The Angel's Samurai set his bag on a washing machine and turned
to Kiwi as concerned eyes watched closely. He made a slight bow. "Hello,
my name is Ukko. It is an honor to finally meet you, Ms. Kiwi."

Kiwi found herself speechless. Not knowing whether she should
reply to his greeting with a bow, she awkwardly held out her hand. The
mysterious man's large hands enveloped hers, and, again with a slight
bow, he gently shook her sweaty palm.

She noticed the elegant yet powerful dragon and tiger tattoos on his
muscular forearms. "Please, just call me Kiwi."

Ukko was taken aback. *Where have I met this woman before?* he pondered.

"As you wish, Kiwi. Now if you don't mind, may I begin my laundry before we start? I was a bit lazy last week, and unfortunately I'm now out of clean underwear." He chuckled.

Kiwi nodded and immediately liked the man. She felt as if a massive wall had just collapsed and she could finally breathe again. What was it about this mysterious and potentially dangerous man that made her instantly feel at ease?

After he finished loading his laundry, he went to the sink and washed his hands. *And clean, too,* she noted. He went to the front desk and greeted the woman. He spoke to her briefly, and she seemed to be a bit more at ease afterward. He bought two bottles of Coca-Cola and opened them with the bottle opener.

"Watch him carefully. Make sure he doesn't slip anything into her drink," the senior guard ordered.

Ukko walked back to Kiwi and handed her a Coke. She thanked him, and before a guard could intercept it to sample the beverage first, she unhesitatingly took a large gulp and smiled. Ukko returned the smile and took a big swig of his. She shooed the guard away, assuring him everything was okay.

Ukko sat down in the seat across from Kiwi's. She took a deep breath and exhaled. "Well now, where to begin?"

"Something about *you* would be a great start," Ukko said with a grin.

Three short hours and six Cokes later—apparently the charismatic assassin loved Coke—Ukko thanked her for sharing such a personal and tragic part of her life with him. He assured her the evil senator would be "taken care of," and she would never be tormented by the likes of him again.

At that moment, the totality of what was going to happen hit Kiwi like a tsunami. She became lightheaded. Never in her life had she thought she would be capable of asking someone to take the life of another. Did she really want to do this? Would it solve anything? The room began to spin. Ukko seemed to sense what was happening. He came and sat next to Kiwi and placed his hand on top of hers.

"There is no other way, Kiwi. This man tried to take your life, drove his son to suicide, had your father murdered, and now is a threat to you and your little brother, *if* he's still alive. No one should have to bear such misery. This is the only way. This evil senator, like everyone else, must face his Karma."

Kiwi shook her head, covered her face with her hands, and began to cry. "I'm sorry, I can't do this. It's all been a mistake. I don't know what came over me. I shouldn't have asked you to come here. I can't allow myself to become a monster like him. I'm not a killer. I'm sorry, Ukko. Please forgive me."

Three guards swept in to check on her, and she waved them away.

Ukko seemed to know it was pointless to try to change her mind. "I understand. Your heart is too pure to allow hate to overcome it, and I respect you all the more for it."

Kiwi nodded her head.

"I have a son. His name is Falcon, and he is not yet one year old. Sometimes I'm certain he is wiser than I'll ever be. I can only hope someday he will have a heart such as yours. He reminds me so much of my baby sister. Her name was Chouko."

"That's a beautiful name. What does it mean?" Kiwi asked.

"It means 'butterfly child.' The name was quite fitting; she adored them."

Kiwi's eyes lit up. "Really? I also loved butterflies when I was a child. I still do. In fact, I have a tattoo of one on the nape of my neck." Kiwi turned her head and lifted her long hair.

Ukko's reaction on the exterior was tranquil and unwavering. But on the inside his mind was reeling and his heartbeat doubled. *How can this be? The butterfly on this woman's neck is the one that came to me when I was ready to commit seppuku. It is the same butterfly that is on my chest above Chouko's name!*

"It's beautiful," Ukko heard his calm voice say.

"Thanks," Kiwi replied. She sensed a bit of confusion in the man. "Are you okay?"

"Yes, yes, sorry. I will honor your wishes, Kiwi. I give you my word that the senator will not be killed. But if you don't mind, I would like to ask a great favor of you."

Kiwi wiped her tears away. "Of course. Please tell me what I can do for you."

Ukko cleared his throat and bowed his head. "A long time ago, in my homeland of Japan, I lost the three most important people in my life to men such as this senator. Had it not been for such ignorant, cowardly, and evil men, my mother, little sister, and fiancée would still be with me today. Ever since then, it has been my life's purpose to rid our world of these diseases. It is my way of honoring my loved ones. If you allow me to, I promise you, without taking his life, I will ensure he will never hurt anyone else again."

Kiwi placed her hand to the nape of her neck and thought about what Ukko had asked of her. After a few moments, she gave him her answer. "Ukko, I'm so sorry for the loss of your family. I can't imagine the suffering you must face every day. I really appreciate your honesty and your willingness to help my family and me, but I can't in good conscience ask you to harm someone as a way for me to resolve my issues. It's only now that I realize how I allowed my anger to fill my heart with hate, blinding me with the thirst for vengeance; and it's only now that I finally hear what my heart has been trying to tell me, that there is a better way, a more effective and permanent way to resolve these issues.

"My dear friend Lawrence was right when he quoted Mahatma Gandhi to me, who said, 'An eye for an eye makes the whole world blind.' At the same time, I know all of us see the world through our own eyes, and we each have to deal with this world in the only way we know how. I wish only the best for you, Ukko. I feel I've known you all my life and that, somehow, you've always been my protector. I know this sounds silly, but that's how I feel. Please, take good care of yourself. I pray the Great Spirits will give you peace in your heart. *Miigwech Nisaye*; thank you, older brother."

Ukko bowed his head even lower and seemed to be in deep thought. *This woman is truly a special spirit. Her voice is the one that has spoken to me since I was a child. My God, it was her voice in the red butterfly too! Is this possible? And the butterfly on her neck—but how could this be? Can she really be the reincarnation of Chouko?...My heart tells me she is.*

Still, my destiny has led me here for a purpose, and now I must do what my mind tells me, just as she must do what her heart tells her.

Ukko lifted his head and wrapped both his hands around Kiwi's. His eyes misted with tears as he looked into hers. "*Doumo arigatou Imouto;* thank you very much, little sister. I, too, appreciate your honesty and wish you and your family good luck and harmony. May the Buddha bless you with joy and happiness. Please forgive me for my simplicity. It is the only way I know."

Kiwi saw and heard the heartfelt sincerity in Ukko's eyes and in his voice. She felt a pang in her heart because she knew that, no matter what, for the remainder of his days, he would serve his purpose, his duty, as the Angel's Samurai.

CHAPTER 23

UKKO VERSUS THE SENATOR

———◆———

THE NEON SIGN ABOVE THE run-down motel was missing half its light-bulbs and pitted with rust holes. The sky was overcast, and the only light came from the flickering sign. *Poor visibility is an ally to the prepared*, Ukko thought as he pulled out his military-grade night-vision scope.

He'd been tracking the senator for almost three weeks and was now sitting in a banged up Lincoln Continental on the outskirts of Washington, DC. The half-dozen junked cars in the parking lot of the abandoned gas station across the street provided the perfect camou-flage for his stakeout.

That a prominent, egotistical man like the senator would check into a dilapidated motel in such an undesirable area was an obvious prelude to something no good…and Ukko knew it. He'd been waiting patiently for an opportunity just like this. The target was out of his element and alone.

Ukko watched the senator step out of his SUV and head for the office. Ten minutes later, he left the office and went back to his vehi-cle. He removed a large briefcase and walked around to the side of the single-level brick building. His deliberate movements suggested he'd been here before and knew exactly where he was going. The building was laid out in the shape of a horseshoe, with one side next to the street and the other alongside a thickly vegetated ravine and wooded area.

Ukko skirted the low ground of the ravine and crouched down at an ideal observation point. He watched curiously as the senator unlocked and entered four different rooms. He noticed that all the doors had two deadbolts and were constructed of a heavy-grade steel.

Manually breaking down the doors is not going to be an option, Ukko noted.

The four rooms were adjoined and had no windows. They also faced the wooded area and ran parallel to the ravine. The scrupulous man seemed to be inspecting each room. After entering the last room at the end of the horseshoe, he didn't come back out.

There were only three other cars in the parking lot besides the senator's blue SUV. The other occupants appeared to be in rooms on the street side of the motel.

Only hours earlier, Ukko had watched as the senator, sporting a glass eye instead of his customary eye patch, a fake mustache, sunglasses, and a cowboy hat, walked from his high-rise condo to a bus stop, taking a bus to a used-car lot in downtown DC. He walked onto the car lot. Within fifteen minutes, he'd picked out a vehicle and paid the man cash without signing any paperwork. Then he drove the SUV straight to the motel.

It was exactly 12:17 a.m. when the motel sign went dark. The only light now was from the door lights above each room. None of the four rooms the senator checked into had that light on. The nearest light to the senator's room was four doors away.

Ukko decided the opportune time had arrived to close in on his target. He put his night scope back into its case, tucked it under a bush, and camouflaged it with leaves. He did a quick equipment check, pulling at the black ropes crisscrossed around his chest and back, then ran his hands over the scabbards of his swords to make sure they were still secured tightly to his body. He looked inside his satchel to ensure the C-4 explosives and blasting caps were properly rigged and ready to go. Just as he stood to make a dash to a tree near the senator's room, he heard the sound of an approaching car. A black Cadillac Coupe Deville, with windows black as night, turned the corner and flipped off its lights before stopping three doors down from the senator's room.

Ukko slowly made his way back to his night scope, low-crawled back into his observation position, placed the scope to his eye, and flipped the switch. The green glow, separated by tiny black dots, quickly revealed the silhouette of the Cadillac.

The car sat idling for about five minutes before the driver door opened. An obese man heaved his weight out of the seat. He stood and pulled his tight flannel pants back over his rotund gut, adjusted his round glasses, and waddled around to the trunk of the car. The nervous man looked left and right, and then opened the truck. He reached in and seemed to be struggling with something inside and began slapping at it. Then he pulled out what appeared to be a zipped-up sleeping bag with tape around one end. Something or someone was thrashing about inside the bag. The big man tossed the bag over his shoulder and waddled to the senator's door. Before his fat fingers could knock, the door cracked open.

When the senator confirmed who the visitor was, he unchained the door and opened it wide. He held out his arms impatiently to receive the package, but the big man didn't hand it over. The senator went back into the room and came back with a paper sack. He handed the big man the sack, yanked the sleeping bag off the fat man's shoulder, then slammed the door in his face. The big man appeared irate as he waddled back to his car. Ukko turned off the scope and allowed his eye to adjust to the darkness. He knew he had little time to lose.

The big man sat sideways in his car with his door wide open. He was counting the stacks of twenty-dollar bills inside the bag when the blurry black object crashed down on him and cinched the rope tightly around his fat throat. The big man tried to scream, but nothing came out. As the man lay gasping for air, Ukko quickly slipped another noose around his hands and secured them to the bottom of the steering wheel. He made sure the passenger door was unlocked, pushed the man all the way into the car, shut the driver door, and entered the car through the passenger side. The man's face was a whitish-blue and reflected that he was on the brink of unconsciousness.

Ukko loosened the rope around his neck; the man gagged, coughed, and drooled all over himself. Ukko pulled out his dagger. "You have exactly three minutes to tell me everything, or you will lose your head."

The man desperately tried to regain his voice, but it was too hoarse to be intelligible.

"Two minutes," said Ukko.

"Okay, okay...I sell children. I sold her to the man in there," the fat man coughed out.

"Has this man bought from you before?" Ukko asked.

"Yes, all the time."

"What will happen to the child?"

"I don't know. I don't ask. It's none of my business," the big man stammered.

Ukko smashed the hilt of his dagger into the side of the fat man's head. The man groaned in pain. "Shit! Okay! Okay! This man, we call him Glass-eye, he's known to torture and kill his girls."

"You know this, and yet you keep bringing him children? Give me one good reason why you deserve to live."

"Oh God, please don't kill me! Have mercy on me, sir! Please don't kill me! I'll do anything you ask. I want to go to jail. I deserve to go to jail for what I've done." The fat man began crying uncontrollably.

"Shut up and listen. You will do exactly as I say, or I will do the honor of sending you to hell myself!"

The knocking on the door startled the senator and sent him scrambling for his guns. *Who the hell is that?* he thought in panic. *Nobody knows I'm here. What if someone found out? Is this the police? Oh God, I'm ruined! After all these years, it's finally happened. There's no way I'm going to prison marked as a child molester...I'll die before I do that! Wait, could this be that fat-ass supplier of mine? He doesn't usually come back after the delivery, though.*

The senator tiptoed to his door in his boxer shorts and pistol in hand. He carefully peeked through the peephole. The child trafficker's fat face came into focus.

"What the hell do you want now, asshole?" the senator demanded. There was no reply. "I said, 'What the hell do you want?'"

The trafficker's face turned to the left and then to the right, and then he held up a stack of twenties against the peephole. "You short-changed me five hundred bones!" he replied.

"Ah, for Christ's sake, I know I gave you the right amount, shithead!"

"I'm not leaving until you pay me."

Enraged, the senator stomped to his briefcase and searched through his wallet, then walked back to the door. "All I have is four hundred. Now, will you take that and get the hell out of here?"

"That'll work," the child trafficker said in a shaky voice.

The dead bolts clicked, popped, and slid, and then the door cracked open just enough for an ash-gray eye to be seen. Four one-hundred-dollar bills slipped through the door.

There was a blur of motion, followed by a terrific transfer of energy from a powerful leg, to a hardened foot, to the center of the door. The senator's nose exploded like a juicy red tomato. The door met his face with the force of a Mack truck. His glass eye shot from its socket like a cannon ball across the room, and his fake mustache was propelled inside the large gash above his upper lip. He was thrown backward, slamming into the far wall. Stunned, he watched as the fat man stumbled forward through the doorway straight at him. The senator raised his revolver and got off two rounds before 380 pounds of blubber collapsed on him.

Ukko had rolled to the side before the first round was fired, and at the moment the fat man fell on the senator, he was already next to both men. The senator moaned as he tried to regain his breath and struggled to push the bleeding whale off of him. In an instant, a vise gripped his hand and removed the gun; a black rope cinched tight around his neck. Ukko kicked the fat man off the senator and, within seconds, had the senator hog-tied. He secured the stunned man's hands and feet behind his back. He then removed the rope from the senator's neck so he could breathe, but he'd already slipped into unconsciousness.

Ukko made a quick assessment of the room: *target secured and unconscious; trafficker on the floor with fatal wounds; child still alive; handgun on floor and another gun in briefcase on the table; other potential threats unknown.*

He secured the guns with his gloved hands and systematically checked the main room and bathroom for any other potential danger. *Room cleared,* he concluded. He closed the door, locked the dead bolts, and sheathed his sword. Pinned up on all four walls of the shabby room were large confederate flags and pictures of Hitler.

The terrified child lay partially naked on the bed with her arms and legs tied to the bedposts. Her mouth was bound with a leather strap and something grotesque and bright pink was on her heaving chest. Ukko saw the electric branding iron on the nightstand, still glowing cherry red, and the capital letters "KKK" seared into the young child's chest.

The brown-skinned child's eyes were wide as she watched the man in black approach her with a white bed sheet in his hands. The hilt of the swords crisscrossed high above his shoulders looked to her like angel's wings. He gently laid the sheet over her trembling body. When he pulled his black mask off, she just knew. She recognized the strength and compassion in his eyes. The guardian angel she'd been praying for had finally come to save her. She relaxed her knotted muscles, closed her eyes, and surrendered. With trembling lips, she whispered, "Thank you, God."

Ukko carefully removed the strap from the child's mouth and cut the ropes off her bleeding hands and feet. He wrapped her in the sheets and then gently picked her fragile body off the bed. Their eyes met as she lay in his powerful arms. "Everything's okay. You're safe now," Ukko assured her.

"I know," the child replied weakly. Ukko squatted down and gathered the child's clothes.

Lying on his side, his lung quickly filling with blood, the child trafficker raised his arm and looked at the child. A wheezing sound escaped his mouth as he exhaled his final breath: "I'm…sorry."

Ukko took the child to the bathroom and sat her on the toilet seat. He set her clothes on the sink. He filled a plastic cup with tap water, smelled it, and then tasted it. He put the cup to her lips. She thirstily drank every drop, and he gave her more. He reached into the small satchel strapped around his waist and removed a tube of special pain-numbing ointment. "This will make the pain go away." He gently applied the anesthetic and placed the tube back in the satchel.

A loud roar came from the living room. The child began to shake uncontrollably, and Ukko knelt down beside her.

"Don't worry. I promise you that he will never hurt you again."

The child sat trembling as screams reverberated through the walls. Ukko calmly looked into the child's big brown eyes and told her, "You must stay here for a short time. I have one more thing to do, and then we will leave, okay?"

Tears ran down her cheeks as she nodded. He stood up, slid the black mask over his face, and then strode into the hallway. The eerie sound of razor-sharp blades being released from their cages sent chills down the child's spine.

"Who the hell are you? Do you know who I am? Cut me loose right now, you son of a bitch!" the senator barked. Ukko picked up the white rope used to tie the child's legs, made a noose, and then calmly walked to the hog-tied man.

"Stop, goddammit! I'm a US senator and about to become the next president of the United States of America...I'll have your ass crucified for this! Cut me loose—now!"

Ukko replaced his black ropes with the senator's white ropes. He made a noose and slid it around the struggling man's neck. Then he pulled the end of the rope through the senator's arms and legs, tying it tightly. The man let out a groan as his head thrust backward toward his hands and feet.

"Don't do this. You don't have to do this," the senator pleaded. "What do you want? Name it and it's yours. Just let me go, and we'll call it even. You hear me, boy?"

Ukko stuck his arms through the senator's bound arms and legs, then lifted him onto the bed. The man let out another painful groan and began gagging. Ukko pulled up a chair next to the man's head and sat down. He laid his swords on the bed.

"So, it seems you are very proud of your brotherhood with this KKK," Ukko stated.

The senator looked hard at Ukko and snarled, "You bet your ass I am. And let me guess; you're one of them Negro lovers ain't you?'"

Ukko calmly stood up, walked over to the nightstand, and picked up the red-hot branding iron. He grabbed the man's gray hair and spun him around so he could see the glowing red KKK on the iron. The senator started kicking and thrashing. Ukko placed a knee on the man's neck. Smoke rose as the sizzling sound of burning flesh was drowned out by the senator's screams, then again and again. The man lay gasping for air. His only functioning eye rolled to the back of his head as he struggled to remain conscious. Across his forehead and on both cheeks was seared the affiliation the senator was so proud of.

Ukko sat back down in his chair facing the branded man and picked up his short sword. "I hear you are a corrupt politician, one who speaks with a forked tongue. I knew of politicians like you once. They cost me everything."

The branded man opened his eye and glared at him. He began to shout something in protest, and a silver blade whipped into his mouth, took out two bottom teeth, split his tongue down the middle, and then exited before the man even knew he was cut. The forked-tongued man screeched in horror as blood poured from his mouth.

"Now you can look the part of a snake whenever you speak," said Ukko.

After a few minutes, the blood coagulated and the bleeding slowed. The forked-tongued man's evil gray eye burned into his captor as he lay quivering.

"It appears you're a man who sees what he wants in life and, instead of earning it, steals from others what's not rightfully his."

The forked-tongued man slowly nodded as thick blood trickled from the side of his mouth. A sound like that of a pencil being snapped in two echoed off the walls of the room. Black, ink-like liquid spewed from the senator's only good eye. He squealed like a pig as he witnessed his world became forever night. Ukko pulled off his black mask and secured it in a pouch at the small of his back. After ten minutes, the blind man fell silent. Only the sound of his labored breathing could be heard.

"Last but not least," Ukko said with a sting in his voice, "it seems you cannot control your sexual desires, that somehow you believe you can just cause pain and suffering to women and children at your pleasure. But what you failed to realize, Mr. Senator, is that someday you would choose to make a victim of a woman who was stronger than you, smarter than you, and more courageous than you would ever be…and that this woman would see to it that you—and lowly creatures of your kind—would face their due justice."

The blind man was silent for a while, and then he completely lost his mind. It suddenly dawned on him what he would lose next. He began kicking his legs hysterically and growling like a wild animal. He spat his blood in the direction of his captor's voice. His raw, primal instincts for self-preservation consumed him. He no longer cared if he lived or died; all that mattered to him was to defend and protect the body organ responsible for reproduction, the organ that influenced his every thought and drove his every action to conquer, dominate, and kill in order to maintain control of the female of the species.

Ukko waited for the man to wear himself out. When the insane blind man became motionless, Ukko brought the sword down with the precision of a surgeon, and in an instant, the senator's manhood detached from his body. The castrated man began shaking, sobbing, and convulsing uncontrollably.

Ukko stood next to the defeated man and said, "I don't claim to be an angel or free from my own demons. I know the errors of my ways and accept what awaits me in the afterlife. The difference between you and me is that I take vengeance on my demons not for myself, but for others, those who cannot defend themselves from animals like you. You, however, are a coward of the lowest class. You take vengeance on your demons upon the innocent and the weak, upon people who, unlike you, have the courage to face their fears every day with dignity as they lead their 'quiet lives of desperation,' as your American writer Thoreau would say. And therefore, unlike you, they still have a chance at salvation."

The senator gave no response.

When Ukko went back into the bathroom, the child was dressed in her blood-spotted clothes and lying in the bathtub balled up in the fetal position. Her small hands were cupped over her ears, and she had somehow managed to fall asleep. Ukko did not want to startle her by picking her up, so he began to whisper over and over, "Everything's okay. It's time to go."

After the third time, the child's eyes opened. He picked her up and said in a soothing voice, "Please cover your eyes until I say you can look."

The senator's body looked small and broken as it lay trembling on the blood-soaked mattress. Before leaving, Ukko tossed the guns on the floor and called the office from the room phone. He told the clerk there was an emergency in room C-45 and asked him to call an ambulance immediately.

The child sat in the passenger seat of the big car as they drove into the night. Ukko looked over at her in amazement. She was nibbling on a cookie and tracing an image of a butterfly into the moisture she'd just breathed onto the window. He recalled what his mother once told him about his little sister: "The ability of a child to quickly forgive and to live only in the moment is what separates heaven from hell."

He remembered seeing several churches earlier when he was following the senator to the motel. It wasn't quite dawn yet as they approached a light glowing behind a large stained glass window. Ukko carried the child to the side door and peeked through the window. A nun was sweeping between the pews. The door was locked, and Ukko knocked firmly. He set the girl down, and she desperately clung to his waist.

"Don't worry," he said. "I promise she will take good care of you. Tell her everything. Now you must let me go. Remember, always look up— somewhere near, a rainbow is present."

The nun made her way to the door. The door opened, and the two pairs of eyes peered into the windows of each other's souls.

CHAPTER 24

AWAKENING

———•———

THICK, FLUFFY SNOW FLOATED LAZILY outside the cabin window, as if its only purpose was to slow down Kiwi's obsessively speeding mind. She had been content with her decision to move from Alaska to Estes Park, Colorado. The majestic beauty of the natural surroundings reminded her of her childhood in Montana. Lawrence had set her up with more than enough money to live on for the rest of her life. Her cozy little cottage in the mountains was perfect. She'd resolved to have as little contact with the outside world as possible: no television, no radio, no newspapers—just her poems and her books.

Most times, she had her groceries brought to her by a store clerk. It seemed lately her only goal was to make it through the day. Thoughts of Johnny-Bear and Connor hardly ever left her mind. Somehow, in her heart, she knew her little brother was still alive. But as for Connor, she wasn't so sure. *What are the odds that two people survived such a horrific fall?* she pondered. Still, she prayed every day the men were alive. Terrible thoughts of grizzly bears eating Johnny-Bear and Connor constantly tortured her mind. So far, there had been no sign of either of them, and winters in the Rocky Mountains are unforgiving.

Kiwi wanted desperately to return to her tribe, but she knew it would only endanger more family and friends. It was obvious it was best if everyone believed she was dead. This was more depressing to her than anything else. *This is insane*, she thought, *because of the father of the man I love, I have to remain dead so that others might live.*

She dreaded each approaching nightfall. It meant she was in danger of falling asleep, which meant the risk of having the dream. She'd had the dream twice, and she was afraid that if she dreamed it again, she wouldn't be able to go on.

The nightmare was always the same. Connor was wearing his plaid shirt, and he was standing at the edge of the cliff with his back to her. The sky was almost dark. She wanted to shout his name, but was afraid it would startle him, causing him to slip and fall. She carefully walked up to him from behind.

Two eagles were perched on a twisted pine tree, watching her as she approached him. She stopped and reached out her hand. Before she could touch him, he turned. His eyes lit with joy. She felt a rush of deeply passionate love, the kind she felt when they had first met.

The feeling was warm and powerful, overcoming them both. They embraced, cried, kissed...then cried some more. They looked into each other's eyes the same way they had when they met at the Salvation Army center. It was a look of relief and the indescribable feeling that came with knowing that finally, against all odds, they'd each met "the one"— they'd each met their soul mate. They kissed passionately and held each other so tight...as if they were afraid to ever let go again.

Somewhere in the distance, a bear growled into the night. One of the eagles screeched and flew away. They looked up to watch it disappear into the trees. Kiwi turned back to Connor. Tears streamed down his face. He said to her, "It's lonely here. Why do you keep me waiting? Why'd you let me die for nothing?" He pushed her away and stepped backward off the cliff.

She lunged forward to grab his arm, but it was too late. Her arm was outstretched over the edge of the cliff as she watched him fall away. The expression on his face sent a dagger through her heart: "Why?"

As always, the hysterical crying would wake her after the dream with a feeling of unbearable guilt, and the pain would crush her so deeply she could hardly breathe. Then she would cry all day and the hallucinations would return. She never knew when Connor would appear. He always wore the same boyish grin—in her kitchen, inhaling everything as if he hadn't eaten for days; outside in the garden, gathering vegetables; in town, strolling down Main Street; lying shirtless beside her in bed, the smell of his aftershave, the tone of his skin so young and soft clinging tightly against his large rippling muscles.

Sometimes she'd get a burst of inspiration and start working on her book. But then the dark past would creep in, pulling her back under the fog. Images of her father, Johnny-Bear, and Connor would take over her mind. *It was all my fault. Had I not challenged the power and authority of the senator, they'd still be alive. Why had I been selfish and ignorant enough to believe I could overcome such evils of this world? Aren't there some things in life you simply have to accept?*

It had been almost a year since she'd last seen Lawrence. She had begged him to allow her to live in seclusion, believing it was her only hope of healing. He had respected her wish. But what he didn't tell her was that he'd paid a retired sheriff, someone she knew as simply one of her neighbors, to keep an eye on her. It didn't take Kiwi long to figure this out. Almost every time they happened to see each other in the yard or in town, the sheriff would give her a concerned look and thumbs-up. She'd smile and reply by giving him a return thumbs-up sign; he would nod his approval, and they'd carry on their merry way.

The phone rang at 5:37 a.m.

Kiwi recognized the voice immediately. "Your age must be showing. Did you forget my birthday isn't for another two months?" she asked sleepily.

"Nope, just giving you fair warning. I'll be there in about three hours to disrupt your tranquil existence," Lawrence said. "I'll pick you up, and we'll make a day of it at the Garden of the Gods. How's that sound?"

"Uh, that sounds great...but what's really going on, Lawrence?"

There was a brief silence, then he said, "There's something very important and urgent I need to tell you." He hung up.

The Garden of the Gods was one of Kiwi's favorite places in Colorado. She felt a spiritual connection to the massive red rocks jutting skyward out of the fault lines in the earth. She wasn't the only one. Archaeological evidence showed that humans had been gathering at the site for more than three thousand years.

They walked the trails all day. Lawrence decided to wait until nightfall to tell her what was so urgent.

They sat together on a sandstone boulder. The night air was crisp and still. The moon was exceptionally bright, casting long shadows behind the large red pillars. Somewhere in the pine trees, an owl made its presence known.

Kiwi broke the awkward silence. "Lawrence, this thing you're needing to tell me, I'm not sure I want to know. I mean, I know you're trying to look out for me, and I truly appreciate it. But I don't think I'm ready for more of your profound knowledge. Maybe I never was."

They sat in silence for a while before Lawrence cleared his throat.

"I remember feeling the same way a long time ago. The world had become unbearable, and I wanted nothing more to do with its lessons. But then I realized there's something happening all around us, a greater good unfolding in the background—and that I was simply a part of that, whether I liked it or not. I realized it's not about what I feel. Feelings and emotions are like the weather; they come and go. It is all about what I do, and it's only in doing this greater good that the world becomes bearable."

After more silence, Kiwi conceded. "As usual, you're right. Please tell me."

"Remember when I told you about my beloved friend and mentor from India?"

"Umm, yes. Rama the sandal maker, right?"

"Yes. Well, there was something else he told me during our spiritual reunion on the country road that evening."

"Okay…"

Lawrence looked away. "I purposely excluded this part because, at the time, I wasn't sure if you really were the one."

A jolt of dread shot through Kiwi as she recalled the title bestowed upon her since childhood by her tribal members.

"But now I realize the time has come for you to know." Lawrence turned to Kiwi, and their eyes locked.

"What Rama told me on the road that evening was what you might call a revelation from the future. Amazingly, I can still remember the encounter with stunning clarity. It's as if the occurrence is a permanent three-dimensional recording in my brain." Lawrence closed his eyes and then spoke as if he were reading from a book in his mind. "This is the way it happened," he began.

"Rama sat down next to me and said, 'My dear Lawrence, I'm so glad to see you. I've traveled a long way to tell you of a most wonderful discovery. It's very important that you listen carefully, as my time here is limited, and I'm counting on you to share this discovery with a special spirit whom you will soon meet in this world.'

"'I've experienced many worlds since I left this one, and although those worlds were fascinating, this one, even with all its flaws, has remained the closest to my heart. For thousands of years, I've worked at figuring out how to get back here to you before it was too late. I know this doesn't make sense to you right now, so I'm asking that you trust me and act with complete faith.'

"'Of course,' I said. 'It's in *you* that I have completed faith, my friend.'

"'Thank you, and I in you,' Rama said. 'I've personally experienced two possibilities for this planet, and these possibilities both exist and do not exist at the same time. Being a physicist with knowledge of quantum mechanics, you can, I know, understand and appreciate what I'm saying.'

"I nodded my head.

"'In other words, one of the two possibilities for this planet must consciously be chosen. The thoughts concerning it must be imagined and replicated over and over in the mind in the greatest detail so that the subconscious may gather the unlimited resources of the universe and prepare the necessary circumstances for its manifestation into physical form. This mental action is called "the world within." Then, once the mental soil has been prepared, the physical soil must be cultivated and seeded. This is done through physical action—passionate, courageous, faithful action—and this is called "the world without."'

"'What are the two possibilities of this world that you've experienced?' I eagerly asked my mentor.

"He smiled and said, 'One possibility is breathtakingly magnificent. It is when human beings awaken to their purpose and become balanced with one another and with the natural laws of the universe. In this way, human beings will mentally and physically evolve light-years closer to their already evolved spirit. It is one where human beings realize their infinite potential and embrace their role as the caretakers of all life on earth. Men and women will recognize and accept one another as equal halves of the whole and realize their physical and spiritual interdependence. All men will finally treat all women with the respect and admiration women deserve. They will work together as one body, one mind, and one spirit. The results of these actions will be so incredible, they will never return to their previous, flawed way of thinking. With these achievements, human beings finally earn their right to move among the stars, and a new infinite universe opens up to them.'

"My eyes lit with excitement and enthusiasm as I heard this wonderful news. But then I saw the expression on Rama's face change.

"'Unfortunately,' he said, 'the other possibility I experienced for this world is not so promising. It's where the human race continues the self-destructive course it's currently on now, a course where the preservation of the individual is more important than that of the whole, a course where humans continue to be ignorant of how their minds and bodies work, thus remaining hostages. It's a course where ignorant men continue to dominate and suppress women, not realizing they are actually destroying the equal half of what makes a human being. They fail to realize it's only in the hearts, minds, and souls of women that men can be complete and at peace.'

"'Unfortunately, in this reality, I witness men destroy one another and the planet with their false selves, the ego, and their weapons of choice will be hate, greed, and self-imposed ignorance. The end result is that the human race will become extinct forever.'

"Rama and I sat in silence for a while before an urgent sense of purpose came over me. 'Please tell me,' I pleaded. 'What do we need to do to choose the first possibility, where we live in peace and harmony and travel to the stars?'

"He chuckled and said to me, 'I thought you'd never ask, my friend!

"'Listen carefully and remember these words always: A child's heart shall enlighten all women and save humanity.'

"I repeated his words, 'A child's heart shall enlighten all women and rescue humanity.'

"Rama nodded and continued. 'The possibility you so desire will require an extraordinary amount of courage, conviction, and faith, not only from you, but from all the peoples of this world, beginning with the women.'

"I looked curiously at my mentor and asked, 'Beginning with women?'

"'Yes, they are the key. Without them, all is lost. The space-time is soon approaching. A mighty nation will for the first time be afforded a genuine opportunity to elect a woman as the supreme leader. If this opportunity is seized, it will be the beginning of a new Earth. If the opportunity is squandered, there will never be another suitable space-time. The result will be the beginning of the end for the human race.'

"I was thunderstruck. 'Please tell me more about these women,' I asked.

"'The reality most beneficial to the human race,' Rama continued, 'is contingent upon the election of the first woman president of this great nation I speak of. Her election will be a direct result of the monumental actions of tens of millions of women who shall be called the "Red Butterfly Movement." This movement will create the situations and circumstances required to win the freedom of all women on this planet.

"'The actions of the Red Butterfly Movement, consisting of hundreds of millions of women all around the world, will catapult the evolution of mankind to the point where it should have been more than a thousand years ago. It's a possible reality whose time is long overdue. Make no mistake, my friend: there is little clock-time left to waste!'

"My mind was racing to comprehend everything Rama said to me. *What is space-time as opposed to clock-time? What do I need to do? How can I even begin to make this happen?* Just at that moment, Rama reached over and touched my temples with his hands. A flash of lightning shot through my brain. Suddenly, I saw what he had seen, heard what he had heard, and experienced what he had experienced.

"A young girl's voice spoke: 'It's not the soul of man that is the problem; it's his primitive brain that is humanity's greatest affliction. This is not a gender-inequality issue; it's much more serious. This is a brain-inequality issue.'

"Throughout history, we've stood by and watched as our leaders, what some have labeled the 'alpha males,' wielded absolute and exclusive decision-making privileges, the ones whose complete power was unjustly seized by force or was to them given in good faith by trusting peoples. As a result, these people became enslaved by the very power-hungry leaders they elected. What has this exclusivity of power, given predominately to men, brought us? Only more war, famine, and suffering.

"Any person of intelligence who was to conduct a thorough and unbiased study of the history of the human race, and who was to construct a list of the worst atrocities committed against humanity, would come to a clear and undeniable conclusion that behind 99.9999 percent of these atrocities, the primary decision-makers involved were predominately, if not entirely, male. Is this just some sort of fantastic coincidence that happened to repeat itself over and over for many thousands of years? Or is there something else going on, something so obvious most cannot see it?

"As irrefutable and deplorable as this fact is, it's appalling that after hundreds of thousands of years, it still remains an accepted norm in society for men to suppress and force their will upon the misperceived 'lesser woman.' It's inexplicable, reprehensible, and inexcusable how any human claiming to be intelligent could perceive woman as being inferior to man. Are these so-called intelligent men remotely aware of what history and science have unequivocally proven—that a woman's brain is, in fact, more evolved and thus superior to a man's brain in almost every category?

"The conclusion of scientific research and historical investigation has proven that male brains are predominantly hardwired for survival by means of violence, sexual domination, and conquest, thus making them ideal for war. Female brains are predominantly hardwired for survival by means of nonviolence, compassion, and collaboration, thus making them ideal for peace. The human brain, when placed under extreme stress will nearly always resort to their default settings.

"With this revelation, the bold and courageous actions of women, consisting of half the population on the planet, will unite and do what it is their brains were designed to do, and in the process save humanity. They will unequivocally wash clean and permanently correct the evils and injustices perpetrated against them and their children for hundreds of thousands of years!

"Women shall finally realize it is only *through* women, *for* women, and *by* women that all women will be permanently liberated. They will realize that no man, entity, or deity will ever do it for them. Never again will they allow themselves to be paralyzed or held hostage by their pre-conditioned fears. They will realize the only thing they have to fear is conformity!

"Women will witness one of the absolute truths of the universe: women, when united as one, are one of the most powerful forces on the planet. Like hundreds of millions of red butterflies, they will come, women of every nationality, race, and religion. They will wear red headbands to symbolize the truth and sacrifice they make to correct the injustices they've endured and still face.

"Women shall realize the power bestowed upon them by the universe. They will realize and demonstrate that women are the lifeblood of all societies, and that without them, everything will stop—there will be no forward movement, no progress, no life. These beautiful red butterflies shall act as one, moving in one direction and with one purpose. Together, they shall descend upon the governing bodies of their nations.

Their actions will be in strict adherence to Mahatma Gandhi's teachings of nonviolent noncooperation.

"With peaceful repose and soft whispers, these women shall simply sit, and, with unwavering conviction and as individual parts of one body, they will be prepared to go to jail or even die for their cause.

"Their uncompromising demand will be change, immediate and indubitable change, concerning the misrepresentation of their governments. No longer shall women accept the grossly unbalanced gender representation within their governments. These women's fair and just demand will be that for every elected man in a position of power and influence, there must also be an elected woman of equal power and influence. From top to bottom, each and every elected office holding each and every position shall consist of one man and one woman sharing equal power and responsibility to serve the people. Only in doing this can any government claim that it reflects equally the population it serves, a population consisting of half male and half female.

"Never again will decisions of paramount importance, such as declarations of war, appropriations of the nation's funds and resources, and laws governing equal rights for all, be decided by one half of the whole, but instead, by an equal number of men and women. These men and women shall share in the decision-making process concerning such prodigious matters.

"For those with concern regarding the ability of women to make important decisions about the defense of the nation, I ask you, who is more qualified than a mother? Is there a force on this earth more ferocious and determined than that of motherly instincts when it comes to the health and welfare of her children? This powerful instinct is instilled in every woman by nature and cannot be overcome by fear, greed, or self-gratification.

"Would mothers, regardless of nationality, race, or religion, not expend all necessary resources to ensure every option has been explored and tested before sending *any* child or grandchild off to die for a cause, which might have been entirely avoided or resolved, had it not been for the interference of overinflated egos and overactive testosterone levels? Not only would engaging in unnecessary conflicts result in the loss of precious life, it would be an egregious act of irresponsibility and a disservice to the people of the nation by squandering its capital and resources. Imagine if every nation in the world had governments fairly elected and represented equally by both men and women, each with the same power, pay, and opportunities as afforded their counterparts. How quickly, effectively, and efficiently will state, national, and world issues be resolved when these women come together to discuss viable and nonviolent solutions? It will be incredible how much progress will be made with less ego and testosterone in the way! This is the natural way—the way the universe intended it to be.

"Until both men *and* women are treated with the respect they deserve, the world will remain out of balance and the human race in peril. With this powerful knowledge, it's only natural for women to share equally the important responsibilities of governing the people. It's only natural for women to share equally the important task of creating and enforcing laws used to protect and increase the quality of life for the people. If the true purpose of government is to represent the needs and desires of the people, and the demographics of the people consist of equal parts—male and female—does it not make sense for the elected officials who make up this government to also reflect equal parts male and female?

"It is a scientific fact that the brains of men and women differ both physically and neurologically. It is a scientific fact that the thinking processes in men and women also differ. The brains of men and women are so designed by nature to complement each another.

"When there is an unequal number of brains of one gender over the other, there is an imbalance in the overall thinking process. This, of course, cannot help but result in unbalanced decisions concerning the health and welfare of the people and the planet.

"But, when men and women utilize the potential *of the whole brain, as opposed to only half, great advances* will be achieved. Most human-rights issues in the world will be resolved, and a higher quality of life for all people of the world will be experienced. Adequate amounts of food and water will be produced and secured to feed every human being on the planet.

"In medicine, cures for cancer and many other diseases will be discovered. Quality medical treatment will be available to all. Solar and other sources of environmentally safe energy will replace dirty and destructive forms of energy. Great advances in agriculture will provide abundant foods for all people. The ethical treatment of animals will be the expected norm in all societies. Many nations will collaborate in joint efforts in space exploration, resulting in the successful colonization of other planets.

"The achievement of this monumental task will not be easy, but think of the alternative, the failure of humanity to become balanced will result in the inevitable self-destruction of the human race. In this choice, the universe has given every man and woman free will. The time has come. It is inescapable, one way or another, action or no action; every human being *will* make a choice.

"Here ye all: It is declared at this moment that until the governing bodies of every village, town, city, state, and country in the world are represented equally by the same number of women holding corresponding positions as that of men, we women, consisting of half the population of the planet, shall converge upon our governing establishments. We women of the Red Butterfly Movement shall sit in peaceful protest and with unwavering conviction. We women of the earth shall no longer remain idle while our birthright is denied us, but instead, we shall claim what is rightfully ours and what is imperative to the survival of every man, woman, and child on this planet. Every female shall be treated with equal respect and dignity and will be considered of equal value as any other human being, henceforth!"

Lawrence seemed to come out of a trance-like state. He gasped and took a deep breath, as if he'd been submerged under water.

"Are you okay?" Kiwi asked.

"Yes, just a bit exhausted. Were my words intelligible?"

"Yes, but I'm confused. What does all this have to do with me?"

Lawrence looked off into the distance and explained. "Rama came back to me in a dream only twenty-four hours ago. He brought someone with him this time. She was a girl of twelve years. Her eyes were bright emerald green."

"And let me guess, you think that girl was me. There're lots of girls in this world with green eyes, Lawrence."

Lawrence turned to Kiwi, placed his hands lightly on her shoulders, and looked deeply into her eyes. "This girl had a tattoo on the nape of her neck."

Lightning shot through Kiwi's brain. She turned away and cupped her hands over her mouth. *Oh my God, what's happening? Why is this happening to me? Why me, God?*

"It was a red butterfly exactly like yours, and she looked just like you, Kiwi; she *was* you. Can't you see that your elders were right all along? You *are* the Chosen One! Now it's up to you to do what *you* yourself have come back to tell you. I can only imagine the pressure you must feel, and I promise I'll have your back the entire way. We both know what the consequences will be if you don't do this."

Kiwi didn't answer. They sat in silence.

Above, billions of glimmering suns filled the night sky. They seemed touchable and extraordinarily bright on that night. It was as if each had an urgent story to tell…and all seemed to bear down on Kiwi.

Kiwi had a strong urge to get somehow closer to the stars. She left Lawrence and walked up the trail. He watched as she stood at the base of a tall rock formation. Memories of rock-climbing lessons with her father and Johnny-Bear came to her. She recalled what her father once quoted to her by Edmund Hillary, "*It's not the mountain we conquer, but ourselves.*"

Kiwi looked up at the three-hundred-foot rock face. It jutted out from the earth at a slight angle and she knew that it was rated by the Yosemite Decimal System as a class four out of six in level of difficulty. This meant that although a rope is often used it is not required. She also knew that with this grade a fall may be fatal.

She mapped her route and saw that there were plenty of anchor points for her fingers and toes...and enough moonlight to go by if she could manage to stay out of the shadows.

Suddenly a vivid image of the red butterfly she encountered as a child appeared before her. This time the butterfly's words, spoken through a child's voice, were crystal clear and echoed over and over in her mind: *You shall lead the Red Butterfly Movement.* For the first time she recognized her eyes on the butterfly's wings. As if in a trance, she unraveled her red scarf and tied it around her forehead.

The instant she placed her left hand on the rock, an image appeared before her. It was Princess Farashatan, the Arab prince's sister! Kiwi saw the young woman's face clearly. The image seemed to her like a mirage of colored pixels dancing inside waves of fine mist. *She's so beautiful,* Kiwi thought. When Kiwi placed her right hand on the rock, another woman's face appeared. It was the young prodigy student from India Lawrence spoke of. It was an image of her beautiful, radiant face before the acid attack committed against her. *Oh my God,* Kiwi thought. *What's happening here?*

When she placed her right foot into her first foothold, the faces of two radiant women appeared side by side. One was a blonde with unusually big blue eyes, and the other was a brunette with soft amber eyes. They were wrapped in each other's arms and smiling. They raised their hands, revealing matching tattoos on the inside of their wrists. Kiwi couldn't believe what she was seeing. *Those tattoos are identical to the one on my neck! But how could this be?*

Then the image of the red butterfly reappeared in Kiwi's mind, but this time it was her mother's and Me'me's voices she heard: *Have faith, child, and embrace your destiny; you shall lead the Red Butterfly Movement.* Something warm and unimaginably powerful poured into Kiwi. She didn't resist, but surrendered to it. When the energy of the universe was done renewing every cell in her body, she wiped the tears from her face and began her ascent. With every step toward the stars, she saw a new face of yet another beautiful woman who had been victimized, women from all around the world, past to present—girls who'd been drowned to death because of their gender, women oppressed or murdered because they exercised their birthright of freedom to choose, women and children who'd been victims of sexual enslavement. It didn't make Kiwi feel sadness or pity to see them. To her, they were all magnificent souls, and she embraced and loved them as her own. And in return, they gave her more and more strength, strength she knew she would need for the battle ahead. Somehow the women before her not only gave her strength, but also guided the movement of her hands and feet to all the right places. *They already know the way,* Kiwi realized. *All that's required of me is unwavering faith.*

She recalled the vow she'd made what seemed like a lifetime ago: *Someday I'll help put an end to these senseless atrocities against women. I'll create change, by force if necessary. I'll achieve this by doing something unforgettable, something unstoppable. To this I swear!*

On the ground, Lawrence stood mesmerized by what he was witnessing. There were tense moments when Kiwi disappeared into the crevices and shadows, out of sight of his anxious observation. But then she would reappear again, a little bit closer to the top. After what seemed to Lawrence like forever, she finally pulled herself onto the precipice. She found a spot just wide enough for her to sit cross-legged with her hands on her knees. She watched with fascination as the stars descended, enveloping her. She closed her eyes and was quickly pulled in—and became one with the universe.

The temperature began to drop, and Kiwi felt the cold's bite against her skin nudging her back to the world. When she opened her eyes, somehow everything had changed. She had no idea how long she'd been sitting there, but she knew where she was and where she was going. She knew, like she'd never known before, who she was and what she would do. She watched as a meteor blazed across the starry sky. It left a trail of red fire in its wake, casting light on everything around it.

Kiwi sprang to her feet and raised her arms to the heavens. With a renewed spirit in her heart and fire glimmering in her emerald-green eyes, she called out, "*We women* are the chosen ones! The place is *here*! The time is *now*!"

THE END

(Book One)

My beautiful granddaughter Safina

My country kiddo's Chase and Faith

My wonderful son Robby

My niece Carissa and her daughter McKenzie

Mom and dad and sisters and brother. I'm on top right

Mom and Dad. "We didn't have much but we had
each other – and that was enough"

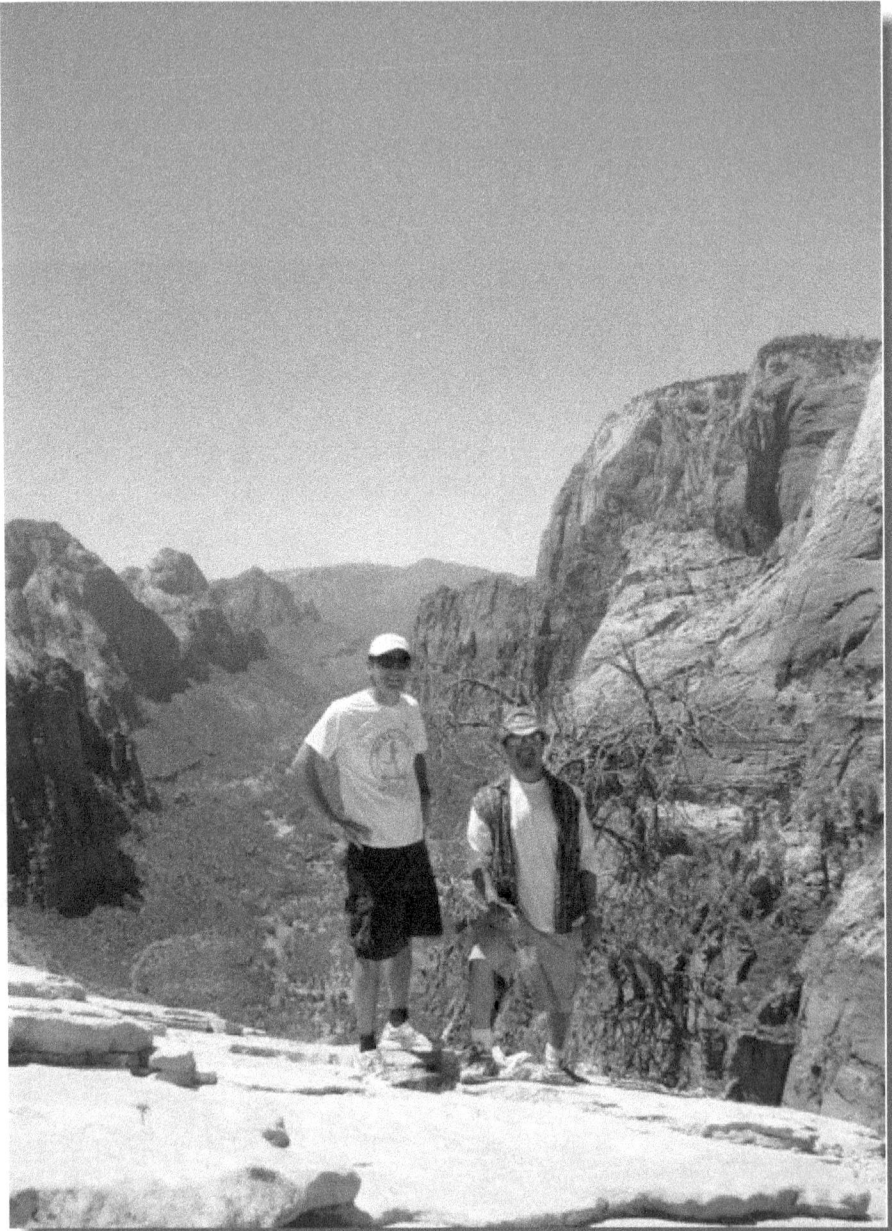

Me (on left) and "The man, the myth, the legend"
Johnny Baravong at Zion National Park, Utah

ABOUT THE AUTHOR

ROBERT WAS BORN IN VIETNAM during the war. After the fall of Saigon, he and his mother and three siblings became part of the massive sea of refugees fleeing the country for their lives. He and his siblings were half

American and it was almost a certainty that they would be one of the first to be slaughtered by the North Vietnamese Army. All the money his father had given his mother to use as bribe money had been stolen by Vietnamese police and checkpoint guards.

His father, a Navy veteran was ordered to immediately evacuate Vietnam without his family because his mother was not a U.S citizen. In America his father lived in agony waiting for his wife and children. He begged politicians to help him; he went to the local newspapers and news stations and told his story with little consequence.

Over many months of unimaginable suffering, his courageous mother, with a child on each hip and two more clinging to her shirttails, managed to navigate her family across perilous borders from camp to camp until finally arriving in America.

Robert grew up in Las Vegas, Nevada where he met his childhood friend Johnny Baravong. Johnny and his family too had been casualties of war, having been refugees from Laos and Thailand. Together the boys had managed to build a reputation for never taking no for an answer, and using ingenuity and unrelenting perseverance to achieve their goals.

Upon graduating from high school Robert immediately shipped out to Army basic training. He served twenty years and retired honorably as a Master Sergeant. While home visiting his family and friends in Las Vegas, his friend Johnny, who had become an engineer, suggested he do the unthinkable and write a book. After relentless badgering Robert finally conceded. As a result the most unlikely of passions was born.

Robert resides in Oklahoma with his wife and three children.

www.ingramcontent.com/pod-product-compliance
Lightning Source LLC
Chambersburg PA
CBHW060230050426
42448CB00009B/1375